Industrial Locomotives
of South Western England

INDUSTRIAL LOCOMOTIVES of SOUTH WESTERN ENGLAND

HANDBOOK H

COMPILED BY ROGER HATELEY

General Editor, the Handbook Series – BRIAN RUMARY

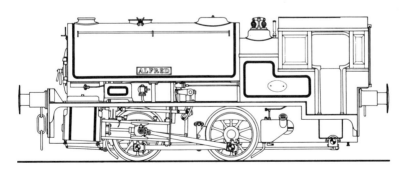

Bagnall 3058 of 1953 – drawing by Roger West

INDUSTRIAL RAILWAY SOCIETY

Published by the INDUSTRIAL RAILWAY SOCIETY
at 44 Hicks Avenue, Greenford, Middlesex

© INDUSTRIAL RAILWAY SOCIETY 1977

ISBN 0 901096 23 7

Printed in Great Britain by AB Printers Ltd , Leicester

Distributed by IRS Publications, 44 Hicks Avenue, Greenford, Middlesex

Contents

Introduction

'Industrial Locomotives of Southern England', Pocket Book B, was published in 1958 and has been unobtainable for a number of years. In this volume an attempt has been made to revise and update the information last published in Book B and to amplify it towards the standards of Book F, North Wales, published in 1968. The consequent introduction of descriptive and historical notes, National Grid references, details of some lines not worked by locomotives and some maps has so greatly increased the bulk of the work that it is now intended to cover the geographical area of the old Book B in two sections. This first section includes the south-western counties of England.

The local government reorganisation of April 1974 has necessitated some alterations. Locations are listed under the administrative county existing from April 1974, even if the rail system was no longer extant at that date. Footnotes detailing locomotive transfers record the county name appropriate at the time of transfer. In this volume the main areas altered are those formerly of North Somerset and South Gloucestershire which have formed the new county of Avon. Additionally Dorset now includes Bournemouth and an area around formerly in Hampshire.

The information for each county is set out in three sections. Firstly industrial locomotive worked systems, minor public railways and preservation sites; secondly known details of non-locomotive worked systems of sufficient size to be of interest; and thirdly known details of locomotives used on civil engineering contracts. In the first section passenger carrying minor railways are included if they were to a gauge less than 4ft8½in, or if they were of 4ft8½in gauge and remained independent until closure or until or after the grouping of 1923. Miniature railways of gauge less than 1ft6in have been excluded unless used for industrial purposes. Selection for the second section has been governed by available information and by the size of the system. Information on contractors locomotives is often scanty and so that which has been found has been kept apart from the basic industrial lists to give a third section for each county.

My thanks are due to many enthusiasts for information included in this work. In particular to Allan Baker, Ray Fox, Geoffrey Horsman and Russell Wear (for the dimensional data in the indices), Chris Down (for help with Avon and Somerset), Michael Messenger (for help with Cornwall and Devon), Jim Peden and the Industrial Locomotive Society (for much of the information relating to contractors locomotives), Derek Stoyel (for permission to publish photographs from the collection of the late George Alliez), Pete Nicholson (for data on narrow gauge locos) and to the many others who have supplied photographic illustrations. Also to G.W.Green, K.Plant, E.S.Tonks and W.K.Williams for patiently continuing to supply their expert information and trying to remedy deficiencies in my work. Responsibility for the remaining errors, omissions and defects remains of course with me.

Comments on and corrections to any information given in this volume will be most welcome, as will additional information, maps or layout diagrams, in order that any future edition may be more complete than this work. Similarly it is hoped soon to produce the second section to cover the south-central counties listed in the old Book B which have been excluded from this section and information for this work would be helpful to enable it to be of a good standard.

35, Daneshay,
   Northam,
    BIDEFORD,
     Devon EX39 1DG

August 1976

Roger Hateley.

Explanatory notes

GAUGE: The gauge of the railway system is given at the head of the locomotive list. If slight uncertainty exists a gauge may be quoted as, for example, "2ft" , which is to be understood as meaning " 2ft 0in approximately ". Metric measurements are used where the equipment is thought to have been designed to these units.

NUMBER and NAME: A number or name formerly carried is shown in brackets ( ) ; one unofficially bestowed and used by the staff but never carried by the locomotive is shown by inverted commas " " . A dash indicates that no title is carried.

TYPE: The Whyte system of wheel classification is used in the main, but when the driving wheels are not connected by outside rods but by chains (as in "Sentinels" and some diesels) they are shown as 4w, 6w, as the case may be. The following abbreviations are used:-

T	Side tank or similar – denotes a tank positioned externally but fastened to the frame, and includes such variants as Wing Tank.
CT	Crane Tank - a T type loco fitted with load lifting apparatus.
PT	Pannier Tank - Side tanks not fastened to the frame.
ST	Saddle tank
WT	Well tank - a tank located between the frames below the level of the boiler.
VB	Vertical boilered locomotive
D	Diesel locomotive; unknown transmission system
DM	Diesel locomotive; mechanical transmission
DE	Diesel locomotive; electric transmission
DH	Diesel locomotive; hydraulic transmission
P	Petrol or Paraffin locomotive; unknown transmission system
PM	Petrol or Paraffin locomotive; mechanical transmission
PE	Petrol or Paraffin locomotive; electric transmission
PH	Petrol or Paraffin locomotive; hydraulic transmission
R	Railcar - a vehicle primarily designed to carry passengers
BE	Battery powered electric locomotive
RE	Third rail powered electric locomotive
WE	Overhead wire powered electric locomotive
F	Fireless steam locomotive

CYLINDER POSITION:
IC	Inside cylinders
OC	Outside cylinders
3C	Three cylinders
4C	Four cylinders
VC	Vertical cylinders
G	Geared transmission (used with IC, OC or VC)

In the case of non-steam locomotives this column is left blank

MAKERS: Abbreviations used to denote the makers are listed on page

MAKERS NUMBER and DATE: The first column shows the works number, the second shows the date which appears on the works plate, or the date the loco was built if there is no date on the plate.

REBUILDING DETAILS: These are recorded only if they caused considerable alteration to the appearance of the locomotive, or were recorded on plates displayed on the locomotive.

SOURCE OF LOCOMOTIVE: "New" indicates that the locomotive was delivered from the makers to this location; a transfer from elsewhere is denoted by a bracketed letter, the full details being given in a footnote. The date of arrival is shown in the footnote where this information is known.

DISPOSAL OF LOCOMOTIVE: A locomotive transferred to another location is shown by a bracketed number and footnote, the date of departure being given in the footnote if it is known. In other cases the following abbreviations are used:

OOU   Loco noted to be permanently out of use on the date shown
Dsm   Loco both OOU and incomplete on the date shown
Scr   Loco broken up for scrap on the date shown
s/s   Loco scrapped or sold; disposal unknown

Many sales of locomotives have been effected through dealers and contractors and abbreviations used for some of these are included in the list below. If the dealers name is followed by a location, e.g. Abelson, Sheldon, it is to be understood that the loco went to Sheldon depot before resale. If no location is shown, the loco either went direct to its new owner or else definite information on this point is lacking. If a direct transfer is known to have been effected by a dealer, the word "per" is used.

GENERAL ABBREVIATIONS: c   circa; i.e. about the time of the date quoted
                         f   formerly, previously
                         orig originally
                         Reb   Rebuilt
                         ret   returned

FOOTNOTE ABBREVIATIONS: In addition to the abbreviations listed below, the abbreviations used to denote the various locomotive builders and main line railway companies are also used in footnotes where appropriate.

Abelson	– Abelson & Co (Engineers) Ltd, Sheldon, Birmingham
APCM	– Associated Portland Cement Manufacturers Ltd
BPCM	– British Portland Cement Manufacturers Ltd
BQC	– British Quarrying Co Ltd
Bungey	– G.W.Bungey Ltd , Heston (Hayes until /1953)
Cohen	– George Cohen Sons & Co Ltd
contr	– Contractor or Contractors
ECC	– English China Clays Ltd
ECLP	– English Clays Lovering Pochin Ltd
ICI	– Imperial Chemical Industries Ltd
MoD	– Ministry of Defence
MoD.AD	– Ministry of Defence, Army Department
MoD.AFD	– Ministry of Defence, Air Force Department
MoD.ND	– Ministry of Defence, Navy Department
MoM	– Ministry of Munitions
MoS	– Ministry of Supply
MSC	– Manchester Ship Canal
NCB	– National Coal Board
Nuttall	– Edmund Nuttall Sons & Co (London) Ltd
Pugsley	– J.Pugsley & Sons Ltd , Stoke Gifford, Glos
RAF	– Royal Air Force
ROD	– Railway Operating Department
ROF	– Royal Ordnance Factory
RNAD	– Royal Naval Armament Depot
RNCF	– Royal Naval Cordite Factory
SLP	– Sir Lindsay Parkinson & Co Ltd
SWGB	– South Western Gas Board
TWW	– Thos W Ward Ltd
USATC	– United States Army Transportation Corps
Wake	– J.F.Wake Ltd , Darlington
WD	– War Department
WDLR	– War Department Light Railways

DOUBTFUL INFORMATION: Information known to be of a doubtful nature is printed in brackets with a question mark. Thus "P (1244 ?) 1910" denotes that the loco was certainly a Peckett of 1910 vintage and could have been works number 1244.

Locomotive builders

AB	Andrew Barclay, Sons & Co Ltd , Caledonia Works, Kilmarnock
A.C.Cars	A.C.Cars Ltd , Thames Ditton, Surrey
AE	Avonside Engine Co Ltd , Bristol
AP	Aveling & Porter Ltd , Invicta Works, Canterbury, Kent
AtW	Atkinson Walker Wagons Ltd , Preston,Lancs
Austro-Daimler	Austro-Daimler, Wiener Neustadt, Austria
AW	Sir W.G.Armstrong, Whitworth & Co (Engineers) Ltd ,Newcastle upon Tyne
Barclays	Barclays & Co , Riverside Works, Kilmarnock
B&ER	Bristol & Exeter Railway Co Ltd , Bristol
B&S	Bellis & Seekings Ltd , Birmingham
BE	Brush Electrical Engineering Co Ltd , Loughborough, Leics
Bg	E.E.Baguley Ltd , Burton-on-Trent
BgC	Baguley Cars Ltd , Burton-on-Trent
BH	Black, Hawthorn & Co Ltd , Gateshead
BLW	Baldwin Locomotive Works, Philadelphia, USA
BP	Beyer, Peacock & Co Ltd , Gorton, Manchester
BTH	British Thomson-Houston Co Ltd , Rugby
Bton	Brighton Works, British Railways (prev SR and LBSCR)
Cattybrook	Cattybrook Brick Co Ltd , Almondsbury, Glos
C&N	Curwen & Newbury Ltd , Devizes
CE	International Combustion Ltd , Clayton Equipment Works, Hatton, Derbys
CF	Chapman & Furneaux Ltd , Gateshead (succesors to BH)
Crossley	Crossley Engineering Ltd , Trafford Park, Manchester
D	Dubs & Co, Glasgow Locomotive Works, Glasgow
Dar	British Railways, Darlington Works (and predecessors)
DC	Drewry Car Co Ltd , London
Derby	Derby Works, British Railways (prev LMSR, Midland Railway)
Don	Doncaster Works, British Railways (prev LNER and GNR)
Dtz	Motorenfabrik Deutz A.G., Koln, Germany
EBW	E.B.Wilson & Co , Railway Foundry, Leeds
Eclipse	Eclipse Peat Co Ltd , Ashcott, Somerset
EE	English Electric Co Ltd
EEV	EE, Vulcan Works, Newton-le-Willows, Lancs (succesors to VF)
Electromobile	
FE	Falcon Engine & Car Works Ltd , Loughborough, Leics
Ferrubron	Ferrubron Manufacturing Co Ltd , Hennock, Devon
FH	F.C.Hibberd & Co Ltd , Park Royal, London
FJ	Fletcher, Jennings & Co , Lowca Engine Works, Whitehaven
B.J.Fry	B.J.Fry Ltd , Dorchester, Dorset
FW	Fox, Walker & Co , Atlas Engine Works, Bristol
GB	Greenwood & Batley Ltd , Leeds
GECT	General Electric Co Traction Ltd , Newton-le-Willows, Lancs
Geevor	Geevor Tin MInes Ltd , Pendeen, Cornwall
Gilkes,Wilson	Gilkes, Wilson & Co
Guest	Trevor Guest, Stourbridge, Worcs
H	James & Fredk Howard Ltd , Britannia Ironworks, Bedford
HC	Hudswell, Clarke & Co Ltd , Railway Foundry, Leeds
HCR	Hudswell, Clarke & Rodgers, Railway Foundry, Leeds
HE	Hunslet Engine Co Ltd , Hunslet, Leeds
Hine Bros	Hine Brothers Ltd , Gillingham, Dorset
HL	R & W Hawthorn, Leslie & Co Ltd, Forth Bank Works, Newcastle upon Tyne
HU	Robert Hudson Ltd , Leeds

Jesty	Bedford & Jesty Ltd , Bere Regis, Dorset
JF	John Fowler & Co (Leeds) Ltd , Hunslet, Leeds
Jung	Arn.Jung Lokomotivfabrik G.m.b.H., Jungenthal, Germany
K	Kitson & Co , Airedale Foundry, Leeds
K.Bickle	K.Bickle, Plymouth
KC	Kent Construction & Engineering Co Ltd , Ashford, Kent
KS	Kerr, Stuart & Co Ltd , California Works, Stoke-on-Trent
L	R & A Lister & Co Ltd , Dursley, Glos
LB	Lister Blackstone Traction Ltd , Dursley, Glos
Lewin	Stephen Lewin, Dorset Foundry, Poole
Lill	Lilleshall Co Ltd , Oakengates, Salop
Longhedge	Longhedge Works, London, SE&CR
Lott & Walne	Lott & Walne, Engineers, Dorchester, Dorset
MH	Muir Hill Engineering Ltd , Trafford Park, Manchester
MR	Motor Rail Ltd , Simplex Works, Bedford
MW	Manning, Wardle & Co Ltd , Boyne Engine Works, Hunslet, Leeds
N	Neilson & Co , Springburn Works, Glasgow
NB	North British Locomotive Co Ltd , Glasgow
NSC	National Smelting Co Ltd , Avonmouth, Glos
OK	Orenstein & Koppel A.G., Berlin, Germany
P	Peckett & Sons Ltd , Atlas Locomotive Works, St George, Bristol
Park Royal	
Regent St.Poly	Regent St. Polytechnic, London
RH	Ruston & Hornsby Ltd , Lincoln
RP	Ruston, Proctor & Co Ltd , Lincoln
RR	Rolls Royce Ltd , Sentinel Works, Shrewsbury (succesors to S)
R&R	Ransomes & Rapier Ltd , Riverside Works, Ipswich, Suffolk
RS	Robert Stephenson & Co Ltd , Darlington
RSH	Robert Stephenson & Hawthorns Ltd
RS&J	Ransome, Simms & Jeffries Ltd , Ipswich, Suffolk
RWH	R & W Hawthorn, Forth Bank Works, Newcastle-on-Tyne
S	Sentinel (Shrewsbury) Ltd , Battlefield, Shrewsbury
S&B	Sara & Burgess Ltd , Falmouth,Cornwall
S&H	Strachan & Henshaw Ltd , Ashton, Bristol
St Helens	St Helens Railway Co , Lancs
Schneider	Societe des Forges et Ateliers du Creusot (Usines Schneider), Le Creusot, France
Sdn	British Railways, Swindon Works, Wilts (prev GWR)
Sharp	Sharp Brothers, Manchester
Spittle	Thomas Spittle & Co , Newport, Mon
Stothert & Slaughter	Stothert & Slaughter, Bristol
SS	Sharp,Stewart & Co Ltd , Atlas Works, Glasgow (from /1888),f Manchester
TH	Thos Hill (Rotherham) Ltd , Vanguard Works, Kilnhurst, Yorks
VE	Victor Electrics Ltd , Burscough Bridge, Lancs
VF	Vulcan Foundry Ltd , Newton-le-Willows, Lancs
VIW	Vulcan Iron Works, Wilkes-Barre, Philadelphia, USA
W&B	Whipp & Bourne, Engineers,
WB	W G Bagnall Ltd , Castle Engine Works, Stafford
WkB	Walker Brothers (Wigan) Ltd , Wigan, Lancs
Wkm	D.Wickham & Co Ltd , Ware, Herts
Worcester Engine Co	Worcester Engine Co

Wpn	Wolverhampton Works, British Railways (prev GWR)
WR	Wingrove & Rogers Ltd (British Electric Vehicles), Kirkby, Liverpool
YE	Yorkshire Engine Co Ltd , Meadow Hall Works, Sheffield
9E	Nine Elms Works, London , LSWR

Locomotive index

This index is intended to provide a quick source of reference to the principal
dimensions and characteristics of many of the locomotives listed in this book.
The inclusion of the page number(s) enables the reader to establish the owner
of any loco. It should be remembered that driving wheel diameters decrease
each time that wheels are turned and cylinders were sometimes bored out to a
larger diameter. Diesel engines quoted were those fitted when the loco was new.

Products of the following Builders, not covered by the detailed tables below, will be
found on the page numbers quoted:

AP (37, 55, 103, 107); AtW (35); AW (83); B&ER (46, 77); B&S (129);
BE (91); BTH (2); Bton (29, 60, 74, 106); CE (Numerous); Charles Tayleur
(56, 119, 120); Crewe (60); Crossley (68, 81); D (62, 106); Dar (5);
DC (4, 39, 41, 82, 98, 106); Derby (63); Don (5, 30); EBW (135); EE (69)
Elh (62); GB (Numerous); Gilkes,Wilson (32); H (73); HU (12);
K.Bickle (10); KC (45); L & LB (Numerous); Lewin (40, 125); Lill (31);
Longhedge (28); MR (Numerous); Park Royal (74); R&R (90); RH (*);
S&B (6, 7, 9, 28); St Helens (119); Schneider (68, 70); Sdn (11, 29, 30,
44, 62, 64, 82, 119); Spittle (25, 32); Stothert & Slaughter (50, 77);
VIW (28); WkB (106); Wkm (30, 31); Worcester Engine Co (119); Wpn (89);
WR (Numerous); 9E (28, 55, 65).

*A very large number of RH locos are included. Further details and dimensions of any
RH loco whose works number is known can be obtained by reference to the indices in
'Ruston & Hornsby Locomotives' by E.S.Tonks, Industrial Railway Society, 1974.

WORKS NUMBER	DATE EX WORKS	GAUGE AS BUILT	TYPE		CYLINDERS Bore x Stroke (or POWER)	DRIVING WHEEL DIAM.	RIGID WHEEL BASE	NOTES/ WEIGHT	SEE PAGE
BARCLAYS - BARCLAYS & CO									
229	.76	4ft8½in	0-4-0ST	OC	11x18	3ft0in			52
AB - ANDREW BARCLAY SONS & CO LTD									
185	30. 5.77	4ft8½in	0-4-0ST	OC	10x17	3ft0in			52
702	30.12.91	2ft7¾in	0-4-0ST	OC	10x	2ft6in			114
703	21. 1.93	1ft11½in	0-4-0ST	OC	5x10	3ft0in			53
737	27.11.93	4ft8½in	0-4-0ST	OC	10x18	3ft0in	5ft0in	18T	43 45
761	.95	3ft0in	0-4-0T	OC	6x12	1ft10in			50
853	27.12.99	4ft8½in	0-4-0ST	OC	10x18	3ft0in			52
867	22. 3.00	4ft8½in	0-4-0ST	OC	10x18	3ft0in			52
887	23. 2.01	4ft8½in	0-4-0ST	OC	12x20	3ft2in			52
888	22. 1.01	4ft8½in	0-4-0ST	OC	12x20	3ft2in			52
891	10.12.01	4ft8½in	0-4-0ST	OC	10x18	3ft0in			52
969	23. 3.03	4ft8½in	0-4-0ST	OC	10x18	3ft0in			57
1286	.14	4ft8½in	0-4-0ST	OC	10x18	3ft0in	5ft0in	18T	58
1379	23.10.14	4ft8½in	0-4-0ST	OC	12x20	3ft2in			37
1380	3.11.14	4ft8½in	0-4-0ST	OC	12x20	3ft2in			37
1397	12. 4.15	4ft8½in	0-4-0ST	OC	14x22	3ft5in	5ft6in	28T	37
1398	7. 9.15	4ft8½in	0-4-0ST	OC	10x18	3ft0in		62	102
1406	12. 5.15	4ft8½in	0-4-0ST	OC	14x22	3ft5in			37
1474	13. 6.16	2ft6in	0-2-4F	OC	8x12	2ft4in		11T	122
1475	20. 6.16	2ft6in	0-2-4F	OC	8x12	2ft4in		11T	122
1516	8. 4.19	4ft8½in	0-4-0ST	OC	14x22	3ft5in			37
1570	11. 9.17	4ft8½in	0-4-0ST	OC	12x20	3ft2in	5ft6in	22T	128
1719	23.12.20	4ft8½in	0-4-0ST	OC	10x18	3ft0in		62	102

1828	16. 4.24	4ft8½in	0-4-0ST	OC	12x20	3ft2in					111
1844	26. 8.24	4ft8½in	0-6-0ST	OC	12x20	3ft2in				55 89	111
1845	9.10.24	4ft8½in	0-6-0ST	OC	12x20	3ft2in					111
1846	9.10.24	4ft8½in	0-6-0ST	OC	12x20	3ft2in					111
1855	30. 3.31	2ft0in	0-4-0WT	OC	7x11	1ft10in	3ft11in	6.9T Class E		68	99
2071	2.10.39	4ft8½in	0-4-0ST	OC	12x20	3ft2in	5ft6in				37
2082	12. 2.40	4ft8½in	0-4-0ST	OC	14x22	3ft5in	5ft6in	28T			65
2137	12. 3.42	4ft8½in	0-4-0ST	OC	12x20						37
2221	16.10.46	4ft8½in	0-4-0ST	OC	12x20						37
336	6. 3.38	4ft8½in	0-6-0DM		180HP			29½T			78
349	25. 1.41	4ft8½in	0-4-0DM		84HP	2ft3in	5ft0in	14½T			65
352	.41	4ft8½in	0-4-0DM		84HP	2ft3in	5ft0in	14½T			65
422	1. 4.58	4ft8½in	0-6-0DM		204HP						29
578	30. 3.72	4ft8½in	0-4-0DH		302HP						65
579	7. 4.72	4ft8½in	0-4-0DH		302HP						65

AE - AVONSIDE ENGINE CO LTD

900	1.73	7ft0¼in	0-4-0WT	IC	10x16	3ft0in	7ft0in				53
901	2.73	7ft0¼in	0-4-0WT	IC	10x16	3ft0in	7ft0in				53
1371	.98	4ft8½in	0-6-0ST	OC	14x20	3ft3in	9ft8½in	30T	B2		96
1421	.00	4ft8½in	0-6-0ST	OC	14x20	3ft6in	11ft0in	29T			64
1428	.01	3ft0in	0-6-0ST	OC	7x10	1ft8in	9ft0in	8½T	"Spl"		40
1431	.01	4ft8½in	0-6-0ST	OC	14x20	3ft3in	9ft8½in	30T	B2		96
1565	.11	4ft8½in	0-4-0ST	OC	14x20	3ft3in	5ft6in	25T	SS1:44 99		100
1593	.10	1ft11in	0-4-0T	OC	7x10	1ft8in	3ft6in	5¾T	-	12	95
1655	.13	4ft8½in	0-6-0ST	OC	14x20	3ft3in	9ft8½in	30T	B3		89
1679	.14	4ft8½in	0-6-0ST	OC	14x20	3ft3in	9ft8½in	30T	B3		96
1690	.15	4ft8½in	0-4-0ST	OC	14x20	3ft3in	5ft6in	25T	SS1		37
1701	.15	4ft8½in	0-4-0T	OC	10x16	2ft9in	5ft0in	18¼T	"Spl"		130
1724	.15	4ft8½in	0-6-0ST	OC	14½x20	3ft3in	9ft8½in	35T	B4		96
1725	.15	4ft8½in	0-6-0ST	OC	14½x20	3ft3in	9ft8½in	35T	B5		96
1748	.16	1ft6in	0-4-0T	OC	8½x12	2ft1in	3ft3in	11¼T	-		27
1763	.17	4ft8½in	0-6-0ST	OC	14½x20	3ft3in	9ft8½in	35T	B4		69
1764	.17	4ft8½in	0-6-0ST	OC	14½x20	3ft3in	9ft8½in	35T	B4	80 82	96
											102
1798	.18	4ft8½in	0-6-0ST	OC	14½x20	3ft3in	9ft8½in	35T	B4	83 89	
1799	.18	4ft8½in	0-6-0ST	OC	14½x20	3ft3in	9ft8½in	35T	B4		96
1800	.18	4ft8½in	0-6-0ST	OC	14½x20	3ft3in	9ft8½in	35T	B4		96
1976	2.11.25	4ft8½in	0-4-0ST	OC	13x18	3ft0in	5ft6in	24T	-	121	128
1978	11.6 .28	4ft8½in	0-4-0ST	OC	12x18	2ft11in	5ft0in	21T	D		103
2013	.30	4ft8½in	4wPM		40HP	2ft9in	5ft0in		-	*	85
2061	28.10.31	3ft0in	0-4-0DM		21½/35HP	2ft0in	3ft6in	4½T	-	@	46
2072	30.6. 33	2ft0in	0-4-0T	OC	7½x12	2ft0in	3ft9in	7½T	-	57 68	
2073	6.7. 33	2ft0in	0-4-0T	OC	7½x12	2ft0in	3ft9in	7½T	-	68 99	
2076	13.9. 34	3ft0in	0-4-0DM		26/36HP	2ft0in	3ft6in	4½T	-	@	46

* Brotherhood-Ricardo engine
@ Dorman-Ricardo engine

BgC - BAGULEY CARS LTD

717	31.11.17	600mm	0-4-0PM	10HP	1ft6in	2ft6in	37¾cwt		80
736	18. 3.18	600mm	0-4-0PM	10HP	1ft6in	2ft6in	37¾cwt		83
758	9.10.18	600mm	0-4-0PM	10HP	1ft6in	2ft6in	37¾cwt		27
759	19.10.18	600mm	0-4-0PM	10HP	1ft6in	2ft6in	37¾cwt		2

(Bg/DC) 2104	7.37	2ft0in	4wDM	25HP	1ft6in	3ft0in	(a)	4 25 98
(Bg/DC) 2105	7.37	2ft0in	4wDM	25HP	1ft6in	3ft0in	(a)	4 25 98
2108	10.37	2ft0in	4wDM	16HP	1ft6in	3ft0in	(a)	90
(Bg/DC) 2263	16.11.49	2ft6in	0-6-0DM	102HP	2ft0in	6ft0in	12½T (b)	39
3017	17.2 .38	4ft8½in	2-2-0PMR	28HP	2ft0in	5ft9in	(c)	121
3410	7.2. 55	4ft8½in	0-4-0DM	150HP	3ft6in	5ft6in	(d)	82
(Bg/DC) 2652	15.2. 58	4ft8½in	0-4-0DM	102HP	3ft1½in	5ft6in	(b)	82
(Bg/DC) 2655	29.6. 59	4ft8½in	0-4-0DM	102HP	3ft1½in	5ft6in	(b)	82
(Bg/DC) 2723	11.1. 61	4ft8½in	0-4-0DM	102HP	3ft1½in	5ft6in	(b)	82

(a) Ailsa Craig engine (b) Gardner 6LW engine
(c) Meadows engine (d) Gardner 6L3 engine

BH - BLACK, HAWTHORN & CO LTD

466	.78	4ft8½in	0-6-0ST	OC			116
511	.83	4ft8½in	0-6-0ST	OC			117
576	.80	3ft0in	0-6-0ST	OC	7½x10	1ft8in	40
1059	.92	4ft8½in	0-4-0ST	OC	12x19	3ft3in	40

BLW - BALDWIN LOCOMOTIVE WORKS

15965	5.98	2ft0in	2-4-2T	OC	10x16	2ft9in	5ft0in	22T	36
	.16	2ft0in	0-4-0DM						1

BP - BEYER, PEACOCK & CO LTD

248	.61	4ft8½in	2-4-0	IC	17x24	6ft2in	8ft6in	34T	73
249	.61	4ft8½in	2-4-0	IC	17x24	6ft2in	8ft6in	34T	73
1736	3. 9.77	4ft8½in	0-4-0ST	OC					86 114
1881	.79	4ft8½in	4-4-0T	OC	17x24	5ft10in		46½T	73

CF - CHAPMAN & FURNEAUX LTD

1105	.95	4ft8½in	0-6-0ST	OC			117
1161	.98	4ft8½in	0-6-0T	OC	12x20	3ft7in	66

Dtz - MOTORENFABRIK DEUTZ A G

9898	600mm	0-4-0DM	69
88153	600mm	0-6-0DM	68 100

EEV - ENGLISH ELECTRIC CO LTD, VULCAN WORKS

D1124	.66	4ft8½in	0-4-0DH	305HP	34T	(a)	87
D1280) 3987)	.70	4ft8½in	0-4-0DH	272HP			34

(a) Cummins NHRS 6 B1 engine

FH - F C HIBBERD & CO LTD ("PLANET")

1833	15. 8	.33	2ft0in	4wDM	20HP			3½T				28
1834	8	.33	4ft8½in	4wPM	60HP			15T	"Howard"			29
1887	9	.34	2ft0in	4wDM	20HP	1ft5in	3ft6in	2½T	"Simplex"		124	132
1896	11.34		2ft0in	4wDM	20HP	1ft5in	3ft6in	2½T	"Simplex"		8	132
1987	6	.36	2ft0in	4wPM	8HP			Ford		60	61
2048	5	.37	2ft0in	4wPM	8HP			Ford			60
2054	3	.38	4ft8½in	4wDM	54HP					123	131
2115	3	.38	2ft0in	4wPM	10HP			Ford		60	61
2161	30.11.38		2ft6in	4wDM	25HP		(c)		"Simplex Rebuild"	39
2326	5	.40	2ft0in	4wPM	10HP			1½T Ford		60	61
2337	7	.40	2ft6in	4wDM	20HP			2¾T			122
2401	5	.41	2ft0in	4wDM	20HP			3½T	"Simplex"	1	16
2798	3	.44	2ft0in	4wDM	20HP			3½T	"Simplex"		60
2914	9	.44	4ft8½in	4wDM				6T	"Simplex"		105
3057	1	.46	4ft8½in	4wDM				11T		41	102	105
3061	2	.46	2ft0in	4wDM				1½T Y Type		60	71
3281			4ft8½in	4wDM							29
3424		.49	1ft8in	4wPM	8HP	1ft3in	2ft6in	1½T Ford			61
3677	11.53		4ft8½in	4wDM				18T	(b) SC		87
3737	3	.55	4ft8½in	4wDM	c150HP	3ft2in	5ft6in	23T	(a) AD	38	37
3741	5	.55	4ft8½in	4wDM	c150HP	3ft2in	5ft6in	23T	(a) AD		37
3744	7	.55	4ft8½in	4wDM	c150HP	3ft2in	5ft6in	23T	(a) AD		37
3746	8	.55	4ft8½in	4wDM	c150HP	3ft2in	5ft6in	23T	(a) AD		37
3747	8	.55	4ft8½in	4wDM	c150HP	3ft2in	5ft6in	23T	(a) AD		37
3773-6	2-3	.55	4ft8½in	4wDM	c150HP	3ft2in	5ft6in	23T	(a) AD		37
3790		.56	2ft0in	4wDM							127
3816	5	.56	4ft8½in	4wDM	c150HP	3ft2in	5ft6in	23T	(a) AD		37
3831	2	.58	2ft6in	4wDM	75HP			13T	(b) SCN		39

(a) Foden engine
(b) Dorman 4DL engine
(c) Paxman 2RQT engine

FJ - FLETCHER, JENNINGS & CO

46		.65	4ft8½in	0-4-0T	OC				50
47		.65	4ft8½in	0-4-0T	OC				55
58		.66	4ft8½in	0-4-0T	OC	12x20	3ft4in		84
129		.73	3ft0in	0-4-0	OC	9x16	2ft9in		40
139		.74	3ft0in	0-4-0	OC	9x16	2ft9in		40
150		.75	3ft0in	0-4-0	OC	9x16	2ft9in		40

FW - FOX, WALKER & CO

159	11.5	.72	4ft8½in	0-4-0ST	OC	10x18	2ft8in	5ft0in	16T	D	127
180	14.1	.73	4ft8½in	0-6-0ST	OC	13x20	3ft7in	10ft0in	28T	B	96
242		.74	4ft8½in	0-6-0ST	OC	13x20	3ft7in	10ft0in	28T		82 102
280		.75	4ft8½in	0-6-0ST	OC	13x20	3ft7in	10ft0in	28T	B1	96
281		.75	4ft8½in	0-4-0ST	OC	14x20	3ft2in	5ft6in	24T	S	85
286	11.75		4ft8½in	0-6-0ST	OC	13x20	3ft5in	10ft0in	28T	B	85
326		.76	4ft8½in	0-6-0ST	OC	13x20	3ft7in	10ft0in	28T	B1	84
328		.77	4ft8½in	0-6-0ST	OC	13x20	3ft7in	10ft0in	28T	B1	92

HCR - HUDSWELL, CLARKE & RODGERS

153	23.6	.74	4ft8½in	0-6-0ST	OC	14x20	3ft6in		69 72

302	11. 6.88	4ft8½in	0-4-0ST	OC	8x15	2ft6in	5ft0in	12T		105
327	16.10.89	4ft8½in	0-6-0ST	IC	13x20	3ft3in				115
336	28. 6.89	4ft8½in	0-4-0ST	OC	10x16	2ft9in	5ft6in	15T	130	133
369	23.10.90	2ft8½in	0-6-0ST	OC	7½x12	2ft0in				108
402	3. 7.93	4ft8½in	0-4-0ST	OC	10x16	2ft9in				79
442	2. 9.95	4ft8½in	0-6-0ST	IC	12x18	3ft0in	10ft6in	21½T		89
444	5. 8.95	4ft8½in	0-4-0ST	OC	10x16	2ft9in				117
464	29.12.96	4ft8½in	0-4-0ST	OC	13x18	3ft0in	5ft6in	22½T		108
495	27. 5.98	3ft0in	0-4-0ST	OC	10x16	2ft9in				15
546	18. 1.00	2ft8½in	0-6-0ST	OC	8x12	2ft0in				108
639	31. 1.02	600 mm	0-4-2ST	OC	9x15	2ft6in				8
640	31. 1.00	600 mm	0-4-2ST	OC	9x15	2ft6in				8
645	29. 1.03	3ft6in	0-4-0ST	OC	12x18	3ft1in				13
650	30. 3.03	4ft8½in	0-4-0ST	OC	10x16	2ft9in				50
654	10. 8.03	4ft8½in	0-6-0ST	IC	13x20	3ft3in				115
656	17. 7.03	4ft8½in	0-4-0ST	OC	10x16	2ft9in				79
671	23. 3.04	4ft8½in	0-6-0ST	IC	13x20	3ft3in				115
823	4. 6.08	4ft8½in	0-6-0ST	OC	14x20	3ft7in	9ft8in	29½T		106
1029	30. 5.13	4ft8½in	0-6-0ST	IC	12x18	3ft1in	10ft6in	21½T	93	101
1045	10.14	4ft8½in	0-4-0ST	OC	14x20	3ft3in	5ft6in	28T		100
1246	21. 9.16	4ft8½in	0-6-0T	IC	15½x20	3ft4in	10ft3in	34T	89	91
1298	31. 7.17	600 mm	0-6-0WT	OC	6½x12	1ft11in	4ft2in	6⅞T		65
1314	5. 6.18	600 mm	0-6-0WT	OC	6½x12	1ft11in	4ft2in	6⅞T	33 50	115
1323	24. 4.18	4ft8½in	0-6-0T	OC	16x24	3ft9in	10ft0in	42T		96
1377	31. 5.19	600 mm	0-6-0WT	OC	6½x12	1ft11in	4ft2in	6⅞T		81
1378	31. 5.19	600 mm	0-6-0WT	OC	6½x12	1ft11in	4ft2in	6⅞T		81
1525	11. 4.24	4ft8½in	0-6-0ST	IC	12x18	3ft1in	10ft6in	21½T		114
1539	23. 7.24	4ft8½in	0-6-0ST	IC	13x20	3ft3in				78
1586	30. 8.27	4ft8½in	0-6-0ST	IC	13x20	3ft3in				78
1608	14. 6.34	4ft8½in	0-6-0ST	IC	13x20	3ft3in				78
1609	29. 7.34	4ft8½in	0-6-0ST	IC	13x20	3ft3in				78
1632	19. 2.29	4ft8½in	0-4-0ST	OC	14x22	3ft9in	5ft6in	28½T		9
1669	31. 8.36	4ft8½in	0-6-0ST	IC	13x20	3ft3in				114
1674	11. 3.37	4ft8½in	0-6-0ST	IC	13x20	3ft3in				114
1697	28. 6.38	4ft8½in	0-6-0ST	IC	13x20	3ft3in				114
1749	21. 6.46	4ft8½in	0-6-0ST	IC	13x20	3ft3in				114
1750	19. 7.46	4ft8½in	0-6-0ST	IC	13x20	3ft3in				114
1815	4.10.48	4ft8½in	0-6-0T	OC	16x24	3ft9in	10ft0in	42T		89

D754	.52	4ft8½in	0-6-0DM	300HP		Crossley	96
D755	.52	4ft8½in	0-6-0DM	300HP		Crossley	96
D756	.52	4ft8½in	0-6-0DM	300HP		Crossley	96
D757	.52	4ft8½in	0-6-0DM	300HP		Crossley	96
D760	.51	4ft8½in	0-6-0DM	204HP	3ft6in	36T Gardner 8L3	96
D761	.51	4ft8½in	0-6-0DM	204HP	3ft6in	36T Gardner 8L3	96
D774	.50	4ft8½in	0-4-0DM	200HP			80
D851	.55	4ft8½in	0-6-0DM	204HP	3ft6in	36T Gardner 8L3	96
D894	.54	4ft8½in	0-4-0DM	100HP		Gardner 6LW	96
D915	.56	4ft8½in	0-6-0DM	204HP	3ft6in	36T Gardner 8L3	96
D916	.56	4ft8½in	0-6-0DM	204HP	3ft6in	36T Gardner 8L3	96
D917	.56	4ft8½in	0-6-0DM	204HP	3ft6in	36T Gardner 8L3	96
D918	.56	4ft8½in	0-6-0DM	204HP	3ft6in	36T Gardner 8L3	96
D919	.56	4ft8½in	0-6-0DM	204HP	3ft6in	36T Gardner 8L3	89 96
D1009	.56	4ft8½in	0-4-0DM	153HP		Gardner 6L3	84
D1171	.59	4ft8½in	0-6-0DM	204HP	3ft6in	36T Gardner 8L3	96
D1172	.59	4ft8½in	C-6-0DM	204HP	3ft6in	36T Gardner 8L3	96
D1192	.60	4ft8½in	0-6-0DM	204HP	3ft6in	36T Gardner 8L3	96
D1193	.60	4ft8½in	0-6-0DM	204HP	3ft6in	36T Gardner 8L3	89 96

HE - HUNSLET ENGINE CO LTD

3	23.10.65	4ft8½in	0-6-0ST	IC	12x18	3ft1in	10ft6in			53
17	22.12.66	4ft8½in	0-4-0ST	OC	10x15	2ft9in	4ft9in			116
29	2.11.68	4ft8½in	0-4-0ST	OC	10x15	2ft9in	4ft9in			116
63	7. 7.71	4ft8½in	0-6-0ST	IC	13x18	3ft1in	10ft6in			117
65	26. 9.71	4ft8½in	0-6-0ST	IC	12x18	3ft1in	10ft6in			116
137	1. 7.75	4ft8½in	0-4-0ST	OC	10x15	2ft9in	4ft9in			116
152	10. 2.76	4ft8½in	0-6-0ST	IC	12x18	3ft1in	10ft6in			52
161	27. 3.76	4ft8½in	0-6-0ST	IC	12x18	3ft1in	10ft6in			116
219	7. 2.79	1ft11in	0-4-0ST	OC	6x10	1ft8in	3ft3in	5¾T		12
220	4. 3.79	1ft11in	0-4-0ST	OC	6x10	1ft8in	3ft3in	5¾T		12
242	12. 1.81	4ft8½in	0-6-0ST	IC	12x18	3ft1in	10ft6in	18½T		116
266	29.11.81	4ft8½in	0-6-0ST	IC	12x18	3ft1in	10ft6in	18½T		117
279	9. 1.82	2ft8½in	0-4-0ST	OC	7x10	1ft8in	3ft3in			108
282	27. 6.82	4ft8½in	0-4-0ST	OC	12x18	3ft1in	5ft4in	17½T		80 99
287	2.11.83	4ft8½in	0-4-0ST	OC	10x15	2ft9in	4ft9in	13½T		51 115
365	18. 9.85	4ft8½in	0-4-0ST	OC	10x15	2ft9in	4ft9in	13½T		53
367	9. 3.85	4ft8½in	0-4-0ST	OC	9x14	2ft8in	4ft6in	12T		117
400	5. 7.86	4ft8½in	0-4-0ST	OC	11x15	2ft6in	4ft6in			117
409	9.10.86	1ft10¾in	0-4-0ST	OC	7x10	1ft8in	3ft3in	6T		8
450	24. 4.88	4ft8½in	0-4-0ST	OC	12x18	3ft1in	10ft6in	18½T		117
545	26. 6.91	4ft8½in	0-6-0ST	IC	12x18	3ft1in	10ft6in	18¾T		116
571	21.11.92	4ft8½in	0-6-0ST	IC	13x18	3ft1in	10ft6in	23T		117
573	13. 1.93	4ft8½in	0-6-0ST	OC	11x15	2ft6in	9ft6in	17¾T		117
574	20. 2.93	4ft8½in	0-6-0ST	OC	11x15	2ft6in	9ft6in	17¾T		117
578	29. 3.93	4ft8½in	0-6-0ST	IC	13x18	3ft1in	10ft6in	23T		117
579	16. 6.93	4ft8½in	0-6-0ST	IC	13x18	3ft1in	10ft6in	23T		117
580	6. 3.93	4ft8½in	0-6-0ST	OC	11x15	2ft6in	9ft6in	17¾T		117
581	28. 4.93	4ft8½in	0-6-0ST	OC	11x15	2ft6in	9ft6in	17¾T		117
584	25. 7.94	4ft8½in	0-6-0ST	IC	13x18	3ft1in	10ft6in	23T		117
585	17. 9.94	4ft8½in	0-6-0ST	IC	13x18	3ft1in	10ft6in	23T		117
* 586	5. 7.93	4ft8½in	0-6-0T	IC	11x15	2ft9in	9ft6in	22¾T		117
* 587	5. 8.93	4ft8½in	0-6-0T	IC	11x15	2ft9in	9ft6in	22¾T		117
593	19. 9.93	4ft8½in	0-6-0ST	OC	11x15	2ft6in	9ft6in	17¾T		117
594	28. 9.93	4ft8½in	0-6-0ST	OC	11x15	2ft6in	9ft6in	17¾T		117
607	29. 4.95	4ft8½in	0-6-0T	IC	15x20	3ft4in	12ft0in	29T		117
625	20. 4.95	4ft8½in	0-6-0T	IC	11x15	2ft9in	9ft6in	22¾T		117
626	22. 5.95	4ft8½in	0-6-0ST	IC	13x18	3ft1in	10ft6in	23T		117
627	21. 6.95	4ft8½in	0-6-0ST	IC	13x18	3ft1in	10ft6in	23T		117
628	30. 5.95	4ft8½in	0-4-0ST	OC	10x15	2ft10in	4ft9in	13½T		117
713	6. 4.00	4ft8½in	2-4-2T	OC	12x18	3ft3in	5ft0in	27T		27
714	21.4 .00	4ft8½in	2-4-2T	OC	12x18	3ft3in	5ft0in	27T		27 89 91
715	2. 5.00	4ft8½in	2-4-2T	OC	12x18	3ft3in	5ft0in	27T		27
901	29. 5.06	1ft11½in	2-6-2T	OC	10¾x15	2ft4in	5ft6in			125
1246	15.12.16	600mm	4-6-0T	OC	9½x12	2ft0in	5ft6in	14T	WAR OFFICE	90
1428	29. 4.22	3ft0in	0-4-0ST	OC	9x14	2ft6in	4ft6in	12½T		15
1659	5. 9.30	4ft8½in	0-6-0ST	IC	14x20	3ft4in	9ft6in	29T		121
1684	24. 8.31	4ft8½in	0-4-0T	OC	12x18	3ft4in	5ft6in	23½T		93 102
1840	15.12.36	4ft8½in	0-4-0DM		40/44HP	2ft9in	5ft6in	10T		54
2207	25. 3.41	2ft0in	4wDM		20HP	1ft6in	2ft11in	3¼T	HUDSON/HUNSLET	88
2242/3	21. 5.41	2ft6in	0-4-0DM		50HP	2ft0in	4ft0in	8½T	MINES	39
2244/5	22. 7.41	2ft6in	0-4-0DM		50HP	2ft0in	4ft0in	8½T	MINES	39
2246/7	9.12.40	2ft6in	0-4-0DM		25HP	1ft8in	3ft0in	4½T	MINES	39
2384	30.6. 41	2ft0in	0-4-0ST	OC	6x 9	1ft8in	3ft0in	4¼T	WREN	90
2665/6	9. 2.42	2ft0in	4wDM		25HP	1ft6in	2ft11in	3¾T	HUDSON/HUNSLET	1 42
2805	2. 9.43	2ft0in	4wDM		20HP	1ft6in	2ft11in	3¾T	HUDSON/HUNSLET	107
3133	30. 8.44	4ft8½in	0-4-0DM		93/102HP	3ft4in	5ft6in	21T		38
3810	26. 2.54	4ft8½in	0-6-0ST	IC	18x26	4ft3in	11ft0in	48T	AUSTERITY	83
4524	16. 3.54	1ft6in	0-4-4-0DM		88HP	1ft8in	3ft0in	13¾T		27
6263	30.12.64	4ft8½in	0-4-0DH		195HP	3ft4in	5ft6in	25T		43
6342	22. 5.70	1ft10in	4wDH		28HP	1ft6in	2ft10in	3½T		17
6646	22.11.67	2ft6in	4wDH		60HP	2ft0in	4ft0in	8T		39
6647/8	29. 2.68	1000mm	4wDH		60HP	2ft0in	4ft0in	8T		39
7083	6.10.71	1ft10in	4wDH		28HP	1ft6in	2ft10in	3½T		17

7084	3.12.71	1ft10in	4wDH	28HP	1ft6in	2ft10in	3½T	17
7087	6.11.72	1ft10in	4wDH	28HP	1ft6in	2ft10in	3½T	17
7266/7	21. 3.72	2ft 0in	4wDM	29HP	1ft6in	2ft10in	3½T	112
7270	25. 7.72	2ft 0in	4wDM	29HP	1ft6in	2ft10in	3½T	112
7271	4. 9.72	2ft0in	4wDM	29HP	1ft6in	2ft10in	3½T	112
7272/3	19. 9.72	2ft0in	4wDM	29HP	1ft6in	2ft10in	3½T	112
7312/3	25. 1.73	2ft0in	4wDM	29HP	1ft6in	2ft10in	3½T	112
7317	27. 9.73	2ft0in	4wDM	29HP	1ft6in	2ft10in	3½T	112
7320/1	27. 9.73	2ft0in	4wDM	29HP	1ft6in	2ft10in	3½T	112

* Built as Tunnel Locomotives with removable chimney and canopy to enable the
engine to enter a heading 7ft6in high x 8ft6in wide.

HL - R & W HAWTHORN, LESLIE & CO LTD

2184	.91	4ft8½in	0-4-0ST	OC	12x18	3ft0in	5ft6in	20T	104
2234	.91	4ft8½in	0-4-0ST	OC	12x18	3ft0½in	5ft6in	20T	91
2399	.98	4ft8½in	0-4-0ST	OC	12x18	3ft0½in	5ft6in	20T	37
2400	.98	4ft8½in	0-4-0ST	OC	12x18	3ft0½in	5ft6in	20T	37
2420	.99	4ft8½in	2-4-0T	OC	12x18	3ft3in	11ft0in	24T	106
2599	.04	4ft8½in	0-4-0CT	OC	12x15	2ft10in	7ft0in	34T	37
2695	.07	4ft8½in	0-6-2T	OC	16x24	4ft0in	16ft9in	50T	14
2696	.07	4ft8½in	0-6-2T	OC	16x24	4ft0in	16ft9in	50T	14
2697	.07	4ft8½in	0-6-0T	OC	14x22	3ft10in	10ft0in	36T	14
2820	.10	4ft8½in	0-4-0ST	OC	12x18	3ft0½in	5ft6in	21T	37
2821	.10	4ft8½in	0-4-0ST	OC	12x18	3ft0½in	5ft6in	21T	37
2972	.12	4ft8½in	0-4-0ST	OC	14x22	3ft6in	5ft6in	27T	91
3159	.16	4ft8½in	0-4-0ST	OC	14x22	3ft6in	5ft6in	27T	93
3200	.16	4ft8½in	0-4-0ST	OC	14x22	3ft6in	5ft6in	27T	37
3201	.16	4ft8½in	0-4-0ST	OC	14x22	3ft6in	5ft6in	27T	37
3333	.18	4ft8½in	0-4-0ST	OC	14x22	3ft6in	5ft6in	27T	91
3360	.18	4ft8½in	0-4-0ST	OC	10x15	2ft10in	5ft0in	16T	123
3437	.19	4ft8½in	0-6-0ST	OC					102
3597	.26	4ft8½in	0-4-0ST	OC	12x20	3ft0½in	5ft6in	21T	9
3598	.26	4ft8½in	0-4-0ST	OC	12x20	3ft0½in	5ft6in	21T	9
3648	.26	4ft8½in	0-4-0ST	OC	12x20	3ft0½in	5ft6in	21T	9
3670	.27	4ft8½in	0-4-0ST	OC	14x22	3ft3in	5ft6in	28T	9

JF - JOHN FOWLER & CO (LEEDS) LTD

7958	8. 9.98	2ft0in	4wTG	"Class A4 Compound Geared Loco"					99
19425	11.31	4ft8½in	0-4-0DM	35HP			Petters		67
19645	8.32	4ft8½in	0-4-0DM	100HP		25T	Sanders	57 67	100
22288	2.38	4ft8½in	0-4-0DM	40HP			Sanders	81	98
22917	8.40	4ft8½in	0-4-0DM	150HP	3ft3in	5ft6in	29T	Sanders	34
22920	10.40	4ft8½in	0-4-0DM	150HP	3ft3in	5ft6in	29T	Sanders	128
22928	4.40	4ft8½in	0-4-0DM	80HP				Sanders	40
22935	2.41	4ft8½in	0-4-0DM	150HP	3ft3in	5ft6in	29T	Sanders	128
22986	9.42	4ft8½in	0-4-0DM	150HP	3ft3in	5ft6in	29T	Sanders	65
22998	3.43	4ft8½in	0-4-0DM	150HP	3ft3in	5ft6in	29T	Sanders	101
3900012	8.47	3ft0in	4wDM	40HP				Howard	40
3930037	12.49	3ft0in	4wDM	40HP	2ft0in	4ft0in	7¼T	Marshall	40
3930048	6.51	3ft0in	4wDM	40HP	2ft0in	4ft0in	7¼T	Marshall	46 40
4000001	9.45	4ft8½in	0-4-0DM	80HP					40
4100014	3.49	4ft8½in	0-4-0DM	80HP	3ft0in	5ft6in	25T	Sanders	101
4200021	1.48	4ft8½in	0-4-0DM	150HP	3ft3in	5ft6in	29T	Howard	87
4210005		4ft8½in	0-4-0DM	150HP					
4210082	2.53	4ft8½in	0-4-0DM	150HP					65
4210126	28. 3.57	4ft8½in	0-4-0DM	150HP					65
4210141	.58	4ft8½in	0-4-0DM	150HP					86
4210143	.58	4ft8½in	0-4-0DM	150HP					92
4210144	.58	4ft8½in	0-4-0DM	150HP					92
4210145	.58	4ft8½in	0-4-0DM	150HP					86

Jung - ARN. JUNG LOKOMOTIVFABRIK G.m.b.H

5189		600 mm	4wDM	42 68

K - KITSON & CO

1829	19. 2.72	4ft8½in	0-6-0ST	IC	13x20	3ft6in			106
3799	.98	4ft8½in	0-4-0ST	OC	14x21	3ft2½in	6ft0in	25½T	102

KS - KERR, STUART & CO LTD (Empty)

812	14. 3.03	1ft10in	0-4-2T	OC	7½x12	2ft3in	3ft0in	8¼T	Skylark	3 5
856	16. 7.04	2ft0in	0-4-2ST	OC	7 x12	2ft0in	3ft0in	6 T	Tattoo	68 100
1017	21. 2.08	2ft3in	0-4-0ST	OC	6 x 9	1ft8in	3ft0in	3¼T	Wren	71
1146	27. 1.12	3ft0in	0-4-2ST	OC	7 x12	2ft0in	3ft0in	6¼T	Tattoo	35
1169	22. 5.11	1ft10in	0-4-2T	OC	7½x12	2ft3in	3ft0in	7¾T	Skylark	3 5
1188	4. 1.11	2ft3in	0-4-0ST	OC	6 x 9	1ft8in	3ft0in	3¼T	Wren	71
1190	4. 8.11	2ft0in	0-4-0ST	OC	6 x 9	1ft8in	3ft0in	3¼T	Wren	35
1228	13. 9.11	3ft0in	0-4-2T	OC	9½x15	2ft2in	3ft9in	12½T	Waterloo	35
2390	27. 1.15	2ft0in	0-4-0ST	OC	6 x 9	1ft8in	3ft0in	3¼T	Wren	58
3065	5. 6.18	2ft0in	0-4-2ST	OC	7 x12	2ft0in	3ft0in	6½T	Tattoo	68 57 99
3090	17. 7.17	2ft0in	0-4-0ST	OC	6 x 9	1ft8in	3ft0in	3¼T	Wren	113
3102	18.12.17	2ft0in	0-4-0ST	OC	6 x 9	1ft8in	3ft0in	3¼T	Wren	58
3104	24. 4.18	2ft0in	0-4-0ST	OC	6 x 9	1ft8in	3ft0in	3¼T	Wren	90
3112	3 .9.18	4ft8½in	0-4-0ST	OC	15x20	3ft3in	5ft6in	22½T	Moss Bay	57 99
3123	5.10.18	4ft8½in	0-4-0ST	OC	15x20	3ft3in	5ft6in	22½T	Moss Bay	121
3128	31. 7.18	2ft0in	0-4-0ST	OC	6 x 9	1ft8in	3ft0in	3½T	Wren	90
4161	4. 4.21	2ft0in	0-4-0ST	OC	6 x 9	1ft8in	3ft0in	3½T	Wren	44
4250	31. 1.22	2ft0in	0-4-0ST	OC	6 x 9	1ft8in	3ft0in	3½T	Wren	31 32
4251	31. 1.22	2ft0in	0-4-0ST	OC	6 x 9	1ft8in	3ft0in	3½T	Wren	31 32 51 55
4255	4. 3.22	2ft0in	0-4-0ST	OC	6 x 9	1ft8in	3ft0in	3½T	Wren	98
4256	8. 3.22	2ft0in	0-4-0ST	OC	6 x 9	1ft8in	3ft0in	3½T	Wren	31 32
4258	9. 3.22	2ft0in	0-4-0ST	OC	6 x 9	1ft8in	3ft0in	3½T	Wren	31 32 51 55
4260	27. 3.22	2ft0in	0-4-0ST	OC	6 x 9	1ft8in	3ft0in	3½T	Wren	32
4265	27. 3.22	2ft0in	0-4-0ST	OC	6 x 9	1ft8in	3ft0in	3½T	Wren	32 51 55
4426	21.11.29	1ft8in	4wDM		30HP	2ft0in	3ft0in	5T	DX.1 (a)	1 81
4427	3. 8.29	2ft0in	4wDM		30HP	2ft0in	3ft0in	5T	DX.1 (a)	68
4468	24. 4.30	2ft0in	4wDM		30HP	2ft0in	3ft0in	4T	DX.1 (a)	1

(a) McLaren engine.

MH - MUIR HILL ENGINEERING LTD

	.25	4ft8½in	4wPM	3ft4in		2¼T	Fordson eng.	106
	.25	2ft0in	4wPM					33
A110	.25	2ft0in	4wPM	1ft7in	3ft3in		Fordson eng.	33
A125	.25	2ft0in	4wPM					62
A131	.25	2ft5½in	4wPM					19
A137	.26	4ft8½in	4wPM	3ft4in		4T	Fordson eng.	106
27	.27	4ft8½in	4wPM					98
33	.27	4ft8½in	4wPM					124

MW - MANNING WARDLE & CO LTD

16	31.10.60	4ft8½in	0-6-0ST	IC	11x17	3ft1in	10ft 3in	16T	'old I'	113
21	22. 1.61	4ft8½in	0-6-0ST	IC	11x17	3ft1in	10ft3in	16T	'old I'	114
50	20. 6.62	4ft8½in	0-6-0ST	IC	12x17	3ft1in	10ft3in	16T	'old I'	54
51	28. 6.62	4ft8½in	0-6-0ST	IC	12x17	3ft1in	10ft3in	16T	'old I'	113 119
66	30. 1.63	4ft8½in	0-6-0ST	IC	12x17	3ft1in	10ft3in	16T	'old I'	119
79	17. 6.63	4ft8½in	0-4-0ST	OC	9½x14	2ft8in	4ft9in	11T	E	78
128	23. 8.64	4ft8½in	0-6-0ST	IC	11x17	3ft1in	10ft3in	16T	'old I'	78
156	16. 2.65	4ft8½in	0-4-0ST	OC	9½x14	2ft8in	4ft9in	11T	E	78

213	9. 8.66	4ft8½in	0-4-0ST	OC	9½x14	2ft8in	4ft9in	11T	E			67
379	10. 1.72	4ft8½in	0-4-0ST	OC	9½x14	2ft8in	4ft9in	11T	E			54
461	29. 7.74	2ft6in	0-6-0	OC	7 x12	1ft8in	10ft0in	6½T	Special			13
503	1. 7.75	4ft8½in	0-4-0ST	OC	13x18	3ft0in	5ft6in?	19½T	I			135
594	15. 3.76	4ft8½in	0-4-0ST	OC	9x14	2ft9in	4ft9in	11T	E			54
595	5. 4.76	4ft8½in	0-6-0ST	IC	12x17	3ft1in	10ft9in	18½T	K			117
628	8. 9.76	4ft8½in	0-4-0ST	OC	9x14	2ft9in	4ft9in	11T	E			54
713	23. 1.79	4ft8½in	0-4-0ST	OC	9x14	2ft9in	4ft9in	11T	E			6
714	24. 1.79	4ft8½in	0-4-0ST	OC	9x14	2ft9in	4ft9in	11T	E			52
731	4. 5.81	4ft8½in	0-6-0ST	IC	13x18	3ft0in	11ft3in	19½T	L			106
746	26. 4.80	4ft8½in	0-6-0ST	IC	15x20	3ft9in	12ft0in	22½T	O			119
767	12. 5.81	4ft8½in	0-4-0ST	OC	10x16	2ft9in	4ft9in	15T	F			28
786	19. 8.81	4ft8½in	0-4-0ST	OC	9x14	2ft9in	4ft9in	11T	E			111
817	30.11.81	4ft8½in	0-6-0ST	IC	12x17	3ft1in	10ft9in	18½T	K			114
855	30.11.82	4ft8½in	0-4-0ST	OC	9x14	2ft9in	4ft9in	11T	E			52
891	29. 5.83	4ft8½in	0-6-0ST	IC	12x17	3ft1in	10ft9in	18½T	K			119
941	28. 3.85	4ft8½in	0-4-0ST	OC	8x14	2ft8in	4ft6in	10T	D			18
951	7. 1.85	4ft8½in	0-6-0ST	IC	14x20	3ft4in	12ft0in		Q			52
967	1. 4.85	4ft8½in	0-6-0ST	IC	12x17	3ft1in	10ft9in	18½T	K			18
994	28. 5.86	2ft6in	0-6-0	OC	7½x12	1ft8in	10ft0in		Special			13
999	1. 9.86	2ft8in	0-6-0ST	OC	7½x12	2ft4in	7ft6in	12½T	Special			129
1005	15. 6.87	4ft8½in	0-6-0T	IC	13x18	3ft0in	11ft6in	22½T	Special	M		115
1018	9. 5.87	4ft8½in	0-4-0ST	OC	10x16	2ft9in	4ft9in	15T	F			52
1036	3.11.87	4ft8½in	0-4-0ST	OC	10x16	2ft9in	4ft9in	15T	F			52
1049	15. 2.88	4ft8½in	0-6-0ST	IC	12x17	3ft0in	10ft9in	18½T	K		40	50
1051	28. 1.88	4ft8½in	0-4-0ST	OC	10x16	2ft9in	4ft9in	15T	F			52
1068	21. 6.88	4ft8½in	0-6-0ST	IC	12x17	3ft0in	10ft9in	18½T	K			116
1079	19.12.88	4ft8½in	0-6-0ST	IC	12x18	3ft0in	11ft3in	19½T	L			77
1087	1. 7.89	4ft8½in	0-4-0ST	OC	9x14	2ft9in	4ft9in	11T	E			51
1090	19.12.88	4ft8½in	0-4-0ST	OC	12x18	3ft0in	5ft4in	19½T	H			52
1134	21. 4.90	4ft8½in	0-6-0ST	IC	12x17	3ft0in	10ft9in	18½T	K		106	113
1135	21. 4.90	4ft8½in	0-4-0ST	OC	9½x14	2ft9in	4ft9in	11T	E			117
1153	7. 4.90	4ft8½in	0-6-0ST	IC	12x18	3ft0in	10ft9in	19½T	L		50	91
1196	21. 8.90	4ft8½in	0-6-0T	IC	14x22	3ft9in	12ft0in	35T	Special			117
1228	25. 3.95	4ft8½in	0-6-0ST	IC	12x18	3ft0in	10ft9in	19½T	L			121
1235	16.10.91	4ft8½in	0-6-0ST	IC	12x17	3ft0in	10ft9in	18½T	K			46
1237	20. 6.92	4ft8½in	0-6-0ST	IC	12x17	3ft0in	10ft9in	18½T	K			78
1279	5. 4.95	4ft8½in	0-4-0ST	OC	9x14	2ft9in	4ft9in	11T	E			117
1300	8. 5.95	4ft8½in	0-4-0ST	OC	10x16	2ft10in	4ft9in	15T	F			117
1302	22. 5.95	4ft8½in	0-6-0ST	IC	12x18	3ft0in	10ft9in	19½T	L			117
1306	29. 4.95	4ft8½in	0-4-0ST	OC	9x14	2ft9in	4ft9in	11T	E			117
1342	4. 6.97	4ft8½in	0-4-0ST	OC	10x16	2ft9in	4ft9in	15¾T	F			52
1361	11.11.97	1ft11½in	2-6-2T	OC	10½x16	2ft9in	6ft0in	27¼T	Special			36
1362	11.11.97	1ft11½in	2-6-2T	OC	10½x16	2ft9in	6ft6in	27¼T	Special			36
1363	11.11.97	1ft11½in	2-6-2T	OC	10½x16	2ft9in	6ft6in	27¼T	Special			36
1365	30. 3.98	4ft8½in	0-6-0ST	IC	12x18	3ft0in	10ft9in	19½T	L			130
1392	13.10.98	4ft8½in	0-6-0ST	IC	13x18	3ft0in	11ft6in	22½T	M			115
1400	13. 3.99	4ft8½in	0-6-0ST	IC	12x17	3ft0in	10ft0in	19T	K			26
1420	17. 9.99	4ft8½in	0-4-0ST	OC	10x16	2ft9in	4ft9in	15¾T	F			31
1425	24.11.98	4ft8½in	0-6-0ST	IC	12x18	3ft0in	10ft9in	19½T	L			98
1484	1. 3.01	4ft8½in	0-6-0ST	IC	13x18	3ft0in	11ft6in	22½T	M			78
1547	16.12.01	2ft6in	0-6-2ST	OC	7½x12	1ft8in	6ft0in	10T	Special			13
1552	21. 1.02	3ft6in	0-4-0ST	OC	9½x14	2ft6in	4ft6in	11T	Special			125
1555	28. 2.02	4ft8½in	0-6-0ST	IC	14x20	3ft6in	12ft0in		Q			116
1579	30.9. 02	4ft8½in	0-6-0ST	IC	12x18	3ft0in	10ft9in	20½T	L			111
1584	20.10.02	4ft8½in	0-6-0ST	IC	12x18	3ft0in	10ft9in	20½T	L			111
1585	1.12.02	4ft8½in	0-6-0ST	IC	12x18	3ft0in	10ft9in	20½T	L			111
1586	1.12.02	4ft8½in	0-6-0ST	IC	12x18	3ft0in	10ft9in	20½T	L			111
1587	13.10.02	4ft8½in	0-4-0ST	OC	10x16	2ft9in	4ft9in	15¾T	F			111
1588	15.10.02	4ft8½in	0-4-0ST	OC	10x16	2ft9in	4ft9in	15¾T	F			111
1592	16.12.02	4ft8½in	0-6-0ST	IC	12x18	3ft0in	10ft9in	20½T	L			111
1593	22.12.02	4ft8½in	0-6-0ST	IC	12x18	3ft0in	10ft9in	20½T	L			111
1601	8. 5. 03	4ft8½in	0-6-0ST	IC	12x18	3ft0in	10ft9in	20½T	L			111

1620	22.12.03	4ft8½in	0-6-0ST	IC	13x18	3ft0in	11ft6in		'Spl M'	121
1691	10. 7.07	4ft8½in	0-6-0ST	IC	12x18	3ft0in	10ft9in	20½T	L	78
1726	9. 1.08	4ft8½in	0-6-0ST	IC	13x18	3ft0in	11ft6in	22½T	M	115
1733	25. 5.08	4ft8½in	0-6-0ST	IC	13x18	3ft0in	11ft6in	22½T	M	78
1793	26. 2.12	4ft8½in	0-6-0ST	IC	12x18	3ft0in	10ft9in	20½T	L	77
1854	17. 8.14	2ft8in	0-4-0ST	OC	9½x14	2ft4in	4ft6in	15T	'Spl'	129
1954	8. 6.18	4ft8½in	0-4-0PM		180HP	3ft0in	6ft0in	28T	(a)	67 69
1966	22. 5.18	4ft8½in	0-6-0ST	IC	14x20	3ft6in	12ft0in		'Spl Q'	77
1970	17. 4.19	4ft8½in	0-6-0ST	IC	12x18	3ft0in	10ft9in	20T		106
2042	23. 7.25	1ft11½in	2-6-2T	OC	10½x16	2ft9in	6ft6in	27¾T	'Spl'	36
2046	13. 7.26	4ft8½in	0-6-0ST	IC`	13x18	3ft0in	11ft6in			89

N - NEILSON & CO

81	.54	4ft0in	0-4-0ST	OC	11x18	3ft6in		13T	15
82	.54	4ft0in	0-4-0ST	OC	11x18	3ft6in		13T	15
370	.56	4ft8½in	0-4-0ST	OC	11x18	3ft6in		13T	73
540	.59	4ft0in	0-6-0ST	OC	12x18	3ft6in			15
1660	.71	3ft6in	0-4-0ST	OC	10½x18	3ft1in	5ft0in	13T	14
1661	.71	3ft6in	0-4-0ST	OC	10½x18	3ft1in	5ft0in	13T	14

OK - ORENSTEIN & KOPPEL A G

		1ft8in	0-4-0WT	OC						2
		2ft0in	0-4-0WT	OC						1
4470	.31	2ft	4wPM		8½HP	1ft6in	2ft7½in	2.3T	M	126
4586	.32	2ft	4wPM		8½HP	1ft6in	2ft7½in	2.3T	M	4 5
5674	.34	2ft	4wDM							16
5677	.34	2ft	4wDM							1 16
6191		2ft	4wDM							107
7736	.38	2ft	4wDM							103
9239		2ft	0-6-0WT	OC						124
10408		2ft	4wDM							1
20777	.36	1ft11½in	0-4-0DM		35HP	1ft6in	3ft3½in	7T	RL.3	125
21160	.38	1ft11½in	0-4-0DM		35HP	1ft6in	3ft3½in	7T	RL.3	125

P - PECKETT & SONS LTD

449	22. 4.86	4ft8½in	0-4-0ST	OC						117
451	31. 5.86	4ft8½in	0-4-0ST	OC	10x14	2ft6in	5ft0in	16T	M3	104
459	23.12.87	4ft8½in	0-6-0ST	OC	14x20	3ft7in	10ft0in	33T	B1	96
466	31. 1.89	4ft8½in	0-6-0ST	OC	14x20	3ft7in	10ft0in	33T	B1	96
505	8. 2.93	4ft8½in	0-4-0ST	OC	10x14	2ft6in	5ft0in	17T	M4	25
520	8. 6.91	4ft8½in	0-4-0ST	OC	12x18	3ft0in	5ft3in	21T	R1	85 86 101
526	28.12.93	4ft8½in	0-6-0ST	OC	14x20	3ft7in	10ft0in	33T	B1	96
528	14. 6.93	4ft8½in	0-4-0ST	OC	12x18	2ft10in	5ft3in	21T	xL	127
581	28.12.94	4ft8½in	0-4-0ST	OC	14x20	3ft2in	5ft6in	25T	W4	105
686	.98	4ft8½in	0-4-0ST	OC	12x18	2ft11in	5ft3in	21T	R1	128 135
687	24. 2.98	4ft8½in	0-4-0ST	OC	12x18	2ft11in	5ft3in	21T	R1	128 135
690	14. 2.98	4ft8½in	0-4-0ST	OC	14x20	3ft2in	5ft6in	25T	W4	117
709	15. 4.98	4ft8½in	0-4-0ST	OC	10x14	2ft9in	5ft0in	17T	M4	96
718-23	.98	4ft8½in	0-6-0ST	OC	14x20	3ft7in	10ft0in	34T	B1	117
729-30	.98	4ft8½in	0-4-0ST	OC	10x14	2ft6in	5ft0in	17T	M4	117
737	10. 8.99	4ft8½in	0-4-0ST	OC	14x20	3ft2in	5ft6in	25T	W4	99
751	18.11.98	4ft8½in	0-6-0ST	OC	14x20	3ft7in	10ft0in	34T	B1	135
783	24. 3.99	4ft6in	0-4-0ST	OC	10x14	2ft6in	5ft0in	17T	M4	20 34 36
784	6. 4.99	4ft6in	0-4-0ST	OC	10x14	2ft6in	5ft0in	17T	M4	34 36 40
808	19. 2.00	4ft8½in	0-6-0ST	OC	14x20	3ft7in	10ft0in	34T	B1	96

No.	Date	Gauge	Type	Cyl			Wt	Name/Class	Refs
825	5. 4.00	4ft8½in	0-6-0ST IC	16x22	4ft0in	11ft9in	38T	'Judith'	84
864	24.10.01	4ft8½in	0-4-0ST OC	14x20	3ft2in	5ft6in	25T	W4	104
920	29. 7.02	4ft8½in	0-4-0ST OC	14x20	3ft2in	5ft6in	25T	W4	127
1006	.04	4ft8½in	0-6-0ST OC	14x20	3ft7in	10ft0in	34T	B1	96
1021	.04	2ft6in	0-4-0ST OC	9 x14	2ft3in	4ft3in	13½T	9"	66
1030	.04	2ft0in	0-4-0ST OC	7 x10	1ft8in	3ft6in	7¼T	7"	70
1041	15. 1.06	4ft8½in	0-6-0ST IC	16x22	3ft10in	11ft9in	38T	x	84 93
1067	29. 7.05	4ft8½in	0-6-0ST IC	14x20	3ft2in	10ft6in	30T	C	94
1093	9. 8.07	4ft8½in	0-6-0ST OC	14x20	3ft7in	10ft0in	34T	B2	96
1163	.08	4ft8½in	0-4-0ST OC						60 64
1191	8. 8.10	4ft8½in	0-4-0ST OC	10x15	2ft9in	5ft0in	18T	M5	101
1221	25.1. 11	4ft8½in	0-4-0ST OC	10x15	2ft9in	5ft0in	18T	M5	104
1243	10.11.10	4ft8½in	0-6-0ST OC	15x21	3ft7in	12ft0in	36½T	FA	96
1244	24.11.10	4ft8½in	0-6-0ST OC	15x21	3ft7in	12ft0in	36½T	FA	96
1264	1. 8.13	4ft8½in	0-6-0ST OC	14x20	3ft7in	10ft0in	34T	B2	96
1267	24. 6.12	4ft8½in	0-4-0ST OC	10x15	2ft9in	5ft0in	18T	M5	103
1301	27.11.12	4ft8½in	0-4-0ST OC	10x15	2ft9in	5ft0in	18T	M5	43
1377	2.10.14	4ft8½in	0-6-0ST OC	14x20	3ft7in	10ft0in	34T	B2	96
1412	22.10.15	2ft0in	0-6-0ST OC	7 x10	1ft8in	6ft6in	7½T	'Jurassic'	65
1448	30. 3.17	4ft8½in	0-4-0ST OC	10x15	2ft9in	5ft0in	18T	M5	12
1530	15.12.19	4ft8½in	0-4-0ST OC	14x20	3ft2in	5ft6in	28T	W5	9
1545	20.10.19	4ft8½in	0-4-0ST OC	12x18	3ft0in	5ft3in	23T	R2	89
1546	14. 1.20	2ft8½in	0-4-0ST OC	9 x14	2ft3in	4ft3in	13½T	9"	108
1611	26. 3.23	4ft8½in	0-4-0ST OC	14x20	3ft2in	5ft6in	28T	W5	80 104
1612	4.10.22	4ft8½in	0-4-0ST OC	7 x12	2ft0in	4ft6in	11½T	'Yorktown'	105
1636	.29	4ft8½in	0-6-0ST OC						102
1692	16. 7.25	2ft8in	0-4-2ST OC	10x15	2ft6in	(9ft8in)	21T	Spl M5	129
1717	19. 4.26	4ft8½in	0-6-0ST OC	12x18	3ft0in	10ft0in	26T	Spl R2	46
1721	13. 7.26	4ft8½in	0-6-0ST OC	15x21	3ft7in	12ft0in	36½T	FA	96
1788	10. 9.29	4ft8½in	0-4-0ST OC	12x20	3ft0in	5ft3in	23T	R3	93 102 108
1808	28. 2.30	2ft8in	0-4-2ST OC	8 x12	2ft3in	(8ft10in)	18T	Spl 8"	129
1877	3.10.34	4ft8½in	0-6-0ST OC	15x21	3ft7in	12ft0in	36½T	FA	96
1878	22.10.34	4ft8½in	0-6-0ST OC	15x21	3ft7in	12ft0in	36½T	FA	96
1904	.36	4ft8½in	0-4-0ST OC	10x15	2ft9in	5ft0in	18T	M5	58
1940	.37	4ft8½in	0-6-0ST OC	15x21	3ft7in	12ft0in	36½T	FA	82 96 102
1967	.39	4ft8½in	0-4-0ST OC	14x22	3ft2in	5ft6in	29T	W6	104
2012	.41	4ft8½in	0-4-0ST OC	7 x12	2ft0in	4ft6in	11½T	'Yorktown'	128
2031	.42	4ft8½in	0-4-0ST OC	10x15	2ft9in	5ft0in	18T	M5	29 43
2035-38	.43	4ft8½in	0-6-0ST OC	15x21	3ft7in	12ft0in	36½T	FA	96
2074	.46	4ft8½in	0-4-0ST OC	10x15	2ft9in	5ft0in	18T	M5	43
5000	.56	4ft8½in	0-4-0DM	200HP	3ft2in	5ft6in	32T	G20	80
5002	.57	4ft8½in	0-4-0DM	100HP	3ft0in	5ft0in	17T	G10	80

R&R - RANSOMES & RAPIER LTD

73	21. 5.36	2ft0in	4wDM	26HP					90

RP - RUSTON, PROCTOR & CO LTD

(50823	7. 6.15?)	1000mm	4w PM	10HP	1ft3in	2ft5½in	4T		8
52124	20.3.18	2ft6in	4w PM	10HP	1ft3in	2ft5½in	4T		122

RR - ROLLS ROYCE LTD

10217	15. 4.65	4ft8½in	0-6-0DH	325HP	3ft6in	9ft8in	48T	(a)	96
10218	11. 5.65	4ft8½in	0-6-0DH	325HP	3ft6in	9ft8in	48T	(a)	96
10219	16. 6.65	4ft8½in	0-6-0DH	325HP	3ft6in	9ft8in	48T	(a)	96
10220	29. 6.65	4ft8½in	0-6-0DH	325HP	3ft6in	9ft8in	48T	(a)	96
10221	29. 7.65	4ft8½in	0-6-0DH	325HP	3ft6in	9ft8in	48T	(a)	96

(a) Rolls-Royce C8SFL engine.

RS - ROBERT STEPHENSON & CO LTD

No.	Date	Gauge	Type	Cyl arr	Cyl size	Driver	Length	Wt	Refs
619	.47	4ft8½in	0-6-0	IC	15x24	5ft6in			25 135
620	.47	4ft8½in	0-6-0	IC	15x24	5ft6in			135
2383	.79	4ft8½in	0-6-0T	IC	14x18	3ft6in	10ft6in	21T	51 106 120
3894	.25	4ft8½in	2-8-0	OC	21x28	4ft7in	17ft6in	111T	102

RSH - ROBERT STEPHENSON & HAWTHORNS LTD

No.	Date	Gauge	Type	Cyl arr	Cyl size	Driver	Length	Wt	Refs
7169	.44	4ft8½in	0-6-0ST	IC	18x26	4ft3in	11ft0in	48T	62
7544	.49	4ft8½in	0-4-0ST	OC	10x15	2ft10in	5ft0in	17T	123
7645	.49	4ft8½in	0-4-0ST	OC	10x15	2ft10in	5ft0in	17T	123
7921	.57	4ft8½in	0-4-0DM	156HP				(DC 2588)	82

RWH - R & W HAWTHORN

No.	Date	Gauge	Type	Cyl arr	Cyl size	Driver	Refs
2040	.85	4ft8½in	0-4-0ST	OC	12x18	3ft0in	105

SS - SHARP, STEWART & CO LTD (and predecessors)

No.	Date	Gauge	Type	Cyl arr	Cyl size	Driver	Length	Wt	Refs
995	.57	4ft8½in	0-6-0ST	IC	16x24	4ft6in	13ft0in		73
1017	.57	4ft8½in	2-2-2WT	IC	14x18	5ft7in	15ft0in	23T	106
1677	.66	4ft8½in	0-6-0ST	IC	17x24	4ft7in	12ft8in	36T	73
1707	.66	4ft8½in	2-2-2WT	IC	15x18	5ft7in	15ft0in	26T	106
2262	.72	4ft8½in	0-6-0ST	IC	17x24	4ft7in	12ft8in	36T	73
2578	.76	4ft8½in	2-4-0T	IC	14x18	4ft6in	12ft5in	24½T	106
3472	.88	4ft8½in	0-6-0T	IC	13x20	3ft0in			115
3478	.88	4ft8½in	0-6-0T	IC	13x20	3ft0in			52

S - SENTINEL (SHREWSBURY) LTD

No.	Date	Gauge	Type	Drive	Cyl	a	b	Wt	HP	Trans	Refs
5644	.23	(4ft8½in)	2-2-0VBT	VCG							44
6090	.25	4ft8½in	4wVBT	VCG(4)	6¾x9		7ft0in	30T	200HP	DE	57 67
6219CH	c.27	4ft8½in	0-4-0VBT	VCG							69 100
6520	.27	4ft8½in	4wVBT	VCG	6¾x9			12T		BE	6
7492	.28	4ft8½in	4wVBT	VCG	6¾x9	2ft6in	4ft9in	17T	100HP	BE	84 87
9374	.47	4ft8½in	4wVBT	VCG	6¾x9	2ft6in	4ft9in	24T	100HP	BE57	69 102
9386	.48	4ft8½in	4wVBT	VCG	6¾x9	2ft6in	4ft9in	24T	100HP	BE	57
9387	.48	4ft8½in	4wVBT	VCG	6¾x9	2ft6in	4ft9in	24T	100HP	BE	57 64
9391	.49	4ft8½in	4wVBT	VCG	6¾x9	2ft6in	4ft9in	24T	100HP	BE	57 100
9398	.50	4ft8½in	4wVBT	VCG	6¾x9	2ft6in	4ft9in	24T	100HP	BE	69
10005	8. 9.59	4ft8½in	4wDH		256HP	3ft2in	6ft6in	34T	CD	(a)	89
10023	.60	4ft8½in	4wDH		256HP	3ft2in	6ft6in	34T	CD	(a)	89
10048	15.12.60	4ft8½in	4wDH		256HP	3ft2in	6ft6in	34T	CD	(a)	89
10148	24.10.63	4ft8½in	0-6-0DH		325HP	3ft6in	9ft8in	48T	SR	(b)	96
10149	10.12.63	4ft8½in	0-6-0DH		325HP	3ft6in	9ft8in	48T	SR	(b)	96
10150	19.11.63	4ft8½in	0-6-0DH		325HP	3ft6in	9ft8in	48T	SR	(b)	96
10151	26.11.63	4ft8½in	0-6-0DH		325HP	3ft6in	9ft8in	48T	SR	(b)	96

(a) Rolls-Royce C6SFL engine
(b) Rolls-Royce C8SFL engine

TH - THOMAS HILL (ROTHERHAM) LTD

114V	6. 2.62	4ft8½in	4wDH	170HP	3ft2in	5ft3in	30T	A	(a)	91
125V	26.8. 63	4ft8½in	4wDH	170HP	3ft2in	5ft3in	28T	A	(a)	27
133C	31.12.63	4ft8½in	4wDH	178HP	2ft6in	4ft9in	25T	1SDC	(a)	57
136C	2. 3.64	4ft8½in	4wDH	178HP	2ft6in	4ft9in	25T	1SDC	(a)	57
152V	27. 5.65	4ft8½in	4wDH	178HP	2ft6in	4ft9in	25T	*	(a)	57
200V	25.11.68	4ft8½in	4wDH	210HP	3ft2in	5ft3in	34T	-		57

* Low Bridge Type Light V

(a) Rolls-Royce C6NFL engine

VF - VULCAN FOUNDRY LTD

798	.76	4ft8½in	0-4-0ST	OC	11x17	3ft0in				57 100
4195	.27	4ft8½in	0-6-0T	IC	18x26	4ft7in	16ft6in	49½T		62 102
D 77	.47	4ft8½in	0-4-0DM						(DC 2251)	82
D 98	.49	4ft8½in	0-4-0DM						(DC 2269)	41
D297	.56	4ft8½in	0-4-0DM						(DC 2583)	82

WB - W G BAGNALL LTD

300	1.80	2ft0in	0-4-0T	IC	5 x7½				58
566	12.83	3ft0in	0-6-0T	OC	7½x10				40
970	4.88	1ft11½in	0-4-2T	OC	5 x7½	1ft3in	3ft0in		53 122
1432	2.95	4ft8½in	0-4-0ST	OC	12x18	3ft0in	5ft6in	17¾T	86
1434	11.94	3ft0in	0-4-0ST	OC	8 x12	2ft0in			50
1480	9.97	3ft0in	0-4-0ST	OC	8 x12	2ft0in			50
1493-6	12.96	4ft8½in	0-4-0ST	OC	10x15	2ft9in	5ft0in		123 128 130 135
1663	11.02	1ft11in	0-4-0ST	OC	6½x10	1ft8in			12
1701	4.03	2ft6in	0-4-0ST	OC	7½x12	1ft10in			66
1725	6.03	2ft0in	0-4-0ST	OC	6 x 9	1ft7in			65
1760	5.06	1ft10¾in	0-4-0ST	OC	7 x12	1ft9in	3ft6in	7¾T	8
1884	.08	4ft8½in	0-4-0ST	OC	12x18	3ft0in	5ft0in	18T	93 101
2043	.18	2ft0in	0-4-0ST	OC	6 x 9	1ft7in	3ft0in	5¼T	56
2044	.18	2ft0in	0-4-0ST	OC	6 x 9	1ft7in	3ft0in	5¼T	80
2049	.18	2ft0in	0-4-0ST	OC	6 x 9	1ft7in	3ft0in	5¼T	80
2473	.32	4ft8½in	0-4-0F	OC	18½x18	3ft0in	5ft6in	25T	102
2572	.37	4ft8½in	0-4-0ST	OC	10x16	2ft9in	5ft0in	16½T	6
2596	.38	4ft8½in	0-4-0ST	OC	14x22	3ft6in	5ft6in	27T	121
2668	5.42	4ft8½in	0-6-0ST	OC	15x22	3ft4in	10ft0in	38½T	102
2962	.50	4ft8½in	0-4-0ST	OC	14½x22	3ft6in	5ft6in	27T	11 37
2994	.50	4ft8½in	0-6-0ST	OC	18x26	4ft3in	11ft0in	55½T	74
2996	.51	4ft8½in	0-6-0ST	OC	18x26	4ft3in	11ft0in	55½T	74
3058	1.54	4ft8½in	0-4-0ST	OC	10x16	2ft9in	5ft0in	16¾T	6
3121	5.57	4ft8½in	0-4-0F	OC	18½x18	3ft0in	5ft6in	25T	34

YE - YORKSHIRE ENGINE CO LTD

757	23.11.03	2ft6in	2-6-2ST	OC	6 x14	2ft6in	5ft6in	11T		13
2719	7. 7.58	4ft8½in	0-6-0DE		400HP			49T	Janus (a)	88
2725	21.11.58	4ft8½in	0-6-0DE		400HP			49T	Janus (a)	88
2741	20. 3.59	4ft8½in	0-6-0DE		400HP			49T	Janus (a)	88

(a) Two Rolls-Royce C6SFL engines per loco

Location index

This index is intended to provide a quick means of locating the entry relevant to any operator or location which is listed in this book. Both latest and former titles are listed as are the names of quarries and other works, where these differ from the title used by the operators. All titles are abbreviated. Numbers given below refer to page numbers H.37 , etc.

Cornwall

Locomotive worked systems

S.ANDREW & SON,REDRUTH

1   An old established steel stock holder and plant dealer (at SW 703412).

Gauge: 2ft 0in

-	4wPM	(MR?)	(a) (1)

(a) ex   ?   (1) to South Crofty Ltd ,hire,c/1950;retd;
                                         sold c/1968

A.R.C.(SOUTH WESTERN) LTD

2   Penlee Quarries,Newlyn (f.Penlee Quarries Ltd)

Quarrying commenced in the 1890's;the tramway was laid c/1900. Stone from a
cliffside quarry was loaded into a crushing plant which discharged the crushed
stone into wagons on the tramway below.These were then hauled along the sea wall
for about ¾ mile to the quayside to discharge into vessels.Traffic was heavy when
a ship was at the quay.
Track was single from the storage hopper to a secondary loading point,thence
double to the quay.The quarry itself may have been rail served at an earlier time.
Stone from Castle-an-Dinas quarry (4 miles north of Penzance) was brought down
by lorry to the crushing plant also.
Rail traffic ceased from 31/7/1972,the system being replaced by a conveyor belt.
The loco shed is at SW 467281.

   Ref: IRR 20 (8/1968), p269ff

Gauge: 2ft 0in

(PENLEE)	(KOPPEL until c1916)	0-4-0WT	OC	OK		c1900	New	Pvd on site
	-	0-4-0DM		BLW		c1918	(a)	Scr c/1951
	-	4wDM		KS	4426	1929	(b)	(1)
"LM 1"	-	4wDM		KS	4468	1930	New	(2)
	-	4wDM		OK	5677			(3)
"LM 4"	-	4wDM		OK	10408			(4)
"LM 2"	-	4wDM		HE	2665	1942	(c)	(2)
"LM 3"	PENLEE	4wDM		HE	2666	1942	(d)	(5)
"LM 37"	-	4wDM		RH	177643	1936	(e)	s/s
LM 38		4wDM		FH	2401	1941	(f)	(6)
"LM 40"	J.W.JENKIN	4wDM		RH	375315	1954	New	(8)
LM 39	T.W.LEWIS	4wDM		RH	375316	1954	New	(8)
"LM 28"	-	4wDM		RH	229655	1944	(g)	(7)
"LM 24"	-	4wDM		RH	175412	1936	(h)	(2)
"LM 42"	No.2	4wDM		RH	200748	1940	(j)	(8)
"LM 30"	-	4wDM		RH	229656	1944	(k)	
"LM 44"	(YARD No.AD574)	4wDM		RH	246793	1947	(m)	s/s
"LM 45"	(YARD No.AD573)	4wDM		RH	213848	1942	(n)	
"LM 46"	-	4wDM		RH	221592	1943	(o)	s/s
"LM 47"	-	4wDM		RH	287664	1951	(p)	
	-	4wDM		RH	264240	1949	(q)	Scr c/1972
	-	4wDM		RH	224310	1943	(q)	Scr c/1972
	-	4wDM		RH	213858	1942	(q)	Scr c/1972
	-	4wDM		RH	221591	1943	(q)	Scr c/1972

Note: The "LM xx" series of running numbers are alloted in the ARC records,but few of
      the locos appeared to carry them.
      In the following footnotes "Malvern Works" refers to the ARC central plant
      workshops and depot at Malvern,Worcs.

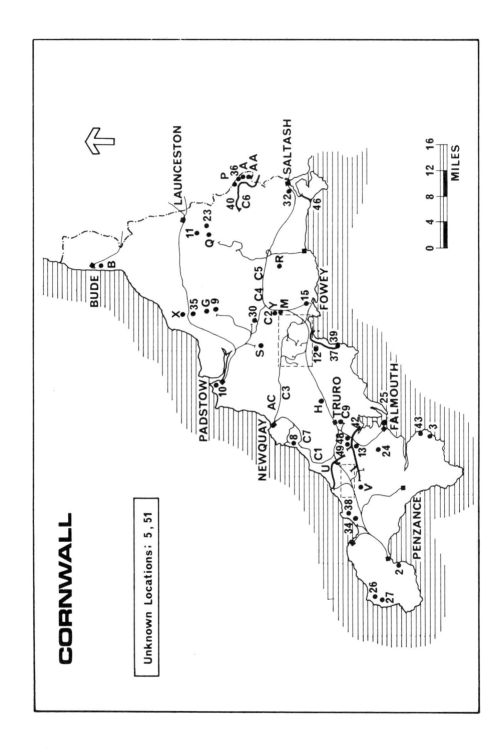

CORNWALL

Unknown Locations: 5, 51

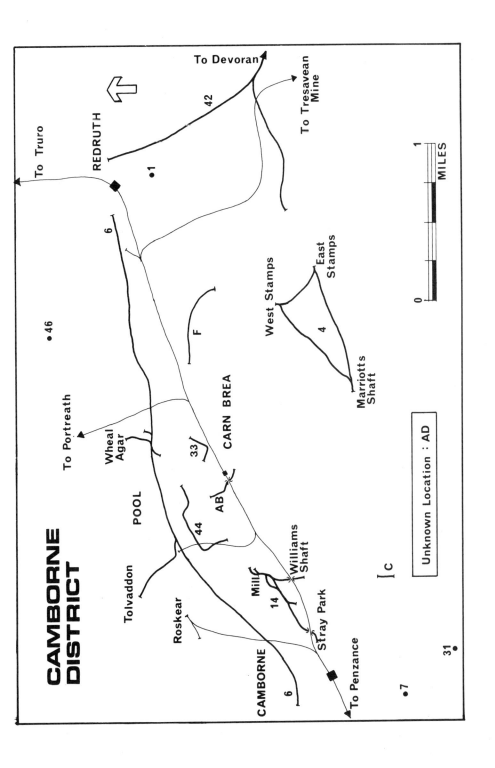

CAMBORNE DISTRICT

To Truro

To Devoran

To Tresavean Mine

REDRUTH

•1

42

•46

6

To Portreath

West Stamps

East Stamps

Marriott's Shaft

4

F

Wheal Agar

POOL

Tolvaddon

33

CARN BREA

AB

44

Roskear

Mill

Williams Shaft

14

Stray Park

CAMBORNE

6

To Penzance

•7

31 •

Unknown Location : AD

0   1
MILES

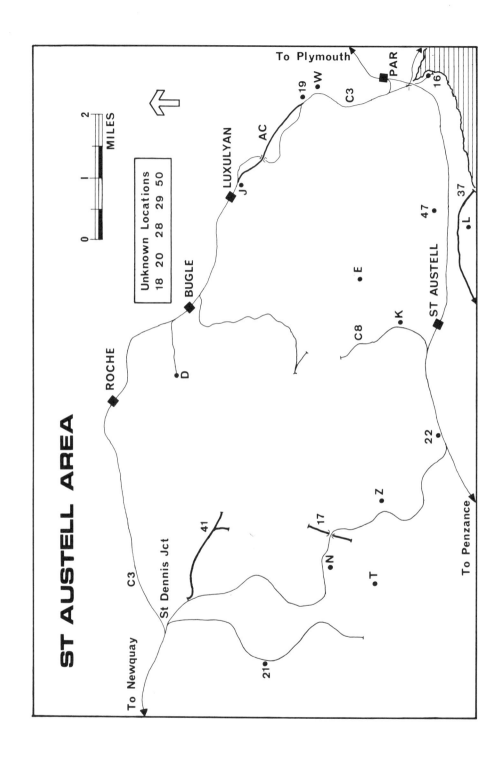

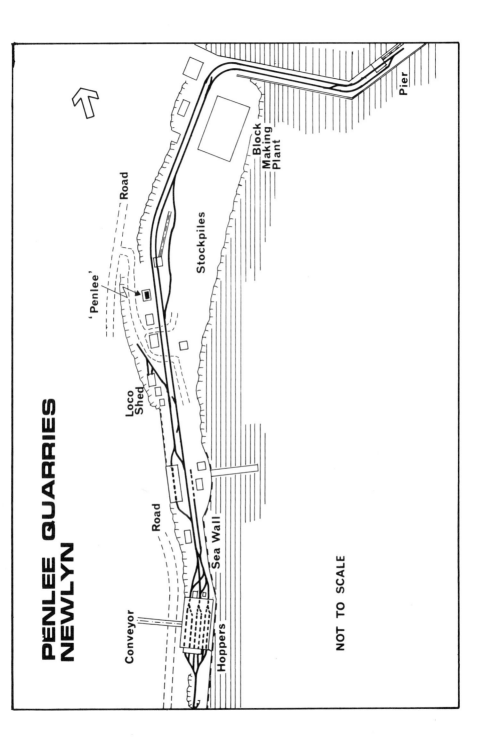

PENLEE QUARRIES NEWLYN

Conveyor

Road

Hoppers

Sea Wall

Loco Shed

'Penlee'

Road

Stockpiles

Block Making Plant

Pier

NOT TO SCALE

(a) ex WDLR,via Honeywill Bros Ltd,10/1924
(b) ex J.Arnold & Sons Ltd,Chipping
    Sodbury,Glos ,10/1947
(c) ex Tarslag Ltd,Winslow,Bucks,1/1947
(d) ex Tarslag Ltd,Winslow,Bucks,1/1947;
    to Malvern Works,5/1954;thence to
    BQC Lydd,Kent;ex Lydd,/1958
(e) ex St.Keverne & Associated Quarries Ltd,
    Porthoustock,/1949
(f) ex ARC Carreg-y-Llam Quarries,Caerns, .
    7/1951;to Malvern Works,/1954;thence
    to St.Keverne,3/1956;ex St.Keverne
    9/1961
(g) ex ARC Borough Green Quarry,Kent,9/1955
(h) ex ARC Borough Green Quarry,Kent,via
    Malvern Works,10/1956
(j) ex Malvern Works,7/1961;f.Bessacarr
    Gravel Co Ltd,Yorks WR
(k) ex Malvern Works,9/1961;prev.at St.Keverne
(m) ex MacSalvors Ltd,Pool,11/1962;f.
    Admiralty
(n) ex MacSalvors Ltd,Pool,11/1962;f.
    Admiralty,Carfin
(o) ex MacSalvors Ltd,Pool,c8/1963;prev.
    H.Orchard & Sons,dealers,Par;f.
    ECLP Park Works,St.Neot
(p) ex Geo Wimpey & Co Ltd,contrs,12/1964
(q) ex South Crofty Ltd,Pool,/1971

(1) to Malvern Works for scrap,c/1957
(2) Scr 3/1965 and parts sold to Meyer
    Newman & Co Ltd,St.Erth station
(3) to St.Keverne,loan & return;to Malvern
    Works
(4) to Malvern Works,1/1953;scr /1953
(5) to C.T.Shears,Winkleigh Aerodrome,
    Devon for preservation,8/1967
(6) to ? ,Redruth,for scrap c/1966
(7) to Malvern Works,5/1958;to Bredonvale
    Products Co Ltd,Defford,Worcs,11/1959
(8) to Llanberis Lake Railway Co , Gwynedd,
    2/1975

Rosenython Quarry,St.Keverne (f.West of England Road-Metal Co.Ltd.)

3   A short line about 40 yards in length for transferring stone from the hoppers to
      the tops of the storage bins;there are two lines in the form of a cross. The
      hoppers supply either road vehicles or ships (SW 810215)
      Ref: IRR 20 (8/1968) p269

Gauge: 2ft 0in
                (NEDDY)   4wDM(f.4wPM) L 30947 1947 (a)
      LM 41   4wDM   L 51509 1960 New

Parts of L 30202 ex St.Keverne & Associated Quarries Ltd were used to repair L 30947,
(a) ex L, 4/1948   c/1959

BASSET MINES LTD.,REDRUTH

4   An amalgamation in 1/1896 of South Frances United and Wheal Basset. A lengthy
      tramway connected Marriott's shaft (SW 680374) with East Basset Stamps (SW 690398)
      and with West Basset Stamps (SW 688403). The two stamps,on opposite sides of a
      valley,were linked by a third line,thus forming a triangle,which descended to the
      valley bottom and ascended again by a pair of inclines. Much of the routes and
      the mines and stamps buildings remain.The company went into liquidation 31/12/1918

Gauge: 1ft 8in
                KIMBERLEY   0-4-0WT OC OK   New (1)
                           (1) loco sold,c/1919

BOARD OF TRADE,HOME GROWN TIMBER SUPPLY DEPARTMENT,TAMERTON

5   Location of line not known;probably short lived.

Gauge: 2ft 0in
                -                  0-4-0PM   BgC   759 1918 New s/s

CAMBORNE & REDRUTH TRAMWAYS,CAMBORNE (Subsidiary of Urban Electric Supply Co.Ltd.)

6   Passenger traffic was operated between Camborne and Redruth with a fleet of seven
       Milnes/BTH electric tramcars from 1/10/1902 until 29/9/1927. From 1904 mineral
       traffic was worked on branches from East Pool Mine (SW 674415) and latterly from
       Agar Mine (SW 675419) to Tolvaddon Smelting Works (SW 657418) reached via a
       lengthy branch.
       An aerial ropeway from Agar to Tolvaddon was built and commenced operation in
       8/1934 when the tramway was abandoned.

       Ref: 'Cornwalls Electric Tramcars' by L Fisher Barham; Glasney Press 1972.

Gauge: 3ft 6in

| 1 | 4wWE | BTH | c1903 | New | s/s /1934 |
| 2 | 4wWE | BTH | c1903 | New | s/s /1934 |

CAMBORNE MINES LTD.,PENDARVES MINE,LITTLE PENDARVES,CAMBORNE. (Camborne Tin Ltd.

until 1/5/1970)

7   A new tin mine commenced c/1968,reworking in the area of the former Pendarves
       United mines.An extensive rail system is used underground and a network of lines
       on the surface connect the shaft,the charging shed and the fitting shops.
       (SW 647385).

Gauge: 600mm

1	4wBE	CE	5554/1	1968	New
2	4wBE	CE	5554/2	1968	New
3	4wBE	CE	5554/3	1968	New
4	0-4-0BE	WR	J7293	1970	New
5	4wBE	CE	5728	1969	New
6	4wBE	CE	5876	1971	New
7	4wBE	CE	5876	1971	New
8	4wBE	CE	5923	1972	New
9	4wBE	CE	5932	1972	New

C.M.POWDER CO.LTD.,TREAMBLE

8   A works producing Fullers Earth,situated at the end of the GWR Treamble branch
       (off the Newquay- Chacewater line)(SW 785561). The narrow gauge line climbed
       steeply from a quarry to an elevated position above the works.
       The line had closed and the track was lifted in 1942

Gauge: 2ft 0in

| – | 0-4-2T | OC | KS | 812 | 1903 | (a) | Scr |
| – | 0-4-2T | OC | KS | 1169 | 1911 | (a) | Scr |

(a) ex Dolcoath Mine Ltd ,Camborne

CORNISH DE LANK GRANITE QUARRIES CO.,DE LANK QUARRIES,ST.BREWARD,WENFORD BRIDGE
(Subsidiary of Thos.W.Ward Ltd. from 1925)

9   Quarries at SX 101755. A standard gauge line was built c/1880 which connected them,initially via an incline,with Wenford Bridge LSWR (SX 086751).A narrow gauge system was used in the quarries.Both rail systems have been replaced by road transport;much of the route of the standard gauge can be traced still.

Gauge: 4ft 8½in

-	4wPM	MR	1925	1919	(a)	(1)

(a) ex Victors Ltd ,St.Helens,Lancs ,/1926   (1) to TWW,Adderley Park,Birmingham,/1950;
                                                    Scr c/1950

Gauge: 2ft 0in

-	4wPM	OK	4586	1932	(a)	(1)
-	4wDM				(b)	(1)

(a) ex Cornwall County Council,Tregongeeves (1) to Arthur Rowe(Scrap)Ltd ,Bodmin,for
      Quarry,c/1961   scrap,12/1965
(b) ex   ?   ,c/1963

CORNISH ROAD-METAL LTD.,STEPPER POINT QUARRY,PADSTOW (Subsidiary of Amalgamated

Roadstone Corporation Ltd)

10   A quarry on the most northerly and inaccesible part of Stepper Point (SW 914785) Stone was brough from quarries round the point to a crusher on the coast side and thence to a jetty after crushing. The quarry was probably opened c/1918 and was closed c/1948 although the plant was not dismantled for many more years.

      Ref: IRR 20 (8/1968) p269

Gauge: 2ft 0in

-	4wPM	MR	1036	1918	(a)	s/s
-	4wPM	MR	4029	1926	(b)	(2)
-	4wDM	RH	177643	1936	New	(1)

(a) ex WDLR 2757   (1) to St.Keverne & Associated Quarries Ltd
(b) ex Western Contracts & Quarries Co ,   Winford,Somerset,c/1948
    /1935   (2) Scr on site by Birds(Swansea)Ltd ,
                                        c7/1969

CORNWALL COUNTY COUNCIL

11   Tolpetherwin Quarry,Lewannick,near Launceston

      A short tramway ran from a roadstone quarry to the plant (SX 270819). The quarry closed c/1952,the track has been lifted and the site is now a highways depot.

Gauge: 2ft 0in

-	4wDM	DC/Bg	2104	1937	(a)	(1)
-	4wDM	DC/Bg	2105	1937	(a)	(1)
-	4wDM	RH	186317	1937	New	s/s
-	4wDM	RH	186324	1937	New	s/s

(a) ex Lostwithiel By-pass construction   (1) to Pugsley,Bristol, /1949
    contract (New to Cornwall C.C. at
    that location)

Tregongeeves Quarry, near St.Austell

12 An elevated line from the quarry to a roadside tipping dock (SX 000515). Quarry closed; track mostly lifted c/1961 and the site is now a highways depot.

Gauge: 2ft 0in

–	4wPM	MR		(a)	(1)
–	4wPM	HU	1931 New	(2)
–	4wPM	UK	4586 1932 New	(3)

(a) ex Thos.W.Ward, /1934

(1) to J.C.Marsden,Hayle,for scrap
(2) to Roberts & Birt,Truro,for scrap,/1954
(3) to Cornish De Lank Granite Quarries Co, Wenford Bridge, c/1961

CORNWALL TIN & MINING CORPORATION,MOUNT WELLINGTON,TWELVE HEADS,TRURO

13 Exploratory work has taken place at this location (SW 762417) by Thyssen (Great Britain) Ltd. A new shaft has been sunk and levels driven in the direction of United Mine. Locos were used underground but were removed in 1973 when activity was suspended. During 1974 work has recommenced and further rail activity seems likely if production commences in 1975 as planned.

(Please refer to Addenda at end of section for late information)

DOLCOATH MINE LTD.,CAMBORNE

14 Dolcoath was Cornwall's deepest mine;Williams Shaft reached 550 fathoms in 1910. It was active for copper by 1758 but tin took predominance around 1860 as deeper levels were reached and Dolcoath soon became the largest producer in England,employing nearly 1000. The cost book company was converted to one of limited liability in 1895. The majority of the workings closed in 1920 although Roskear sett continued until 1930. The company failed on 21/4/1939 Tramways were in use here in 1826. The 1ft 10in gauge line was more recent and ran from the Stray Park section (SW 654399) of the mine to the stamps and dressing floors (SW 660404). Branches served Williams shaft and Harriots shaft. Locomotives were introduced when the stamps were modernised.

Gauge: 1ft 10in

DOLCOATH	0-4-2T	OC	KS	812	1903 New	(1)
DOLCOATH	0-4-2T	OC	KS	1169	1911 New	(1)

(1) to C.M.Powder Co Ltd ,Treamble

E.C.C.PORTS LTD. (Division of English China Clays Ltd)

15 **Fowey Jetties**

The former BR(WR) jetties at SX 128524 and their connecting lines were leased by ECC in 1968;the line to Lostwithiel is retained for rail traffic,while the trackbed of the line to Par has been converted into a private road for lorries bringing in china clay to be shipped for export.

Gauge: 4ft 8½in

D3452	0-6-0DE	Dar	1957	(a)
D3476	0-6-0DE	Dar	1957	(a)
D3497	0-6-0DE	Don	1957	(b)

(a) ex BR (WR), 9/1968
(b) ex BR (WR), 8/1968

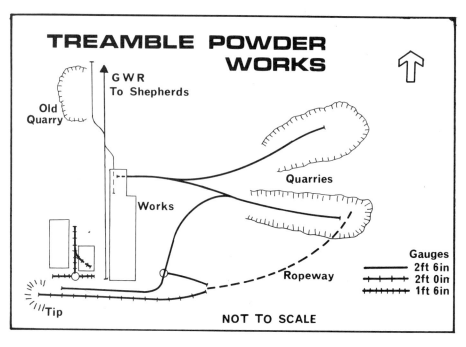

TREAMBLE POWDER WORKS

Old Quarry

GWR
To Shepherds

Quarries

Works

Ropeway

Tip

Gauges
2ft 6in
2ft 0in
1ft 6in

NOT TO SCALE

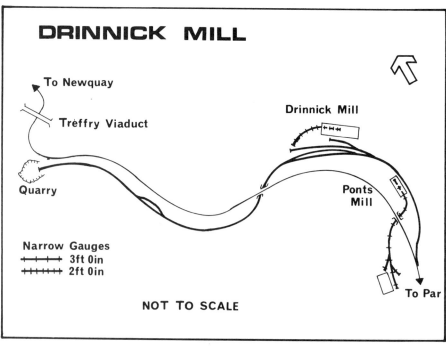

DRINNICK MILL

To Newquay

Treffry Viaduct

Drinnick Mill

Quarry

Ponts Mill

Narrow Gauges
3ft 0in
2ft 0in

To Par

NOT TO SCALE

Par Harbour (Port of Par Ltd. until c/1969)

16 The harbour was constructed 1829-1840 by J.T.Treffry.It has become important for the export of china clay,was leased by English China Clays Ltd in 1946 and was purchased by them in 1964.There is an extensive rail network serving the various quays and at one point the line ran beneath the BR (ex GWR) main line in a low tunnel which has necessitated the use of locomotives specially designed to the required headroom. The loco shed is at SX 076532.

Gauge: 4ft 8½in

–	0-4-0VBT	OCG	S&B		1912	New	Scr /1936
PUNCH	0-4-0ST*	OC	MW	713	1879		
		Reb	Wake	2257		(a)	Scr /1944
(TOBY)	4wVBT	VCG	S	6520	1927	New	Scr 1/1961
JUDY	0-4-0ST	OC	WB	2572	1937	New	
ALFRED	0-4-0ST	OC	WB	3058	1953	New	

* Reb with VB from S&B PUNCH, /1936

(a) ex Wake,/1917;orig.Locke & Co,St.Johns
    Colliery,Normanton,Yorks.

ENGLISH CLAYS,LOVERING POCHIN & CO.LTD. (Formed 12/10/1932 as a division of English China Clays Ltd.)

17 Drinnick Mill Salvage & Disposal Depot,Nanpean
Works at (SW 960557?). The locomotives may have been here for storage only.

Gauge: 2ft 4in

–	4wPM	MR	5456	1935	(a)	(1)
–	4wPM	MR	5404	1932	(b)	(1)

(a) ex Rostowrack Works   (1) to H.Orchard & Sons,Tregrehan Mill,
(b) ex Rostowrack Works, c/1961   Par,for scrap, c/1965

Gauge: 2ft 0in

–	4wDM	RH	235651	1945	(a)	(1)
–	4wDM	RH	235652	1945	(a)	(1)
–	4wDM	RH	221591	1943	(b)	(2)
–	4wDM	MR	7105	1936	(c)	(3)

(a) ex RH ,7/1946 (reconditioned MoS locos)   (1) to Wheal Remfry Works
(b) ex RH,10/1946 (reconditioned MoS loco)   (2) to Western Excavating Co Ltd,
(c) ex Gloucester Tile & Sand Co Ltd,   Charlestown;sold to MacSalvors Ltd,
        Shurdington,Glos   Pool,/1966;to South Crofty Ltd,
                                                  /1970
                                              (3) to Bungey;resold to George Garside Ltd,
                                                  Leighton Buzzard,Beds

Parsons Park Works,St.Neot

18   Rail operation on the tramway serving this works ceased 1/1957

Gauge: 2ft 0in

-	4wDM	RH	221592	1943	(a)	(1)

(a) ex RH,10/1946 (reconditioned MoS loco)   (1) to Western Excavating Co.Ltd,
Charlestown,/1957;to H.Orchard &
Sons,Tregrehan Mill,Par,7/1963;to
MacSalvors Ltd,Pool,c7/1963;to
Penlee Quarries Ltd,Newlyn,c8/1963

Ponts Mill,near Luxulyan (f.Central Cornwall Clay Co.)

19   Standard gauge lines which were a remnant of the Treffry's tramways of 1840
(which see) ran on the east of the BR (ex GWR) St.Blazey- Newquay line. They
served the clay dry of the Central Cornwall Clay Co ,near to which was the loco
shed,and also served the china stone mill at SX 072562 built in 1875 by the
West of England Clay & Stone Co (formed in 1850).Rail traffic ceased c/1965.
The china stone mill was also served by a 2ft 0in gauge tramway,now closed and
dismantled.

Gauge: 4ft 8½in

-	4wPM	MR	1943	1919	New	(1)
-	4wDM*	MR	2032	1920	New	(2)

* Reb from 4wPM, /1948   (1) involved in a crash and returned to
MR, /1933
(2) to H.Orchard & Sons,Tregrehan Mill,
Par,for scrap, 1/1965

Gauge: 2ft 0in

-	VB steam loco (S&B?)	s/s

Rostowrack Works,Nanpean

20   These works were served by a tramway system,initially loco worked,which was
later converted to operation by cable haulage.

Gauge: 2ft 4in

-	4wPM	MR	5456	1935	New	(1)
8	4wPM	MR	5404	1932	(a)	(2)

(a) ex F.J.Moore Ltd,Devon, 1/1949   (1) to Drinnick Mill Depot
(2) to Drinnick Mill Depot, c/1961

Wheal Remfry Works, Retew

21 Rail operation ceased. Track lifted.

Gauge: 2ft 0in

90907	4wDM	RH	235651	1945	(a) (1)
4	4wDM	RH	235652	1945	(a) (2)

(a) ex Drinnick Mill Depot

(1) to Western Excavating Co Ltd ,c/1954; then to H.Orchard & Sons,Tregrehan Mills,Par for scrap

(2) to Western Excavating Co Ltd ;then to J.Howard & Son Ltd ,contrs,Aust, Glos , /1963

Blackpool China Clay Works, Trewoon, near St.Austell

22 Locomotive stored at this works but never used here.

Gauge: 1000 mm

-	0-4-0PM*	RP	(50823 ?)1915	(a) (1)

* Paraffin loco

(a) ex Cotton Powder Co Ltd ,Kent, /1921   (1) to R.P.Morris,Exeter for preservation 12/1963;moved with owner to Longfield,Kent ,2/1965

(Please refer to Addenda at end of section for additional information)

J.J.A.EVANS, TRECARRELL MILL, TREBULLETT, LAUNCESTON

23 A number of locomotives are preserved privately at this site which includes covered storage accomodation and several hundred yards of track on which the working locomotives may be operated (The 'Inny Valley Light Railway'). SX 320772.

Gauge: 2ft 0in

-	4wDM	FH	1896	1935	(a) Dsm

(a) ex Upton Brickworks Ltd ,Poole,Dorset, c12/1968

Gauge: 1ft 10¾in

VELINHELI	0-4-0ST	OC	HE	409	1886	(a)
SYBIL	0-4-0ST	OC	WB	1760	1906	(a)
No.3 -	4wDM		MR	9546	1950	(b)

(a) ex Dinorwic Slate Quarries Co Ltd , Llanberis,Caerns , /1969
(b) ex ECC Quarries Ltd ,Pitts Cleave Quarry, Devon,c9/1970 (Converted here from 2ft 0in gauge)

Gauge: 550 mm

SAN JUSTO	0-4-2ST	OC	HC	639	1902	(a)
SANTA ANA	0-4-2ST	OC	HC	640	1902	(a)*

* At present stored elsewhere

(a) ex San Salvador Spanish Iron Ore Co , Spain, 6/1973

FALMOUTH CORPORATION,ARGAL DAM

24   A tramway serving the site at SW 764328. Line closed and track lifted

Gauge: 2ft 0in

-		4wPM	MR	5072	1930	(a) Scr /1944

(a) ex Rhyl Water Department, 4/1939

FALMOUTH DOCKS AND ENGINEERING CO.,FALMOUTH DOCKS (f. Cox & Son; Falmouth Docks Co until c/1918)

25   Falmouth Docks Co was incorporated in 1859 and the first ship dry-docked in 1861. The company was acquired c/1918 by R.& H.Green & Silley Weir Ltd.,now Silley Cox & Co.Ltd. Extensive sidings serve the docks and connect with the BR (ex GWR) Falmouth branch. They were originally laid to the 7ft 0¼in gauge and were converted to 4ft 8½in gauge by LSWR engineers in 1892 in association with the GWR gauge convertion. The loco shed is at SX 822324.

Gauge: 4ft 8½in

No.1	"BLACKBIRD"	0-4-0VBT OCG S&B		*		Scr /1926
No.2	TORBAY	0-4-0VBT OCG S&B		*(a)		Scr /1926
No.3	"BILLY"	0-4-0VBT OCG S&B		*		Scr c/1926
(No.4)		0-4-0VBT OCG S&B		(b)		(1)
No.3	(No.1 until 3/1955)	0-4-0ST OC HL	3597	1926	New	
No.2		0-4-0ST OC HL	3598	1926	New	(2)
No.1	(No.3 until 3/1955)	0-4-0ST OC HL	3648	1926	New	(2)
No.4		0-4-0ST OC HL	3670	1927	New	Scr 5/1967
No.5		0-4-0ST OC HC	1632	1929	(c)	
No.6		0-4-0ST OC P	1530	1919	(c)	

* Built to 7ft 0¼in gauge;converted to 4ft 8½in gauge by ? in c/1892

(a) ex ? ,Torbay area
(b) construction commenced c/1914 by S&B (who went bankrupt c/1919) and completed in Falmouth Docks workshops c/1920
(c) ex Cooperative Wholesale Society Ltd, Higher Irlam,Lancs, 10/1961

(1) Scr c/1930;boiler preserved at Falmouth Technical School
(2) Sold 15/8/1961 and scrapped on site by Meyer Newman of Hayle, c12/1961

/

GEEVOR TIN MINES LTD.

26   Geevor Mines,Pendeen,near St.Just

These workings were active before 1810 and under the name of North Levant until 1906 when North Levant & Geevor took over. The present company was registered and took over in 1911 and this is one of the two tin mines that have continued working through the present century.

Underground workings are extensive and locos are used on seven of the eight levels. On the surface track connects the shaft and the workshops only (SW 375346) The original WR locos (of which there may have been three including 4884) were to the W217 design;the Geevor built locos are based on this design with improvements and include parts from the original WR locos in the earliest ones and WR supplied motion and wheels in the others.From late 1972 reconstruction of locos with new galvanised chassis has been in hand. The later WR locos are of type WP2072.

Ref: IRR 19 (6/1968) p244.

Gauge: 1ft 6in

1	0-4-0BE	WR	4884	1949	New	Scr c/19 0
1	0-4-0BE	Geevor		1949	New	
2	0-4-0BE	Geevor		1950	New	
3	0-4-0BE	Geevor		1950	New	
4	0-4-0BE	Geevor		1952	New	
5	0-4-0BE	Geevor			New	
6	0-4-0BE	Geevor			New	
7	0-4-0BE	Geevor		1954	New	
8	0-4-0BE	Geevor			New	
9	0-4-0BE	Geevor			New	
10	0-4-0BE	Geevor			New	
11	0-4-0BE	Geevor			New	
12	0-4-0BE	Geevor			New	
13	0-4-0BE	Geevor			New	
14	0-4-0BE	Geevor			New	
15	0-4-0BE	Geevor		1966	New	
No.1	0-4-0BE	WR	H6583	1969	New	
No.2	0-4-0BE	WR	K6915	1971	New	
No.3	0-4-0BE	WR	K6916	1971	New	
No.4	0-4-0BE	WR	L7495	1972	New	
No.5	0-4-0BE	WR	L7496	1972	New	
-	4wBE	CE	5514	1968	New	
-	4wBE	CE	5623		(a)	
-	4wBE	CE	5712		(a)	
-	4wBE	CE	5739		(a)	
-	4wBE	CE	5764		(a)	
-	4wBE	CE	B0163	1973	New	
-	4wBE	CE	B0163	1973	New	
-	4wBE	CE	B0485	1975	New	
-	4wBE	CE	B0485	1975	New	

(a) ex St.Just Mining Services, Levant Mine;
regauged at Geevor from 2ft0in gauge

Levant Mine, St.Just (f St.Just Mining Services Ltd)

27 Very early mines (pre 1820) worked for both tin and copper at various times.
Owned by Daubuz and Batten in 1820. Closed 1871, reopened 5/1874 by a new
company. Worked as a cost book company until closure followed a man engine
disaster in 1919. Taken over by Levant Tin Mines Ltd 1/1/1920, half the shares
being owned by the Geevor company. The upper levels were reopened from 2/1922
until closed again 10/1930. The steam locomotive was intended for use in the
long underground levels but was not a success and was returned to its makers.
Subsequently ponies were used. From 1967 exploration has been made by Geevor
and the Union Corporation of South Africa with a view to reopening using Skip
shaft (SW 368346). The battery locos were used underground during this project
but production has not yet recommenced.

Ref: IRR 34 (12/1970) p365; IRR 38 (8/1971) p116

Gauge: 2ft0in

-	4wBE	CE	5623	New	(1)
-	4wBE	CE	5712	New	(1)
-	4wBE	CE	5739	New	(1)
-	4wBE	CE	5764	New	(1)

(1) to Geevor Mine

Gauge: c. 1ft3in

PIONEER	0-2-2WT	IC	K.Bickle	1892	New	s/s

GOONVEAN & ROSTOWRACK CHINA CLAY CO.LTD.

28　St.Stephen Quarry,Nanpean

Rail system abandoned 1957.

Gauge:2ft 0in

		4wDM	RH	183738	1937	New	(1)

(1) to Great Wheal Prosper Clay Works,
6/1957

Great Wheal Prosper Clay Works,Roche

29　Rail system abandoned c1963

Gauge:2ft 0in

		4wDM	RH	183738	1937	(a)	(1)

(a) ex St.Stephen Quarry,Nanpean,6/1957　　(1) to Goonvean Works,St.Stephen,Nanpean
for scrap c2/1965.

GREAT WESTERN PRESERVATIONS LTD.,BODMIN M.P.D.

30　A preservation group who from 1969 have been using the former BR motive power
depot at Bodmin General station to house locomotives and rolling stock which is
being restored for preservation. (SX 074663)

Gauge:4ft 8½in

1363		0-6-0ST	OC	Sdn	2377	1910	(a)
No.19		0-4-0ST	OC	WB	2962	1950	(b)

(a) ex BR(WR) 8/1964;stored at Totnes until
/1969
(b) ex MoD Navy Dept.,Devonport Dockyard,
Devon,2/1969.

HOLMAN BROS. LTD.,TEST MINE,TROON,CAMBORNE

31　Some 6000 feet of tunnels radiate from a quarry in the granite and are used for
testing Holman's mining products.It was started in the 1930's and the rail system
served most parts until it was removed c1972.A short length including an incline
is still in use by students of the Camborne School of Mines. (SX 657368)

Gauge:2ft 0in.

		4wDM	L	34030	1949	New	Scr/1972

JEFFORD & SONS LTD.,TOR QUARRIES,BURRATON COOMBE,NEAR SALTASH

32　The tramway ran from the quarry at SX 412584 through the village and via an
incline to a quay on Forder Creek (SX 413578). The workings were acquired by
E.C.L.P.&Co.Ltd. in 1948 and closed down immediately. They were later reopened
using road transport only.

Gauge:2ft 0in.

		4wPM	MR				Scr 3/1960
		4wPM	MR	1198	1918	(a)	Scr 3/1960
		4wPM	MR	3842	1926	(b)	Scr 3/1960
		4wPM	MR	4006	1928	New	Scr 3/1960

(a) ex WDLR 2919 by 1/1922
(b) ex MR,new,rebuilt from a WDLR loco.

MACSALVORS LTD.,POOL,NEAR CAMBORNE

33   A plant dealer and scrap merchant with a yard at SW 674415.Narrow gauge diesel
      locomotives have been purchased from time to time and have stood in this yard
      pending scrap or resale for further use.

      Known locomotives include:

Gauge: 2ft 0in

		4wDM	RH	246793	1947	(a)	(1)
-		4wDM	RH	213848	1942	(b)	(1)
-		4wDM	RH	221592	1943	(c)	(2)
-		4wDM	RH	221591	1943	(d)	(3)

(a) ex Admiralty   (1) to Penlee Quarries Ltd , /1962
(b) ex Admiralty,Carfin   (2) to Penlee Quarries Ltd ,c8/1963
(c) ex H.Orchard & Sons,dealers,Par;f ECLP   (3) to South Crofty Ltd ,Pool, /1970
    Park Works,St.Neot
(d) ex Western Excavating Co Ltd ,f ECLP
    Drinnick Mill, c/1966

Gauge: 2ft 6in

		4wDM	RH	268878	1952	(a)	(1)

(a) ex MoD.ND,Ernesettle,Devon,1/1973   (1) to GECT , Vulcan Works, Newton-le-
                                             Willows, Lancs for overhaul & resale,
                                             c 5/1975

NATIONAL EXPLOSIVES CO.LTD.,HAYLE (Subsidiary of Nobel's Explosives Co Ltd)

34   An extensive powder works located in Hayle Towans (SW 576403) which closed in
      1919.Served by standard gauge sidings from the GWR and also by an intricate
      network of 2ft 0in gauge lines connecting the many sections of the works.

Gauge: 4ft 8½in

		0-4-0ST	OC	P	1448	1917	New	(1)

                              (1) to J.C.Hill & Co Ltd ,Cwmbran,Mon ,
                                  /1924

OLD DELABOLE SLATE CO.LTD.,LOWER PENGELLY,DELABOLE,CAMELFORD

35   A very large slate quarry which has been active since the 16th century.The
      present public company was registered 2/6/1898 to acquire the previous private
      company.Four separate workings now form one quarry.A stationary steam engine was
      installed for incline haulage in 1834 and tramroads were certainly in use by 1841.
      In 1907 inclines of up to six roads were in use,but now one incline of two roads
      survives.The rail system has been inactive for some time (SX 075835)

Gauge: 1ft 11in

E.JAGO	0-4-0ST	OC	HE	219	1879	New	Scr c/1930
JOHN ALLEN	0-4-0ST	OC	HE	220	1879	New	Scr c/1930
J.T.FAIRBANK	0-4-0ST	OC	WB	1663	1902	New	Scr c/1930
BROMLEY No.1	0-4-0T	OC	AE	1593	1910	(a)	(1)
-	0-6-0T		HU				Scr c/1930
-	0-4-0T		(OK?)			(b)	Scr c/1930
-	0-4-0T		(OK?)			(b)	Scr c/1930
No.1	4wPM		MR	2094	1922	New	Sold c/1944
No.2	4wDM(f PM)		MR	3739	1925	New	OOU
No.3	4wDM(f PM)		MR	4534	1928	New	Dsm

(a) ex Pensford & Bromley Collieries Ltd , (1) to WD Catterick Camp,Yorks , c2/1915
    Somerset, c1/1913
(b) ex Germany,(/1917?);almost certainly
    OK ('Montania')

36   A line some half mile in length ran from the quarry (SX 431715) to Gunnislake station.It was built to 3ft 6in gauge and converted to 4ft 8½in gauge in 1908 in connection with the regauging of the East Cornwall Mineral Railway. The quarry was closed and the track removed c/1915.

Gauge 4ft 8½in

111	CORNWALL		0-4-0ST	OC	HC	645	1903	New(a)	(1)
-			0-6-0ST	OC	P				s/s c/1917

(a) reb HC from 3ft 6in gauge, /1908   (1) to P.Baker & Co ,Cardiff, /1921;resold
to David Robinson & Co Ltd ,Cardiff

PENTEWAN RAILWAY   (St.Austell & Pentewan Railway,Harbour & Dock Co until /1881;

Pentewan Railway & Harbour Co Ltd until 7/8/1874;Pentewan Railway until 20/2/1873)

37   Opened in 1829 as a horse worked railway to convey china clay from St.Austell to the harbour at Pentewan.Occasional passenger specials were run and locomotive working was introduced in 1874.Continual silting of the harbour and competition from the GWR caused loss of traffic and the last train ran on 2/3/1918. The railway was requisitioned by the Government for military purposes and the track lifted 3-4/1918. The railway had been leased to W.T.Lamb & Sons in 1913 and they sold their premises at Pentewan to the Pentewan Port,Railway & Trading Co Ltd in 1919. Later their successors opened a tramway on the quays,of the same gauge and partly on the same site as the original line in this area. See under Pentewan Sands Ltd for further details. The course of the original Pentewan Railway is still largely discernible.

Ref: 'The Pentewan Railway 1829-1918' by M.J.T.Lewis; D.Bradford Barton,1960
NG 26 (Summer 1960),p20
IRR 30 (4/1970) p250

Gauge: 2ft 6in

PENTEWAN	0-6-0	OC	MW	461	1874	New	(1)	
TREWITHEN	0-6-0	OC	MW	994	1886	New	Scr /1901	
CANOPUS	0-6-2ST	OC	MW	1547	1901	New	(2)	
PIONEER	2-6-2ST	OC	YE	757	1903	(a)	(3)	

(a) ex ? , 5/1912;orig Lodge Hill   (1) Wdn /1886; scr c/1896
  Upnor Rly ,Kent   (2) to WD Sunbury,Middx, 4/1918;noted at
              WD West Drayton,Middx,1/1924;
              Scr c2/1924
             (3) to WD Sunbury,Middx,4/1918;at WD
              Newbury,Berks,by 7/1922 when offered
              for sale; s/s

PENTEWAN SANDS LTD.(Pentewan Dock & Concrete Co.Ltd.until /1965;f Pentewan Dock Ltd.)

The company operated tramways to assist with the extraction of sand at these sites:

38   G - Gwithian   A tramway at SW 585420,three miles north-east of Hayle.Replaced by dumper trucks 10/1958

39   P - Pentewan   A tramway at SX 020472 on the site of the former Pentewan Railway at the harbour.Sand quarrying ceased c/1966 and the site has been used as a caravan camp,although the locomotives have remained in their shed.

Gauge: 2ft 6in

2	4wDM	RH	189992	1938	New	P -G c/1957 -P /1962		
1	4wDM	RH	195842	1939	New	P -G -P /1961	Scr c/1968	
-	4wDM	RH	244558	1946	New	G -P c/1957		

40 A 3ft 6in gauge line,7½ miles long,was built from Kelly Bray (Callington) to East Calstock and thence via an incline down to the level of the Tamar at Calstock Quay. Incorporated in 1869 as the Callington & Calstock Railway,the title was changed to the East Cornwall Mineral Railway before the opening (for mineral traffic only) on 8/5/1872.
The loco shed was at the head of the incline (SX 425695).Branches served the Gunnislake Quarry of S.Pearson & Sons (which see) and Plymouth Works,Gunnislake, while inclined tramways provided connections to Gunnislake Clitters Mine and Kit Hill granite quarries.
The PD&SWJR 'main line' from Lydford to Devonport was opened on 2/6/1890 and was operated by LSWR locos and stock from the outset. The PD&SWJR took over the ECMR on 1/6/1891. Subsequently a standard gauge line was built from Bere Alston to cross the Tamar at Calstock and join the ECMR route near the top of the incline. West of this point the narrow gauge line was regauged to provide a route to Callington (Kelly Bray) where the standard gauge loco sheds and workshops were located (SX 360714). This standard gauge branch was opened to passenger and freight working on 2/3/1908. The PD&SWJR provided its own motive power to work this branch. The line was absorbed into the SR on 1/1/1923.

Ref: 'The Plymouth Devonport & South Western Junction Railway' by A.J.Cheeseman;
Oakwood Press, 1967
'Callington Railways' by Crombleholme,Stuckey & Whetmath; West Country
Handbooks, 1967

Gauge: 4ft 8½in

No.2		0-4-2ST	OC	N	1661	1871	
			Reb	Callington		1907	(a) (1)
No.3	A.S.HARRIS	0-6-0T	OC	HL	2697	1907	New (2)
No.4	EARL OF MOUNT EDGECUMBE	0-6-2T	OC	HL	2696	1907	New (3)
No.5	LORD ST LEVAN	0-6-2T	OC	HL	2695	1907	New (4)

(a) Reb from 3ft 6in gauge 0-4-0ST

(1) to Hundred of Manhood & Selsey Tramway, 7/1912
(2) to SR 756;later BR 30756; Scr 10/1951
(3) to SR 757;later BR 30757; Scr 1/1958
(4) to SR 758;later BR 30758; Scr 2/1957

Gauge: 3ft 6in

No.1	0-4-0ST	OC	N	1660	1871	New (1)
No.2	0-4-0ST	OC	N	1661	1871	New (2)

(1) Wdn /1907;believed scr on site after /1909
(2) Reb to 4ft 8½in gauge, /1907

H.D.POCHIN & CO.LTD.,ST.DENIS TRAMWAY

41   H.D.Pochin purchased the Higher Gothers clayworks in 1879 and promptly built the
two mile tramway from there to Pochins Siding (SW 942592),a tipping dock on the
GWR branch from Burngullow to St.Denis Jct. The original sleepers are said to
have been studded with copper nails having come from one of England's 'wooden
walls'. In 1920 a branch was built to connect with the mica works of C & J Varcoe
and this was in use until 1929. There is photographic evidence that a third
standard gauge rail was added to the line latterly.
The line was closed and most of the track lifted in 1931,but one loco was left
isolated in the engine shed at Gothers (SW 964585)(which still stands)for many
more years.
H.D.Pochin & Co.Ltd. became a constituent of ECLP from 12/10/1932 and much of the
works site has since been occupied by the Gothers Concrete Works of ECLP.

Gauge: 3ft 0in

(GREENFOLD)	0-4-0ST	OC	HE	1428	1922	(a)	Scr c1953	
BROOKE	0-4-0ST	OC	HC	495	1898	(b)	(1)	

(a) ex Fylde Water Board,Stocks Reservoir,   (1) to R.Baillie,contr.,Ladybower Reservoir
    Lancs.   Derbys.
(b) ex Aberthaw & Rhoose Portland Cement
    Co.Ltd.,Glam.

REDRUTH & CHACEWATER RAILWAY

42   One of the earliest railways in Cornwall,built to take the output of the copper
mines in the Redruth area to the port of Devoran,near Truro. Opened for traffic
30/1/1826 with horse traction;locomotives were first used 1/12/1854. Traffic
dwindled as the mines were worked out and the harbour silted up and the railway
was closed 25/9/1915. Some rails were lifted for wartime use and the rest was
dismantled in 1920. The route is traceable almost throughout and some buildings
of railway origin remain at Devoran.

Ref: 'The Redruth & Chacewater Railway,1824-1915', D.B.Barton,Truro 1966.

Gauge: 4ft 0in

MINER	0-6-0ST	OC	N	*	1854		
	(0-4-2ST until 1869;						
	0-4-0ST until 1855)				New	Scr/1919	
SMELTER	0-4-2ST	OC	N	*	1854		
	(0-4-0ST until 1855)				New	Scr/1919	
SPITFIRE	0-6-0ST	OC	N	540	1859	New	Scr/1919

*Works numbers 81 and 82; order not known.

ST.KEVERNE & ASSOCIATED QUARRIES LTD.,PORTHALLOW & PORTHOUSTOCK QUARRIES,ST.KEVERNE

(Subsidiary of ARC(South Western)Ltd.)

43   Quarrying has been carried on here from the 19th century.The rail system was
introduced in 1934 from Porthallow(the most northerly quarry;SW 805231).Stone was
tipped into wagons and hauled out,at first by horses,one mile along the coast to
the processing plant,traversing a small cove and a double track rope worked
incline. Below the crusher there was a further half mile section to Porthoustock
(SW 802819) to a concrete storage silo in the bay and a stock tip in an old
quarry. From the middle level of the crushing plant a short separate line (worked
by the Lister loco)ran into another old quarry,parallel to the main line.
Production ceased towards the end of 1958 and dismantling of the rail system
commenced shortly afterwards.

Ref: IRR 20 (8/1968) p269

Gauge: 2ft 0in

"LM 7"	4wDM	RH	171904	1935	New	(1)
"LM 6"	4wDM	RH	183426	1937	New	(2)
–	4wDM	OK	5674		New	Scr c /1960
–	4wPM	L	30202	1946	New	(3)
"LM 37"	4wDM	RH	177643	1936	(a)	(4)
LM 30	4wDM	RH	229656	1944	(b)	(5)
(LM 26)	4wDM	RH	191642	1938	(c)	(6)
LM 5	4wPM	MR	5094	1931	(d)	(7)
–	4wDM	OK	5677		(e)	(8)
LM 38	4wDM	FH	2401	1941	(f)	(9)
LM 27	4wDM	RH	191643	1938	(g)	(6)

(a) ex Winford Quarry,Somerset, /1949
(b) ex Malvern Works,Worcs , /1952; f BQC
    Allington Quarry,Kent
(c) ex Malvern Works, /1953; f BQC Borough
    Green Works,Kent
(d) ex BQC Borough Green Works,Kent,via
    Malvern Works
(e) ex Penlee Quarries Ltd
(f) ex Malvern Works, 3/1956
(g) ex Malvern Works, 11/1957;f Amalgamated
    Lime Co Ltd ,East Lothian

(1) to Malvern Works,Worcs , /1960;Scr /1961
(2) to Malvern Works, 1/1954; Scr /1954
(3) parts to West of England Road-Metal Co
    Ltd ,c /1959 for spares;frame scrapped
(4) to Penlee Quarries Ltd
(5) to Malvern Works c /1957;retd 11/1957;
    to Malvern Works c /1961;thence to
    Penlee Quarries Ltd, 9/1961
(6) to Cohen for scrap, /1960
(7) to Malvern Works, /1960; scr 9/1961
(8) to Penlee Quarries Ltd , 9/1961
(9) to Penlee Quarries Ltd , 9/1961

SOUTH CROFTY LTD, SOUTH CROFTY MINE, POOL, NEAR CAMBORNE

44   Mines and ore processing plant for the extraction of tin,and formerly arsenic.
The company was formed in 1906 from the South Crofty cost book company which
included several older mines,some dating from the early 18th century. Robinsons
and New Cooks Kitchen shafts were sunk subsequent to this date.
The surface 2ft 0in gauge tramway connected New Cooks Kitchen shaft (SW 664409)
and Palmers and Robinsons shafts (SW 668413) with the ore processing mill. The
section to New Cooks Kitchen shaft was replaced by a conveyor belt in 1968,the
remainder in 1970. This tramway was horse worked prior to the introduction of
locomotives.
The 1ft 10in gauge workings are underground in each mine with surface sidings
and workshops in the vicinity of each shaft. Diesel and electric locos have been
used at Cooks,electrics only at Robinsons. Most of the electric locos from both
mines are brought to the surface daily at 15.00 hours for battery charging.

Ref: IRR 19 (6/1968) p242

Gauge: 2ft 0in

–	4wPM	(MR?)			(a)	(1)
–	4wDM	RH	224310	1944	(b)	(2)
–	4wDM	RH	264240	1949	(c)	(2)
–	4wDM	RH	213858	1942	(d)	(2)
–	4wDM	RH	221591	1943	(e)	(2)

(a) ex S.Andrew & Son,Redruth,hire, c /1950
(b) ex Tampimax Oil Products Ltd ,Force Crag
    Mine, Cumberland
(c) ex Westbere Ballast Pits (Ramsgate) Ltd ,
    Kent, c /1961
(d) ex Scottish Oils Ltd ,Addiewell,
    Midlothian, c /1962
(e) ex MacSalvors Ltd ,scrap merchants,
    Pool, /1970; f ECLP Drinnick Mill

(1) retd to S.Andrew & Son, Redruth
(2) to ARC(South Western)Ltd ,Penlee
    Quarries, /1971; scr c /1972

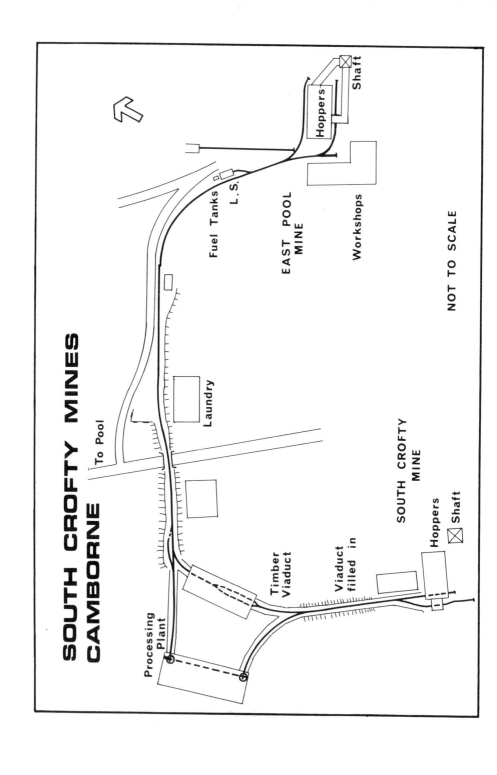

SOUTH CROFTY MINES
CAMBORNE

To Pool

Processing Plant

Laundry

Timber Viaduct

Viaduct filled in

Hoppers

Shaft

SOUTH CROFTY MINE

Fuel Tanks

L.S.

EAST POOL MINE

Workshops

Hoppers

Shaft

NOT TO SCALE

Gauge: 1ft10in

–	4wDM	RH	7002/0865/7	1964	New
–	4wDM	RH	7002/0865/8	1964	New
–	4wDM	RH	7002/0867/5	1967	New
–	4wDH	HE	6342	1970	New
–	4wDH	HE	7083	1971	New
–	4wDH	HE	7084	1971	New
–	4wDH	HE	7087	1972	New*
1	0-4-0BE	WR			
2	0-4-0BE	WR			
3	0-4-0BE	WR			
4	0-4-0BE	WR			
5	0-4-0BE	WR	F7030	1966	New
6	0-4-0BE	WR			
7	0-4-0BE	WR	F7029	1966	New
8	0-4-0BE	WR	J7375	1969	New
9	0-4-0BE	WR			
10	0-4-0BE	WR	F7114	1966	New
11	0-4-0BE	WR			
12	0-4-0BE	WR	J7376	1969	New
13	0-4-0BE	WR	J7374	1969	New
14	0-4-0BE	WR	C6712	1963	New
15	0-4-0BE	WR			
16	0-4-0BE	WR			
17	0-4-0BE	WR			
18	0-4-0BE	WR			
19	0-4-0BE	WR	F7115	1966	New
20	0-4-0BE	WR	F7113	1966	New
21	0-4-0BE	WR			
22	0-4-0BE	WR	J7373	1969	New
23	0-4-0BE	WR	L7526	1971	New
24	0-4-0BE	WR	L7527	1971	New
25	0-4-0BE	WR	L7529	1971	New
26	0-4-0BE	WR	L7528	1971	New
27	0-4-0BE	WR	L7531	1971	New
28	0-4-0BE	WR	L7530	1971	New
29	0-4-0BE	WR	L7533	1971	New
30	0-4-0BE	WR	L7532	1971	New
31	0-4-0BE	WR	4879	1952	(a) s/s?
31	0-4-0BE	WR	7719	1974	New
32	0-4-0BE	WR	7721	1974	New
33	0-4-0BE	WR	7720	1974	New
34	0-4-0BE	WR	7834	1974	New
35	0-4-0BE	WR	7835	1974	New
36	0-4-0BE	WR	7833	1974	New
37	0-4-0BE	WR	7836	1974	New
38	0-4-0BE	WR	7837	1974	New
39	0-4-0BE	WR	7838	1974	New
40	0-4-0BE	WR	7839	1974	New

(a) ex R.P.Morris, Longfield, Kent, /1973   *Used only to provide spares for the
                                                companion locos

Certain WR locos, including No.20, have new main frames built at South Crofty.

WAR DEPARTMENT, TREGANTLE MILITARY RAILWAY

45 Inclines were built in 1859–1860 from the river Lynher to the forts then building at Scraesdon and Tregantle (SX 391531). About 1893 a standard gauge railway was built from Wacker Quay (SX 390552) to Tregantle. This was operated in two sections connected by a cable worked incline with Scraesdon yard at its summit. There was a loco shed here and another at Wacker Quay. The railway was closed c/1903; some track was lifted immediately and the rest during the 1914-18 war. In 1967 the loco shed at Wacker was still in use as a depot by the Cornwall County Council.

A photo exists of 384 allegedly at work on the upper section of the line, which implies that MW 941 worked the lower section. Another source states that the lower section loco remained in its shed until the 1930's when it was broken up for scrap. If this is correct it cannot have been MW 941 which was in Essex in the 1920's.

Ref: SLS.J ,9/1967, p260

Gauge:4ft 8½in

-		0-4-0ST	OC	MW	941	1885	(a) (1)
384		0-6-0ST	IC	MW	967	1885	(a) s/s

(a) ex Lucas & Aird,contrs,Suakin-Berber   (1) to R.Empneirs,contrs,'MONMOUTH';later
    Railway,Sudan   to H.Covington & Sons Ltd ,Tilbury
                                                    Rubbish Shoot,Essex

P.R.WELSH,TOLGUS TIN MINE,PORTREATH ROAD,REDRUTH

46 A museum and display of relics illustrating the Cornish tin mining industry, opened to the public c/1971.

Gauge: 2ft 2in

-	4wDM	RH	371547 1954 (a)

(a) ex British Gypsum Ltd ,Glebe Mines,
    Notts , /1972

WHEAL ELIZA CONSOL MINING CO.,NEAR ST.AUSTELL

47 A prosperous but difficult tin sett at SX 044531 commenced in 1849. Due to being unable to surface on the landowners estate some parts of the mine were half a mile from a shaft. By 1883 there were five miles of underground tramroads and on the surface a small tank engine of 1ft 8in gauge hauled ore from the shafts to the stamps and dressing floors. The mine closed in 1892, there was a sale of plant in 8/1892 and equipment was subsequently scrapped.

WHEAL JANE LTD.,BALDHU,NEAR TRURO (Subsidiary of Consolidated Goldfields Ltd)

Clemows Shaft

48 A reopening from 1968 of old mines. The surface system connects Clemows (f. Clemo's) and No.2 (Thyssens) shafts and the stores,engineering shops,etc. Ore travels on the surface by conveyor. Underground workings connect with those formerly of Nangiles mine. Location of Clemows shaft is SW 772427.

Gauge: 2ft 0in

1		4wBE	CE	5512/1	1968	New	
2		4wBE	CE	5512/2	1968	New	
3	MINER	4wBE	CE	5688/2	1969	New	
4	SMELTER	4wBE	CE	5688/1	1969	New	
5	SPITFIRE	4wBE	CE	5766	1970	New	
6		4wBE	WR	5537	1956	(a)	(1)
7		4wBE	CE	5839A	1971	New	
8		4wBE	CE	5839B	1971	New	
9		4wBE	CE	5839C	1971	New	
10		4wBE	CE	5839D	1971	New	
11		4wBE	CE	5918	1972	New	
12		4wBE	CE	5946/1	1972	New	
12A		4wBE	CE	5957A	1973	New	
14		4wBE	CE	5957B	1973	New	
17		4wBE	CE	0139A	1973	New	
18		4wBE	CE	0139B	1973	New	
		4wBE	CE	B0174	1974	New	
		4wBE	CE	B0466	1975	New	
		4wBE	CE	B0466	1975	New	
		4wBE	CE	B0466	1975	New	

(a) ex Nangiles Mine, c9/1969

(1) to A.M.Keef, Bampton, Oxon, c3/1974;
resold to Dowty R.P.S., Ashchurch,
Glos , c7/1974

Nangiles Mine, Twelveheads, near Truro

49   This shaft was in use in the initial stages of production at Wheal Jane until
the ore could be moved underground to Clemows shaft. Short surface tramways
ran from Engine shaft to the dumps (SW 764420)

Gauge: 2ft 0in

–	4wBE	WR	5537	1956	(a)	(1)

(a) ex Foraky Ltd, contrs on site.

(1) to Clemows shaft, c9/1969

WHEAL REMFRY CHINA CLAY BRICK & TILE CO. LTD., NEAR NANPEAN

(Subsidiary of ECLP after 12/10/1932)

50

Gauge: 2ft 5½in

–	4wPM	MH	A131	c1925	New	s/s

ADDENDA - The following information relevant to Cornwall has
come to hand as this draft is being prepared for press.

CORNWALL TIN & MINING CORPORATION, MOUNT WELLINGTON, TWELVE HEADS, TRURO

Add: The following locos have been delivered by 7/1975, although they had
not been put into traffic by that date.

Gauge: 2ft0in

1	4wBE	CE	BO 444 G	1975	New
2	4wBE	CE	BO 444/6	1975	New
3	4wBE	CE	BO 444 H	1975	New
4	4wBE	CE	BO 444/2	1974	New
5	4wBE	CE	BO 444/1?	1974	New
6	4wBE	CE	BO 444/2?	1974	New
7	4wBE	CE	BO 444/4	1974	New
8	4wBE	CE	BO 444/5	1975	New

ENGLISH CLAYS, LOVERING POCHIN & CO LTD

Add note re the RP locomotive:

The identity of this locomotive is unconfirmed. From the gauge it could be one of
50823, 50861 (1915), 51168, 51207 (1916) of Cotton Powder Co Ltd; or 50878 (1915) of
Explosives Loading Co , both firms operating near Oare in Kent. It is thought to be
50823 but this has not yet been substantiated.

Add entry:

WHEAL MARTYN CHINA CLAY MUSEUM LTD., CARTHEW, ST. AUSTELL

51   A museum of industrial items relevant to the china clay industry, which was
officially opened on 26/3/1975

Gauge: 4ft6in

LEE MOOR NO.1	0-4-0ST OC P	783	1899	(a)

(a) ex Lee Moor Preservation Group, Devon,
17/3/1975

Non-locomotive systems

BAILSWOOD BRICKWORKS,GUNNISLAKE.

A   A tramway connected the clay pits to the works (SX 436712),which were opened c1850 and closed about 1900

BUDE CANAL

B   An early plateway of 4ft gauge was in use by 1825 for about 350 yards from the beach to the canal basin (SS 205064) to carry sand to the canal tub boats. Later (c1920) it was replaced by a 2ft gauge tramway on the same site and most of the track of the latter survives embedded in concrete.

CAMBORNE SCHOOL OF MINES

C   CSM use parts of Great Condurrow Mine,above water level,for teaching purposes. A tramway is installed underground and there is about 100 yards of track on surface connecting the skip shaft with the dump.

CARBIS CHINA CLAY AND BRICK CO.LTD.

D   A tramway ran from the claypit to the brickworks (SS 000596) worked manually. Tramway closed shortly after 1910.

CARCLAZE TIN MINE

E   A very old open working productive in the reign of Henry VI which used an underground canal to remove muck and ore (SX 025547). A tramway was installed by 1827 and extended in 1852 (1ft 11in gauge).Production of tin gave way to china clay in the latter part of the 19th century.

CARN BREA TRAMWAY

F   A tramway,possibly of standard gauge,curved around the north east side of Carn Brea linking a granite quarry with the GWR main line. It appears to have operated sometime between 1884 and 1907.

CORNWALL COUNTY COUNCIL

Michaelstow Quarry

G   A lengthy tramway connected several faces with the crushers and tar plant.Track lifted 6/1970. (SX 088790)

Treworgans Quarry,Ladock

H   A tramway from the quarry (SW 899495) under the GWR main line to a road,traffic being horseworked. Replaced by lorries.

PETER DIXON & SONS LTD.

J   A tramway from Bridges Dry (SX047853) to the nearby Luxulyan station on the GWR Newquay branch. Opened 1924;closed and lifted in the mid 1960's.

MICHAELSTOW QUARRY

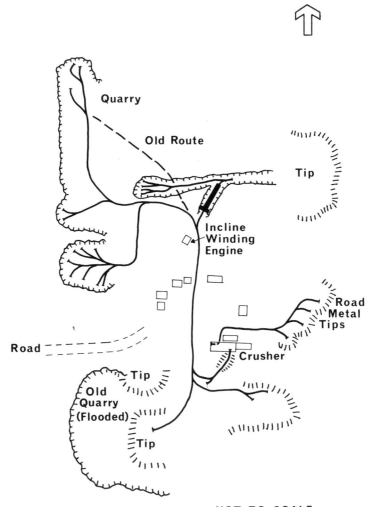

Quarry

Old Route

Tip

Incline
Winding
Engine

Road
Metal
Tips

Road

Crusher

Tip

Old
Quarry
(Flooded)

Tip

NOT TO SCALE

ENGLISH CLAYS LOVERING POCHIN & CO.LTD.

Carlyon Farm Dry

K   Built 1919 and probably one of Cornwall's largest dries. SX 013535.
A large number of 2ft and 2ft 4in gauge tracks ran from the linhay floor onto
pivotted 'draw bridges' over the siding off the Trenance Valley branch of the
GWR.

Charlestown Dry

L   Opened by Lovering & Co in 1908,Charlestown Dry (SX 039519) incorporated a
2ft 4in gauge line which ran underground to the nearby Charlestown Harbour,
wagons discharging into vessels from the wall high above. Instead of the usual
linhay the clay was stored in bins hewn out of the rock and the tramway ran
in a tunnel below these. The present later dry uses a similar principle but
its tramway only runs to an adjacent lorry dock.

FOWEY CONSOLS

M   A rich copper mine (SX 098614) acquired 1813-18 by J.T.Treffry and by 1839
connected to his Par Canal by two inclined tramways both partly in tunnels.
The inclines were powered by waterwheels. Working was abandoned in 1868.

GOONVEAN & ROSTOWRACK CHINA CLAY CO.LTD.,SLIP QUARRY.

N   A china stone quarry at SW 950556 dating back to 1807. A number of 2ft gauge
lines were formerly used in the quarries and some narrow gauge track was
still recently in use here.

GUNNISLAKE CLITTERS MINE

P   A copper mine started about 1820 at SX 425723. Its lower levels were
connected to the river Tamar at Gunnislake by a tramroad from an early date.
This was disused and was replaced by an incline to the East Cornwall Mineral
Railway in 1872.

HALWELL QUARRY

Q   An ochre quarry at SX 305771 active,recently,from 1920 to 1957. A tramway
ran in a straight line for one third of a mile to a tipping dock on the road
at SX 303768. The tipping dock is demolished,but much of the track was still
in situ under the grass.

IMPERIAL CHEMICAL INDUSTRIES LTD.,NOBEL DIVISION,HERODSFOOT POWDER WORKS

R   An intricate system of tracks connected powder mills and stores (SX 205609)
in a pleasant wooded valley,now Forestry Commission.Production ceased c1963
after an explosion.Most of the buildings remain.

MULBERRY OPENWORK

S   A narrow gauge tramway ran in the Deep Adit under the floor of this large
open tin working at SX 019658,the wagons being loaded via ore passes in the
floor. Another tramway in the higher Shallow Adit dropped via an incline to the
stamps and dressing floors. An extension is said to have run to the Ruthern
Bridge terminus of the Bodmin and Wadebridge Railway. Workings have been from
well before 1748 up to 1916

THOMAS OLVER & CO.LTD.,TREGARGUS CHINA STONE QUARRY.

T   A network of 2ft gauge tracks and inclines served the quarry and six mills
at SW 949540 from the 1890's. Work ceased 1965 and scrap merchants cleared
most of the site 12/1968

PORTREATH TRAMROAD

U   A 3ft 6in gauge plateway laid from 25/10/1809 and opened in 1812 by local
mining interests.The final route was from Portreath Harbour (SW 655454)to
Crofthandy (SW 738425) with branches to Scorrier House (SW 725438) and mines
nearby. It was disused by 1866-7 and lifted in the 1880's. A passenger vehicle
survives in the Holman Museum,Camborne.

PORKELLIS MINES LTD.

V   A straight line of tramway connected the shaft (SW 692330) with the stamps and
dressing floors (SW 688327) in the valley below. The route is still clear,
remaining from 1919 when the mine closed for major reconstruction,never
reopening.

PRIDEAUX WOOD DRY

W   A disused 2ft gauge tramway of which the track is still in situ from the
closed dry at SX 073555 to a siding on the GWR Ponts Mill branch.

PRINCE OF WALES QUARRY

X   An old slate quarry at SX 072863 which had a rail system of unknown gauge by
1865. The present small rustic working is at SX 074862 and has a quantity of
2ft gauge track and wagons.

RESTORMEL IRON MINE

Y   A tramway was opened in 1836 from the mine (SX 098614) to riverside quays in
Lostwithiel whence ores were barged to Fowey. The mine was active by 1797 and
closed 1883.

SPICER BROS.LTD.CARPALLA CLAY PIT.

Z   This was the site of the earliest china clay workings and was productive by
1819. The dry was connected to Carpalla siding on the GWR by the Mid-Cornwall
tramway which consisted of two separate portions with a steam winder in between.
The route is traceable and the steam winder remains.

TAMAR FIREBRICK & CLAY CO.LTD.,GUNNISLAKE

AA   A hand worked tramway connected the clay pit and the works,in use 1873 to c1914.

TINCROFT MINE

AB   An industrial estate now occupies the site of the burrows and extensive
tramway of the Tincroft mine. A separate network at Highburrow shaft tunelled
under Carn Brea station.

TREFFRY'S TRAMWAYS

AC   J.T.Treffry built a number of standard gauge railways to develop his properties. These commenced in 1840 with a line from the Ponts Mill (SX 072562) terminus of his Par Canal to Colcerrow Quarry (SX 065579) with the lengthy Carmears Incline worked by a 50ft waterwheel. This line was later (1847) extended over the Treffry Viaduct (SX 057572) to Molinnis (Bugle)(SX 017593). Another line had been built 1846-9 from Newquay Harbour (SW 808620) to Hendra Crazey (SW 954570) and a branch from this line to East Wheal Rose (SW 836553). In 1855 the first line was extended to Par Harbour alongside the canal from Ponts Mill.
The Cornwall Minerals Railway purchased the railways in 1873,connected the two systems in 1874,extended to Fowey,built a number of deviations and branches and introduced locomotives. The CMR was worked by the GWR from 1877 and amalgamated with it in 1896.

WHEAL OWLES

AD   A prosperous tin mine commenced by 1815 and closed by a flood disaster in 1/1893. A surface tramway including two inclines was in use and its remains can be seen. Sometimes known as the Parknoweth Tramway this may have served also adjoining mines including Wheal Boys,Wheal Drea and Parknoweth Mine.

Contractors lines

ARTHUR CARKEEK

C1   Construction of the GWR Chacewater-Perranporth-Shepherds line,   - /1904.

Gauge: ?

	0-6-0ST						s/s

CORNWALL COUNTY COUNCIL

C2   Construction of the Lostwithiel By-pass road, c /1937.

Gauge: 2ft 0in

-	4wDM	DC/Bg 2104	1937	New	(1)
-	4wDM	DC/Bg 2105	1937	New	(1)

(1) to Tolpetherwin Quarry

GRISSEL & PETO

C3   Construction of the Cornwall Minerals Railway, 1873-4.

Gauge: 4ft 8½in

ROEBUCK	?		＼			s/s
CORNWALL	?					s/s
LORD ROBARTES	0-6-0	IC RS	619	1847	(a)	(1)

(a) ex S.M.Peto, 5   (1) to Coode Son & Matthews, Portland,
                                                 Dorset

W.T.JINKIN

C4   Contract, details uncertain, in the Liskeard or Bodmin Road area.

Gauge: 4ft 8½in

BLANCHE	0-4-0ST	OC P	505	1893	New	s/s

J.C.LANG

C5   Construction of the GWR Bodmin Road to Bodmin branch line, c /1886

Gauge: ?

SAM	0-6-0ST	MW		(a)	s/s
NASHETON	0-6-0ST	MW			s/s

(a) MW 106/1864 was an 0-6-0ST IC named SAM but it is not certain that this is the
    SAM of the above contract.

C6   Construction and rebuilding of the PD&SWJR Bere Alston - Kelly Bray line,
        1904-8.

Gauge: 4ft 8½in

	6 wheel loco				(a)	s/s
ADA	0-4-0ST	OC	Spittle 5 c1896		(b)	s/s

(a) ex W.T.Relf,
(b) ex Devon Great Consols, Tavistock, Devon

PITTRAIL LTD.

C7   Lifting of the BR Chacewater- Newquay line, 1964.

Gauge: 4ft 8½in

		DM			(a)	(1)
-						

(a) ex ?   (1) to   ?

ROBERT T. RELF AND SON

C8   Construction of the GWR Trenance Valley (Bojea) branch, St. Austell, c /1920.

Gauge: 4ft 8in

ABER		?						s/s
RELF No.8		0-6-0ST	IC	MW	1400	1899	(a)	(1)

(a) ex Fareham contract, Hants   (1) to Thos W Ward Ltd , Sheffield, Plant
                                            No.36031, c /1925

E. THOMAS & CO. LTD., BUILDING & CONTRACTORS, PONSANOOTH, TRURO

C9   Locomotive kept at this contractors yard when not in use.

Gauge: 4ft 8½in

		4wDM	RH	349041	1953	(a)	(1)
-							

(a) ex Thos W Ward Ltd , Grays, Essex,   (1) to C.Ware, scrap merchants, Carharrack,
        1/1973; f.   , Aden   /1975

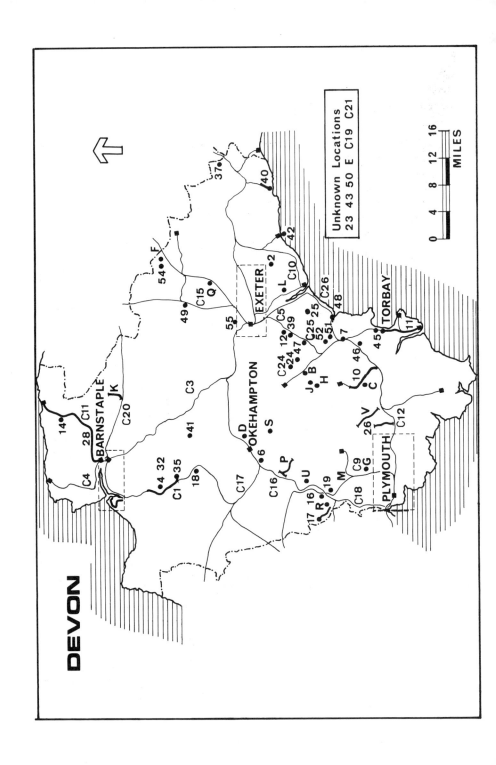

DEVON

BARNSTAPLE

OKEHAMPTON

EXETER

TORBAY

PLYMOUTH

Unknown Locations
23 43 50 E C19 C21

0 4 8 12 16
MILES

One of the Ruston diesels of A.R.C.Penlee Quarries
at work on the quay at Newlyn.   19/8/1963   (R.R.Darsley)

J.W.JENKIN (RH 375315) at A.R.C. Penlee Quarries   13/3/1965
(R.K.Hateley)

The unusual TOBY (S 6520) at Port of Par (now E.C.C)
20/7/1951   (G.Alliez)

ALFRED (WB 3058) also at Port of Par   (R.A.Fox)

One of the Sara & Burgess locos at Falmouth Docks.
(Collection of R.A.Fox)

The more conventional No.4 (HL 3670) at Falmouth
Docks   (R.A.Fox)

5 & 6 , 1¾ Ton class,(both CE 5876) at Camborne
Mines.   4/6/1972   (P.D.Nicholson)

An unidentified 0-4-0BE of the WR W217 type,
one of many at South Crofty Mine   (P.D.Nicholson)

CANOPUS (MW 1547) of the Pentewan Railway
(Collection of F.W.Mabbott)

"11" , 5 Ton class, (CE 5918) at Wheal Jane.
4/6/1972   (P.D.Nicholson)

RH 237897 at E.C.C., Meeth Works. 11/7/1970

(R.K.Hateley)

LORNA DOONE (KS 4250) at Devon County Council,
Wilminstone Quarry.

(F.Jones)

2 (AB 2221) at Devonport Dockyard.
24/6/1965.   (R.K.Hateley)

12 (AE 1690) at Devonport Dockyard.   (F.Jones)

YARD No.5332 (FH 3816) on the passenger train
at Devonport Dockyard. 24/6/1965   (R.K.Hateley)

HUGO (Spittle 3) at Devon Great Consols.
                        (Collection of R.A.Fox)

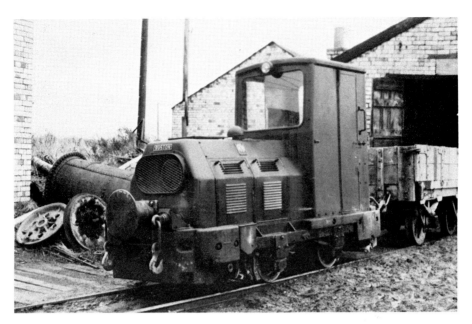

RH 518187 at North Devon Clay, Peters Marland
1/1970 (R.K.Hateley)

EFFICIENCY (RH 446207) at North Devon Clay
1/1970 (R.K.Hateley)

JF 3930037 and 3930048 derelict at North
Devon Clay,   11/7/1970   (R.K.Hateley)

PROGRESS (JF 4000001) at North Devon Clay
1/1970   (R.K.Hateley)

P 2074 at Exeter Gasworks, 7/1961 (R.C.Riley)

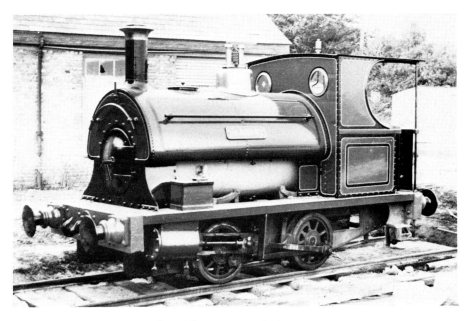

LEE MOOR No.2 (P 784) at Lee Moor Works.
23/8/1967 (M.J.Messenger)

(Ex S.R. 101) at Taylor Woodrow, East Yelland Power
Station contract.   (Collection of R.A.Fox)

E760 EXE (MW 1362) at Pilton Yard, Lynton &
Barnstaple Railway   (Collection of F.W.Mabbott)

L 34758 at Fisons Ltd., Ashcott, Great Plain Works.
29/4/1973   (B.Rumary)

L 51989 at Fisons Ltd., Ashcott, Pools Heath Works
29/4/1973   (B.Rumary)

NIDD (KS 3112) at Roads Reconstruction (now A.R.C.),
New Frome Quarry   (F.Jones)

VF 798 at Roads Reconstruction, New Frome Quarry.
14/8/1949   (G.Alliez)

1 (S 9374) at A.R.C. New Frome Quarry.
13/8/1968   (R.K.Hateley)

1 (TH 133V) and 3 (TH 152V) at A.R.C. New Frome Quarry
29/4/1973 (during the IRS AGM visit)   (B.Rumary)

(TH 200v) with the IRS special train at Great Elm level
crossing, A.R.C. New Frome Quarry. 29/4/1973. (B.Rumary)

2ft0in gauge steam locomotives, including AB 1855, stored
at Roads Reconstruction Ltd., Cranmore Depot. (F.Jones)

Devon

Locomotive worked systems

ASSOCIATED PORTLAND CEMENT MANUFACTURERS LTD.,PLYMSTOCK WORKS

1   A modern cement works,opened c1963,with rail sidings connecting onto the BR Plymstock branch. Loco shed at SX 506542.

Gauge: 4ft 8½in

	-	4wDH	TH	125V	1963	New

BICTON WOODLANDS RAILWAY,BICTON GARDENS,NEAR BUDLEIGH SALTERTON

2   A passenger carrying pleasure line about 1000yards in length in the form of a return loop. Opened 6/4/1963. The depot and terminal station are at SV 073863.

Ref:'The Bicton Woodland Railway' by N.D.G.James ;Rolle Estate 1967.

Gauge:1ft 6in.

No.1	WOOLWICH	0-4-0T	OC	AE	1748	1916	(a)
No.2	BICTON	4wDM		RH	213839	1942	(b)
No.3	CARNEGIE	0-4-4-0DM		HE	4524	1954	(c)
No.4	BUDLEY	4wDM		RH	235624	1945	(d)

(a) ex E.L.Pitt & Co (Coventry)Ltd.,Brackley,
      Northants,4/1962;f. Royal Arsenal,
      Woolwich.
(b) ex M.E.Engineering Ltd.,Cricklewood,
      5/1963;f. Royal Arsenal,Woolwich
(c) ex F.J.Dartnell,Upminster,Essex,2/1966;
      f. Royal Arsenal,Woolwich.
(d) ex W.Morris,Bromyard,Herefords, c6/1974

BIDEFORD,WESTWARD HO AND APPLEDORE RAILWAY

3   A six mile long line opened Bideford - Northam 24/4/1901 and extended to Appledore 1/5/1908. Principally passenger traffic operated,although some goods were carried. Locomotive and carriage sheds were located at Bideford (SS 452271) and still stand.
All services were suspended from 28/3/1917 when the line and locomotives were requisitioned for government use.The track was lifted shortly afterwards.

Ref: 'The Bideford Westward Ho and Appledore Railway,1901-1917' by D.Stuckey; Town & Country Press,1962.

Gauge:4ft 8½in

1	GRENVILLE	2-4-2T	OC	HE	713	1900	New	(1)
2	KINGSLEY	2-4-2T	OC	HE	714	1900	New	(2)
3	TORRIDGE	2-4-2T	OC	HE	715	1900	New	(1)

        (1) to MoM Pembrey,Carms.,8/1917;later
             disposal unknown.
        (2) to MoM Avonmouth,Glos.,8/1917;later to
             National Smelting Co.Ltd.,Avonmouth.

BOARD OF TRADE,HOME GROWN TIMBER SUPPLY DEPT.,TORRINGTON

4   Location of line not known;probably short lived.

Gauge: 2ft 0in.

	-	0-4-0PM	Bg	758	1918	New	s/s

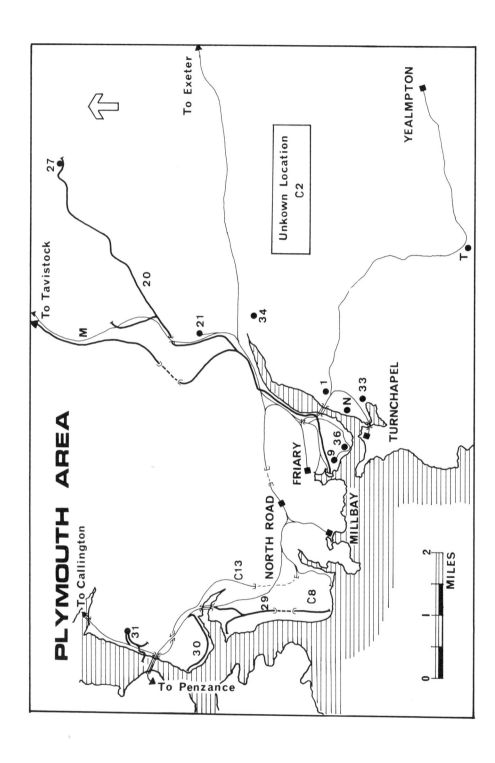

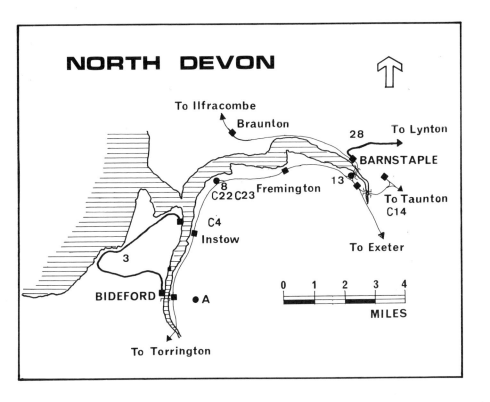

NORTH DEVON

To Ilfracombe

Braunton

To Lynton

28

BARNSTAPLE

13

To Taunton
C14

8
C22 C23 Fremington

C4

Instow

3

To Exeter

BIDEFORD

A

0 1 2 3 4

MILES

To Torrington

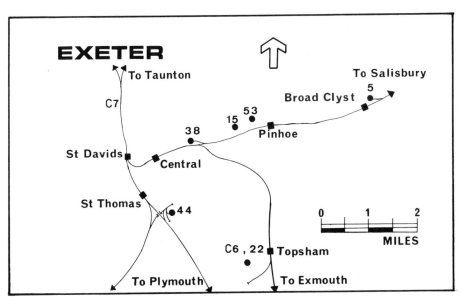

EXETER

To Taunton

To Salisbury

C7

Broad Clyst

5

15 53

38

Pinhoe

St Davids

Central

St Thomas

44

C6 , 22 Topsham

To Plymouth

To Exmouth

0 1 2

MILES

Broad Clyst Permanent Way Depot (Southern Railway until 1/1/1948)

5   A sleeper depot on the north side of the ex-LSWR Exeter-Salisbury line at the east end of Broad Clyst station (SX 992953).Standard gauge sidings served the yard which was closed c/1962. Track lifted and site cleared by 1965.

Gauge: 4ft 8½in

49S		4wPM	?			Wdn 9/1959
DS1169		4wDM	RH	237923	1946	(a)	(1)

(a) ex Engineers Dept,Folkestone Warren, Kent   (1) to Engineers Dept, Taunton,Somerset, c/1964

Meldon Quarry (Southern Railway until 1/1/1948;London & South Western Railway until 1/1/1923)

6   A large quarry at SX 568928,about two miles west of Okehampton,on the south side of the railway line.Production of granite ballast from here commenced about 1895 and has been steadily extended since then. In 1933 the quarry was modernised and new crushing and screening plant installed.
The narrow gauge operated in the quarry in a figure of eight layout and has been superceded and removed for some time. Standard gauge sidings serve the screening plant to transport the output from the quarry;a locomotive shed is available for the quarry locomotive.

Gauge: 4ft 8½in

225S	0-4-0ST	OC	MW	767	1881	(a)	(1)
500S	0-6-0T	IC	Longhedge		1890	(b)	(2)
DS3152	0-6-0T	IC	9E		1898	(c)	(3)
DS 682	0-6-0T	IC	9E		1898	(d)	(4)
DS 234	0-6-0T	IC	VIW	4375	1942	(e)	(5)

(a) ex SER 313 , 3/1927   (1) Wdn 7/1938; Scr at Elh
(b) ex SR A607 , 9/1938   (2) Wdn 11/1949;Scr
(c) ex SR 272 , 6/1950   (3) Wdn 8/1960; Scr
(d) ex BR 30238, 8/1960   (4) Wdn 12/1962;Scr
(e) ex BR 30062, 12/1962; f USATC 1277   (5) Wdn /1967;Scr

Note: Other steam and diesel locomotives numbered in capital stock have been used as regular shunters here.

Gauge: 2ft 0in

–		4wPM	FH	1833	1933	New	s/s
–		4wDM	RH	187073	1938	New	s/s
–		4wDM	RH	198284	1940	New	s/s
–		4wDM	RH	221615	1943	New	(1)

(1) Sold and exported to Egypt

Newton Abbot Station (Great Western Railway until 1/1/1948)

7   A small broad-gauge loco stands preserved on the down platform here (SX 868712)

Gauge: 7ft 0¼in

151	TINY	0-4-0VBWT	VCG	Sara & Co,Penrhyn	1868	(a)

(a) from the South Devon Railway,became GWR 2180;Wdn 6/1883 and used as a stationary engine at Newton Abbot works until preserved, /1927

CENTRAL ELECTRICITY GENERATING BOARD,EAST YELLAND POWER STATION,NEAR BIDEFORD

8   A power station on the Taw estuary opened in 1953.Rail sidings at SS 483324
     connect with the BR Barnstaple-Torrington line but coal is normally brought in
     by sea and rail traffic occurs only under exceptional conditions.

Gauge: 4ft 8½in

-	0-6-0DM	AB	422	1958	(a)	(1)
No.5	4wDM	MR	3966	1939	(b)	

(a) ex Tir John Power Station,Swansea,   (1) to Earley Power Station,Berks, 9/1968
    5/1966
(b) ex Earley Power Station,Berks, 1/1970

COAST LINES LTD.,SHIPOWNERS,VICTORIA WHARF,PLYMOUTH (f. Powell & Hough)

9   Quayside sidings at the end of the BR Cattedown branch. The lines terminate in a
     headshunt in a tunnel at SX 490537 which is used as a loco shed. The sidings
     date from c/1898.

Gauge: 4ft 8½in

ALICIA	0-6-0ST	OC				
	Reb from 0-4-0ST	OC				s/s c/1935
-	4wPM	H				
-	4wPM	FH	1834	1933	New s/s	/1956
-	4wDM	FH	3281			

DART VALLEY RAILWAY CO. LTD.

     A company owning two separate ex-GWR sections of line in Devon on which summer
     passenger services are operated.

     Dart Valley Railway

10   A nine mile branch line from Totnes to Ashburton,built to 7ft 0¼in gauge as a
     subsidiary of the South Devon Railway. Opened to traffic on 1/5/1872,it became
     part of the GWR and was converted to 4ft 8½in gauge on 21-22/5/1892.
     BR withdrew passenger services from 2/11/1958 and freight services from 10/9/1962.
     Renovation of the line and rolling stock by the Dart Valley Co commenced in 1966
     and after the issuing of a light railway order passenger services recommenced on
     the Totnes (Riverside)- Buckfastleigh section 5/4/1969.
     For some years the loco facilities were at Ashburton station (SX 756697) and stock
     movements used the line thereto from Buckfastleigh.The construction of a new dual
     carriageway A38 road on its line necessitated the closure and lifting of this
     section from 11/1971.Present servicing facilities are at Buckfastleigh station
     (SX 746663) and at Staverton Bridge (SX 785638). Stock has also been stored at
     BR Newton Abbot during winter seasons,and at Totnes (Quay branch) prior to 1966.

     Ref: 'The Dart Valley Railway'; Ian Allan, 1967

Gauge: 4ft 8½in

	1369	0-6-0PT	OC	Sdn		1934	(a)
	1420	0-4-2T	IC	Sdn		1933	(b)
	1450	0-4-2T	IC	Sdn		1935	(c)
	1466	0-4-2T	IC	Sdn		1936	(d) (1)
	1638	0-6-0PT	IC	Sdn		1951	(e)
	4555	2-6-2T	OC	Sdn		1924	(f)
	4588	2-6-2T	OC	Sdn		1927	(g) (2)
	5239	2-8-0T	OC	Sdn		1924	(h)
	6412	0-6-0PT	IC	Sdn		1934	(2)
	6430	0-6-0PT	IC	Sdn		1937	(j)
	6435	0-6-0PT	IC	Sdn		1937	(k)
6998	BURTON AGNES HALL	4-6-0	OC	Sdn		1949	(l) (1)
7827	LYDHAM MANOR	4-6-0	OC	Sdn		1950	(m) (3)
	80064	2-6-4T	OC	Bton		1953	(n)
	No.1	0-4-0ST	OC	P	2031	1942	(o)
	No.2 (D2192)	0-6-0DM		Sdn		1961	(p)

	No.2	DINKUM	4wPMR	Wkm	4127		(q)
PWM 3290	No.3	FLOWER	4wPMR	Wkm	4840	1948	(q)
	No.5	BRAMBLE BASHER	4wPMR	Wkm	4146		(q)
	–		4wPMR	Wkm	4149		(q)
PWM 2802			4wPMR	Wkm	4980	c1949	(q)
PWM 3772			4wPMR	Wkm	6651	c1953	(q)
PWM 3944			4wPMR	Wkm	6929	c1954	(q)
PWM 3957	No.4		4wPMR	Wkm	6942	c1954	(q)
PWM 4309			4wPMR	Wkm	7512		(q)
	–		4wPMR	Wkm	946		
900391			4wPMR	Wkm		1932	

Note:Of the petrol trolleys listed above,by 1974 only Wkm 6942 retained an engine;Wkm
6929 was dismantled,Wkm 4146 and several others converted to engineers units.

(a) ex BR(WR),2/1965
(b) ex BR(WR),4/1965
(c) ex BR(WR),6/1965
(d) ex BR(WR),3/1964
(e) ex BR(LMR),4/1967;stored at Tyseley
    until moved here 11/1967
(f) ex BR(LMR),12/1963;stored at Tyseley
    until moved here.
(g) ex Woodham Bros.,Barry,10/1970;renovated
    by BREL Swindon/1971.
(h) ex Woodham Bros.,Barry,6/1973;restored
    at Newton Abbot.
(j) ex BR(WR), /1965.Used for spares.
(k) ex BR(WR),c11/1965
(l) ex BR(WR), 5/1966
(m) ex Woodham Bros.,Barry,7/1970;restored
    at Newton Abbot.
(n) ex Woodham Bros.,Barry, 2/1973
(o) ex S.W.G.B.,Exeter Gas Works,9/1969
(p) ex BR(WR), 8/1970
(q) ex BR(WR).

(1) to Great Western Society,Didcot Depot,
    Berks,12/1967
(2) to Torbay Steam Railway,12/1972
(3) to Torbay Steam Railway, 6/1973

Torbay Steam Railway

11   A six mile line from Paignton to Kingswear. Built to 7ft 0¼in gauge,Paignton to
Churston was opened 14/3/1861 and Churston to Kingswear 16/8/1864. Regauged to
4ft 8½in in 1892 and incorporated in the GWR. Passenger services continued by
BR until .12/1972.
The line was taken over by the Dart Valley Co. and public passenger services
commenced 1/1/1973. After this first year the subsidised winter service has
been discontinued and services operate in the summer only.
A new passenger station and servicing facilities have been built at Paignton
(Queens Park)(SX 890606) on the east side of the BR station.

Gauge: 4ft 8½in

4588		2-6-2T	OC	Sdn		1927	(a)	
6412		0-6-0PT	IC	Sdn		1934	(a)	(2)
7827	LYDHAM MANOR	4-6-0	OC	Sdn		1950	(b)	
4472	FLYING SCOTSMAN	4-6-2	3C	Don	1564	1923	(c)	(1)

(a) ex Dart Valley Railway,12/1972
(b) ex Dart Valley Railway,after renovation
    at BR Newton Abbot,6/1973
(c) ex BR Derby Works,after repainting,
    7/1973.

(1) to Market Overton Depot,Rutland,10/1973
(2) to West Somerset Railway Co Ltd ,
    Minehead, Somerset, 4/1976

DEVON BASALT & GRANITE CO LTD , NEAR CHRISTOW

12   A standard gauge line ran from Christow station (SX 839868) on the GWR Teign
Valley branch across the river Teign and the B3193 road to a point near Bridford
Barytes mine. An incline then ran to the quarry near SX 824866. The quarry
closed c /1932; the track has been lifted and the formation of the incline is
very overgrown.

Gauge: 4ft 8½in

	-	0-4-0ST	OC	MW	1420	1899	(a)	s/s
3	ALDERMAN	0-4-0ST	OC	Lill				s/s ᶜ /1934

(a) ex R.T.Relf & Son, contrs, Fareham, Hants,
    No.11, c12/1911

DEVON CONCRETE WORKS LTD , BARNSTAPLE

13   A siding which connected with the BR Torrington line adjacent to Barnstaple
Junction station ran through the stockyard to the works at SS 555328. The BR
connection was lifted c7/1971 but the siding remains in use internally with
flat trolleys used to move concrete castings about the stockyard. A road lorry
is also used as motive power.

Gauge: 4ft 8½in

PWM 3378	4wPMR	Wkm	5959	c1951	(a)	s/s	/1973
PWM 3379	4wPMR	Wkm	5960	c1951	(a)		
PWM 3380	4wPMR	Wkm	5961	c1951	(a)	s/s	/1973

(a) ex BR (WR) , /1962 (Three units purchased to enable one to be kept in working order)

DEVON COUNTY COUNCIL

14   Beacon Down Quarry, Parracombe

A short tramway connected the roadstone quarry with the crushing plant at
SS667458. This line was not connected to the nearby Lynton & Barnstaple Railway.
The quarry closed in 1958 and the plant and track were removed, as subsequently
was the remaining loco.

Gauge: 2ft 0in

No. 56	LORNA DOONE	0-4-0ST	OC	KS	4250	1922	(a)	(1)
No. 60	MAID OF SKER	0-4-0ST	OC	KS	4251	1922	(b)	(2)
No. 114	PETER PAN	0-4-0ST	OC	KS	4256	1922	(b)	(3)
	ROSE OF THE TORRIDGE	0-4-0ST	OC	KS	4258	1922	(b)	(2)
(No. 493	JOSEPHINE)	4wDM		RH	243388	1946	New	(4)

(a) ex R.H.Neal & Co Ltd , contrs ,
    Barkingside, Essex, 165, by 1/1929
(b) ex Wilminstone Quarry

(1) to Wilminstone Quarry
(2) to Bideford Depot for road widening
    contracts
(3) to C.H.Lambe & Son Ltd , Bromsgrove,
    Worcs , 5/1959; later to Leighton
    Buzzard Light Railway, Beds
(4) to Pinhoe Road Plant Depot, Exeter,
    c /1958; retd c /1960; to ? ,
    dealer, Swindon, Wilts , c /1966;
    resold to A.Keef , Bampton, Oxon ,
    /1968

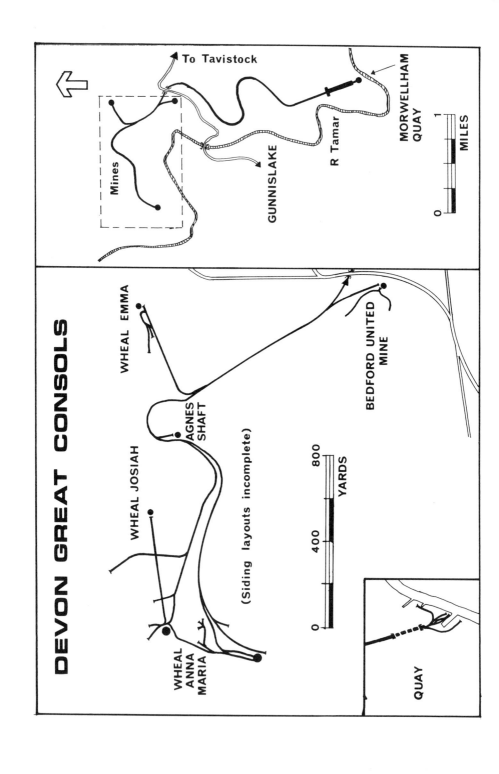

DEVON GREAT CONSOLS

WHEAL EMMA

WHEAL JOSIAH

AGNES SHAFT

WHEAL ANNA MARIA

(Siding layouts incomplete)

BEDFORD UNITED MINE

0   400   800
YARDS

QUAY

To Tavistock

Mines

GUNNISLAKE

R Tamar

MORWELLHAM QUAY

0   1
MILES

Central Vehicle & Plant Repair Depot, Pinhoe Road Trading Estate, Exeter

15   A depot at SS 955941 where locomotives have been stored pending disposal.

Gauge: 2ft 0in

No. 56	LORNA DOONE	0-4-0ST	OC	KS	4250	1922	(a)	(1)
No. 493	JOSEPHINE	4wDM		RH	243388	1946	(b)	(2)

(a) ex Wilminstone Quarry, 12/1955
(b) ex Beacon Down Quarry, c /1958

(1) to C.H.Lambe & Son Ltd , Bromsgrove,
    Worcs , c4/1960; then to Museum of
    Science & Industry, Birmingham,5/1960
(2) retd to Beacon Down Quarry, c /1960

Wilminstone Quarry, Tavistock

16   A roadstone quarry and crushing plant at SX 490755, which was served by an
internal tramway including a short incline. The railway was replaced by road
transport and the track lifted 1952. The quarry has subsequently become disused.

Gauge: 2ft 0in

No. 56	LORNA DOONE	0-4-0ST	OC	KS	4250	1922	(a)	(1)
No. 59	BUNTY	0-4-0ST	OC	KS	4265	1922	(b)	(2)
No. 60	MAID OF SKER	0-4-0ST	OC	KS	4251	1922	(c)	(3)
No.113	PIXIE	0-4-0ST	OC	KS	4260	1922	(d)	(4)
No.114	PETER PAN	0-4-0ST	OC	KS	4256	1922	(d)	(3)
	ROSE OF THE TORRIDGE	0-4-0ST	OC	KS	4258	1922	(e)	(3)

(a) ex Beacon Down Quarry
(b) ex R.H.Neal & Co Ltd,contrs,Barkingside,
    Essex, by 4/1929
(c) ex ? by 4/1929; orig R.H.Neal & Co Ltd
    contrs, Barkingside, Essex, 166
(d) ex Thos.W.Ward Ltd , Grays Depot, Essex,
    /1929; orig R.H.Neal & Co Ltd ,
    contrs, Barkingside, Essex
(e) ex ? by 7/1929; prev Stewart & McDonnell,
    Sutton By-Pass road contract,Surrey

(1) to Pinhoe Road Plant Depot, Exeter,
    12/1955
(2) to Bideford Depot for use on road
    widening contracts

(3) to Beacon Down Quarry
(4) to J.P.Mullett, Berkhamstead, Herts ,
    for preservation by the Industrial
    Locomotive Society, 7/1957; later to
    the Leighton Buzzard Light Railway,
    Beds

DEVON GREAT CONSOLS LTD , TAVISTOCK (Devon Great Consols Co Ltd until /1899)

17   A 4½ mile long line from Wheal Anna Maria (SX 425733) serving other shafts of
this extensive mining complex extending over 160 acres on the east of the Tamar,
about a mile north of Gunnislake,ran to a point above Morwellham Quay. From here
a self acting incline ½ mile long gave access to the quayside sidings (SX 445695).
Mining activities for copper and arsenic commenced in 1844 and were amongst the
largest and richest copper workings in the world in their heyday. Tramways were
in use to connect the shafts with the dressing floors by 1856, while the main
line to Morwellham opened in 1858. Mining ceased in 12/1901, the company going
into voluntary liquidation. Machinery including the railway installations was
sold in 5/1903 and the track lifted for scrap.

    Ref: 'The Mines and Mineral Railways of East Cornwall and West Devon';
        by D.Bradford Barton, Truro, 1964.

Gauge: 4ft 8½in

-	0-4-0T	OC	Gilkes,Wilson		1858	New	s/s
-	0-4-0T	OC	Gilkes,Wilson		1859	New	s/s
HUGO	0-4-0ST	OC	Spittle	3	1882	(a)	(1)
ADA	0-4-0ST	OC	Spittle	5	c1896	(a)	(1)

(a) ex Thos.Spittle Ltd, Newport, Mon   (1) to Thos.Spittle Ltd, Newport,Mon,
/1903.

A (narrow gauge ?) locomotive was built by Messrs Nicholls,Williams & Co,Bedford
Foundry,Tavistock and put into service on the surface tramways in 1856. Its subsequent
fate is not known.

E.C.C.BALL CLAYS LTD.,MEETH WORKS (Hexter & Budge Ltd until 8/1970; Meeth (North Devon)
Clay Co Ltd until /1965)

18   Works opened c/1924 to exploit the extensive ball clay deposits in the area,in
association with the opening of the SR Halwill-Torrington line in 1925. The
narrow gauge line connected several mine shafts (the earlies around SS 528077)
and pits with the drying sheds and standard gauge siding at SS 538086.
In 1965 the workings became part of the ECC group;extensive new opencast
workings were commenced and the railway ceased regular use by c/1968,being
replaced by road transport. The majority of the track and equipment remained
until it was removed in 8/1970.

Gauge: 2ft 0in

	WESTERN LEA	0-6-0WT	OC	HC	1314	1918	(a)	(1)
	-	4wPM		MH	A110	1925		(2)
	-	4wPM		MH				(3)
No.1		4wDM		RH	237897	1945	New	(4)
(No.2)		4wDM		RH	260118	1948	New	(4)

(a) ex P.& W.Anderson,contrs,North Devon &   (1) to P ,c/1929;later to Standard Brick
     Cornwall Jct Light Railway construction   & Sand Co Ltd,Redhill,Surrey,via
                                                 SLP
                                            (2) reb to form a stationary winch inside
                                                 a pithead building;remains to R.P.
                                                 Morris,Longfield,Kent, c12/1970
                                            (3) Dismantled /1965;later s/s
                                            (4) to Pollock Brown & Co Ltd,Northam
                                                 Ironworks,Southampton, 8/1970,for
                                                 scrap

E.C.C.QUARRIES LTD.,PITTS CLEAVE QUARRY,TAVISTOCK (Hoare Bros.Ltd until c/1962)

19   Stone quarries at SX 500760 on the east of the BR (ex-GWR) Tavistock - Launceston
branch. A standard gauge siding connected with this line while a narrow gauge
system at a higher level served the quarries. All rail traffic ceased in 1963
and the track was lifted shortly afterwards.

Gauge: 4ft 8½in

	-	4wDM(f PM)	MR	3793	1927	New	Scr c12/1963

Gauge: 2ft 0in

	-	4wDM	RH	166033	1933	(a)	Scr /1963
	-	4wDM	MR	9546	1950	New	(1)

(a) ex Hillhead Quarries Ltd,Buxton,Derbys   (1) Stored from /1963 until sold to J.J.A.
                                                          Evans,Trecarrell Mill,Trebullett,
                                                          Launceston,Cornwall,for preservation,
                                                          9/1970

ENGLISH CLAYS LOVERING POCHIN & CO.LTD.

Lee Moor Tramway (E.C.C.Ltd.until 12/10/1932;Martin Bros Ltd.until 9/4/1919)

20   A seven mile long tramway from Cattewater (Plymouth) to the Lee Moor Works.The
line crossed the GWR main line on the level at Laira Jct.and included two self
acting inclines at Cann Wood and Torycombe.Locomotives were only used on the
section between the inclines (with the shed at SX 565612),the lower section
being horse worked.
Lee Moor china clay pit (originally known as Morley Clay Works) was opened in
1830 by John Dickens and John Cawley,eventually becoming the Lee Moor Porcelain
Clay Co. in 1850,and purchased by the Martin family on 27/11/1862.
The tramway was connected with the Plymouth and Dartmoor Railway.It was shoddily
built by the South Devon & Tavistock Railway,opened 9/1854 and closed after an
accident 4/10/1854. It reopened after rebuilding 29/9/1858 and worked regularly
until 1939. The upper portion was disused from 11/1945 when a pipeline was
opened for clay slurry from Lee Moor to Marsh Mills Drying Works.Much of the
track remained in situ and occasional horse drawn wagons were operated over
the lower section to maintain the right of way at Laira over the BR main line
until 1960. All track in the Plymouth area was removed 1961-2,and much of the
remainder has been lifted also.

Ref; 'The Lee Moor Tramway' by R.M.S.Hall; Oakwood Press.

Gauge: 4ft 6in

LEE MOOR No.1	0-4-0ST	OC	P	783	1899	New	(1)
LEE MOOR No.2	0-4-0ST	OC	P	784	1899	New	(1)

(1) Wdn.11/1945;remained in their shed,
until in 1964 their preservation
was commenced by the Lee Moor
Tramway Preservation Group (q.v).

Marsh Mills Drying Works.

21   A drying works for clay from Lee Moor served by sidings reached by a steeply
graded line from the BR (ex GWR) Plymouth-Yelverton branch near Marsh Mills
station.Locos stand in the open at SX 521575.

Gauge:4ft 8½in

–	0-4-0DM		JF	22917	1940	(a)	(1)
–	0-4-0F	OC	WB	3121	1957	New	
–	0-4-0DH		EEV	3987*	1970	New	

* Additionally allocated works number D1280 - not shown on plate.

(a) ex R.O.F.Bridgend,Glam./1948   (1) Wdn./1957;to E.L.Pitt & Co.(Coventry)
                                             Ltd.,Brackley,Northants/1964.

EXETER CITY COUNCIL,COUNTESS WEAR SEWAGE WORKS.

22   A sewage treatment works at SX 950888.The tramway served the works and extended
along the river bank almost to the Exeter By-pass at SX 941894. The rail system
was replaced by new internal roadways in 1962 and the track subsequently lifted.

Gauge: 2ft 0in

–	4wPM		L	5098	1933	New	Scr.1949
10	4wPM		MR	9104	1941	(a)	(1)

(a) ex Forestry Commission,Mamhead,9/1946   (1) to C.Shears,Winkleigh Aerodrome for
                                                  preservation,/1968.

LORD EXMOUTH,CANONTEIGN TIMBER ESTATE,ASHTON,NEAR CHRISTOW

23   A forestry tramway,closed 1923 and the track lifted. The estate subsequently
      passed to the Forestry Commission,without any rail system.

Gauge: 2ft 0in

-	4wPM	(Bg?)	c1917	Sold
-	4wPM	(Bg?)	c1917	Sold

FERRUBRON MANUFACTURING CO.LTD.,GREAT ROCKS MINE,HENNOCK,BOVEY TRACEY

24   The mine (at SX 828816) produced micaceous haematite,used in protective paints,
      and was commenced in 1902. It was worked on six levels,five of them being rail
      served.There are also three adits on the opposite side of the hill at Beadon
      Lane (SX 819817) which are connected through the hill.
      The track gauges are 1ft 6in and 2ft 0in on alternate levels. The lowest (No.1)
      level was connected to No.3 by a long 2ft 0in gauge incline. The locos were on
      No.3 (1ft 6in) and No.4 (2ft 0in) levels. The mill was on No.2 level and the
      product was piped to drying sheds at SX 832817.
      The company went into voluntary liquidation on 29/8/1969 and the site has been
      abandoned and partially dismantled.

Gauge: 2ft 0in

-	4wBE	Ferrubron *	New	s/s	c/1969

Gauge: 1ft 6in

-	4wBE	Ferrubron *	New	s/s	c/1969

* One loco built /1957,the other /1959.

FORESTRY COMMISSION,MAMHEAD FORESTRY RAILWAY

25   A line in the area some three miles north-west of Dawlish,exact location unknown.
      System closed by 1946 and dismantled.

Gauge: 2ft 0in

-	4wPM	MR	9104	1941	New	(1)

                         (1) to Exeter City Council,Countess Wear
                             Sewage Works, 9/1946

IVYBRIDGE CHINA CLAY CO.LTD.,BROWN HEATH,DARTMOOR (China Clay Corporation Ltd. until
                                                        /1921)

26   A 7 mile long,3ft 0in gauge,line,the Redlake Tramway,commenced at an interchange
      siding with the GWR near Ivybridge (SX 657565). A cable worked incline gave
      access to the upper,locomotive worked,section which extended to the clay works at
      SX 647670, which was 600 ft above the GWR level.The line was used to convey
      workmen,coal to and sand from the works,the clay being transported by pipeline.
      Opened 9/1911 and closed with the works in 1932,being dismantled in 1933.
      The use made of the 2ft 0in gauge locomotive is not clear.

Ref: 'A Regional History of the Railways of Great Britain,Vol.1' by David St John
     Thomas; David & Charles, 1960.

Gauge: 3ft 0in

C.A.HANSON	0-4-2T	OC	KS	1228	1911	New	Scr /1921
DARTMOOR	0-4-2ST	OC	KS	1146	1912	New	(1)
LADY MALLABY-DEELEY	4wVBT	G	AtW	111	1928	New	(1)

                         (1) to Marple & Gillott Ltd ,Sheffield,for
                             scrap, /1933
Gauge: 2ft 0in

DARTMOOR	0-4-0ST	OC	KS	1190	1911	New	(1)

                         (1) taken by KS in part payment for KS 1146
                             and sent direct to Ship Canal Portland
                             Cement Manufacturers Ltd,Ellesmere
                             Port, Ches, c2/1912

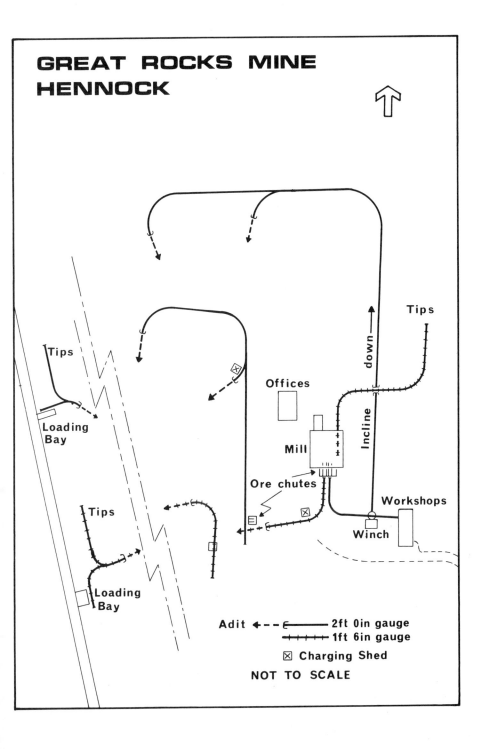

GREAT ROCKS MINE
HENNOCK

Tips

Offices

down

Incline

Tips

Tips

Loading
Bay

Mill

Ore chutes

Workshops

Winch

Tips

Loading
Bay

Adit ◄ – – E——— 2ft 0in gauge
+++++ 1ft 6in gauge
⊠ Charging Shed
NOT TO SCALE

LEE MOOR TRAMWAY PRESERVATION SOCIETY

27 An enthusiasts group which from 5/1964 has been restoring the two locomotives
and other relics of the Lee Moor Tramway at the locomotive shed at Torycombe
(SX 565612) which has been leased from English Clays,Lovering Pochin & Co Ltd.

Gauge: 4ft 6in

LEE MOOR No.1		0-4-0ST	OC	P	783	1899	(a)	(2)
LEE MOOR No.2		0-4-0ST	OC	P	784	1899	(a)	(1)

(a) ex English Clays,Lovering Pochin & Co Ltd (1) to National Trust,Saltram House,
5/1964 Plympton, 7/1970, for display
after completion of external
renovation.
(2) to Wheal Martyn China Clay Museum,
Cornwall, 17/3/1975

LYNTON & BARNSTAPLE RAILWAY

28 A line 19 miles long from Barnstaple (Town) station to Lynton,opened 11/5/1898
for passenger and freight traffic. Locomotive and carriage sheds were at Pilton
Yard,Barnstaple (SS 558337).
The company was absorbed into the Southern Railway on 1/1/1923 and a new
locomotive,and some stock,was provided by the new owners.
The line closed 29/9/1935 and the equipment was auctioned 13/11/1935.
The track was lifted by the SR from Lynton to MP 15½, 9-11/1935,and the
remainder by S.Castle of Plymouth 11/1935 to mid-1936,except Pilton Yard -
Barnstaple Town lifted summer 1937.

Ref: 'The Lynton & Barnstaple Railway' by Brown,Prideaux & Radcliffe;
David & Charles, 1964
'The Lynton & Barnstaple Railway' by L.T.Catchpole; Oakwood Press,

Gauge: 1ft 11½in

E759	YEO	2-6-2T	OC	MW	1361	1897	New	(1)
E760	EXE	2-6-2T	OC	MW	1362	1897	New	(1)
E761	TAW	2-6-2T	OC	MW	1363	1897	New	(1)
E762	LYN	2-4-2T	OC	BLW	15965	1898	New	(1)
E188	LEW	2-6-2T	OC	MW	2042	1925	New	(2)

(1) Scr at Pilton Yard by John Cashmore Ltd,
11/1935
(2) to ? for repairs, 9/1936;then to
F.C.de Vera Cruz,Mexico, /1936

Devonport Dockyard

29   This dockyard dates back to 1691. The Dockyard Railway was opened in 1867,although a tramway may have been in use earlier.The line is some two miles long,from a connection with the BR (ex-GWR) line near Keyham station, serving the main North Yard,and via a lengthy tunnel,to the South Yard. The main loco shed is in the North Yard at SX 448562 but a number of locos are kept semi-permanently in the South Yard. A regular workmen's passenger service was introduced in 1900 over the length of the system but was suspended from 16/5/1966 in connection with road improvements to render the tunnel redundant.

Gauge: 4ft 8½in

–		0-4-0T	G	(AP	450	1869?)New	s/s	
1		0-4-0ST	OC	HL	2399	1898	New	Scr /1948
2		0-4-0ST	OC	HL	2400	1898	New	Scr
3	MIDDLESBROUGH	0-4-0ST	OC	MW+				
		Reb Sir J.Jackson,Keyham			1903	(a)	(1)	
6		0-4-0T*	OC	HL	2599	1904	New	Scr /1955
7		0-4-0ST	OC	HL	2820	1910	New	Scr /1957
8		0-4-0ST	OC	HL	2821	1910	New	Scr c/1955
9		0-4-0ST	OC	AB	1406	1915	(b)	Scr /1957
No.10		0-4-0ST	OC	AB	1379	1914	New	Scr /1957
No.11		0-4-0ST	OC	AB	1380	1914	New	Scr /1957
12		0-4-0ST	OC	AE	1690	1915	New	(6)
No.13		0-4-0ST	OC	AB	1397	1915	New	Scr c/1959
No.14		0-4-0ST	OC	HL	3200	1916	New	Scr /1957
No.15		0-4-0ST	OC	HL	3201	1916	New	Scr /1957
No.16		0-4-0ST	OC	AB	1516	1919	New	Scr c/1955
No.17		0-4-0ST	OC	AB	2071	1939	New	(3)
No.18		0-4-0ST	OC	AB	2137	1942	New	(4)
2	(f No.19)	0-4-0ST	OC	AB	2221	1946	New	(2)
No.19		0-4-0ST	OC	WB	2962	1950	New	(5)
YARD No.4856		4wDM		FH	3737	1955	New(c)	(8)
YARD No.4857		4wDM		FH	3741	1955	New	
YARD No.4858 ++		4wDM		FH	3744	1955	New	
YARD No.4859 ++		4wDM		FH	3746	1955	New	(7)
YARD No.4860 ++		4wDM		FH	3747	1955	New	
YARD No.5197		4wDM		FH	3773	1955	New	
YARD No.5198		4wDM		FH	3774	1955	New	
YARD No.5199 ++		4wDM		FH	3775	1955	New	
YARD No.5200		4wDM		FH	3776	1956	New	
YARD No.5332 ++		4wDM		FH	3816	1956	New	(8)
–		4wD		S&H	7503		New	(9)

+ Works plates read 'Lennox Lange & Co,1883'   * Converted from crane tank
++ Locos which are known to be/have been normally allocated to the South Yard.

(a) ex Sir J.Jackson,contr.,Devonport,c/1907
(b) ex Admiralty,Rosyth,Fife.
(c) to RNAD Ernesettle,c7/1960;returned
    c/1960.

(1) to Wm.Gray & Co,Ltd.,W.Hartlepool,
    Co.Durham,c/1935
(2) to Dowty Preservation Society,
    Ashchurch,Glos.,3/1968
(3) to Small & Lewis,Gloucester,for scrap,
    3/1968
(4) to Small & Lewis,Gloucester,2/1968;
    scr.by Avon Metals Ltd.,Cheltenham,
    3/1968
(5) to Great Western Society,Bodmin,
    Cornwall,2/1969
(6) Adapted as stationary boiler,c/1957;
    scrapped c/1959.
(7) to Wagon Repairs Ltd.,Stoke on Trent,
    Staffs,1/1971.
(8) to Wagon Repairs Ltd.,Gloucester,c/1970.
(9) to Portsmouth Dockyard,Hants.

Royal Naval Armament Depot,Bullpoint

30   A depot on the Hamoaze (at SX 437575 approx) opened 6/1916 with a standard gauge connection to the BR (ex GWR) near St.Budeaux station.The internal narrow gauge tramway was replaced by haulage by road tractors in 1958. The locos were then stored until their disposal.

Gauge: 1ft 6in

4	4wBE	WR		1926		s/s
181	4wBE	WR		1922		s/s
186	4wBE	WR		1932		s/s
229	4wBE	WR		1939		s/s
278	4wDM	RH	200776	1941	(a)	s/s
279	4wDM	RH	200777	1941	(a)	s/s
280	4wDM	RH	200778	1941	(b)	s/s
320	4wDM	RH	243397	1946	New	s/s
321	4wDM	RH	243398	1946	New	s/s
322	4wDM	RH	246810	1947	New	s/s

(a) ex Colwall Tunnel Bomb Store,Herefordshire
(b) ex Hawthorn Tunnel Bomb Store,Cinderford,
    Glos.

Royal Naval Armament Depot,Ernesettle

31   A large depot on the east bank of the Tamar.Standard gauge sidings connect with the BR (ex SR) Plymouth-Bere Alston line at SX 440592 while the narrow gauge system serves the depot,with interchange to the standard gauge,and also serves a jetty on the river at SX 438591.

Gauge: 4ft 8½in

"No.11" (f. No.9)	4wDM	RH	224349	1945	New
-	4wDM	FH	3737	1955	(a) (1)
V3 YARD No.13 (f.YARD No.91)	0-4-0DM	HE	3133	1944	(b)

(a) ex Devonport Dockyard, c7/1960
(b) ex RNAD Lodge Hill,Kent, 1/1962

(1) returned to Devonport, c/1960

Gauge: 1 metre.

There is no system of this gauge at this location;the locomotives may be rebuilt for use on the 2ft 6in gauge.

	YARD No.A497	4wDH	HE	6647	1967	(a)	Stored
	YARD No.A498	4wDH	HE	6648	1967	(a)	Stored

(a) ex Singapore Dockyard,1971.

Gauge: 2ft 6in

		4wDM	FH	2161	1938	New	(1)
1	YARD No.1	0-4-0DM	HE	2247	1940	New	
2	YARD No.2	0-4-0DM	HE	2246	1940	New	(3)
3	YARD No.3	0-4-0DM	HE	2242	1941	New	
4	YARD No.4	0-4-0DM	HE	2243	1941	New	
5	YARD No.5	0-4-0DM	HE	2244	1941	New	
6	YARD No.6	0-4-0DM	HE	2245	1941	New	
7	YARD No.52	4wDM	RH	235737	1945	New	s/s/1972
8	YARD No.53	4wDM	RH	235736	1945	New	s/s/1972
12		4wDM	RH	246794	1947	(a)	(5)
	YARD No.85	0-6-0DM	DC/Bg	2263	1949	(b)	(4)
9	YARD No.689 (f. YARD No.45)	4wDM	RH	268878	1952	(c)	(6)
	YARD No.AD497	4wDM	FH	3851	1958	New	(2)
	YARD No.722	4wDH	HE	6646	1967	New	

(a) ex RNCF Holton Heath,Dorset,c/1956
(b) ex RNAD Lodge Hill,Kent,10/1960
(c) ex RNAD Lodge Hill,Kent,11/1960

(1) to Joseph Arnold & Sons Ltd.,Leighton Buzzard,Beds.
(2) to RNAD Trecwn,Pembs.,6/1959
(3) to Messrs Davies & Cann Ltd.,Laira Bridge Rd.,Plymouth for scrap/1966
(4) to RNAD Broughton Moor,Cumbs.,c/1966
(5) to Messrs Davies and Cann Ltd.,Plymouth /1967;scrapped/1967
(6) to MacSalvors Ltd.,Pool,Cornwall,1/1973

MONMOUTH & SOUTH WALES COLLIERY OWNERS PITWOOD ASSOCIATION,NEAR TORRINGTON

32   A short lived forestry line,location uncertain.

Gauge: 1ft 8in

		4wPM	MR	1291	1918	(a)	(1)

(a) ex MR,/1919 (ordered as WDLR '3012')   (1) to H.Smith,Newport,Mon.,12/1920

F.J.MOORE LTD.,HOOE LAKE QUARRY,NEAR PLYMOUTH

33   An internal tramway serving a quarry (at SX 505531?).The premises were taken over by the U.S.Army in World War II.

Gauge: 2ft 0in

		4wPM	MR	1104	1918	(a)	s/s c/1946
		4wPM	MR	5404	1932	(b)	(1)

(a) ex WDLR '2825'
(b) ex R.R.Paton,12/1937

(1) to ECLP,Rostowrack Works,Cornwall, 1/1949

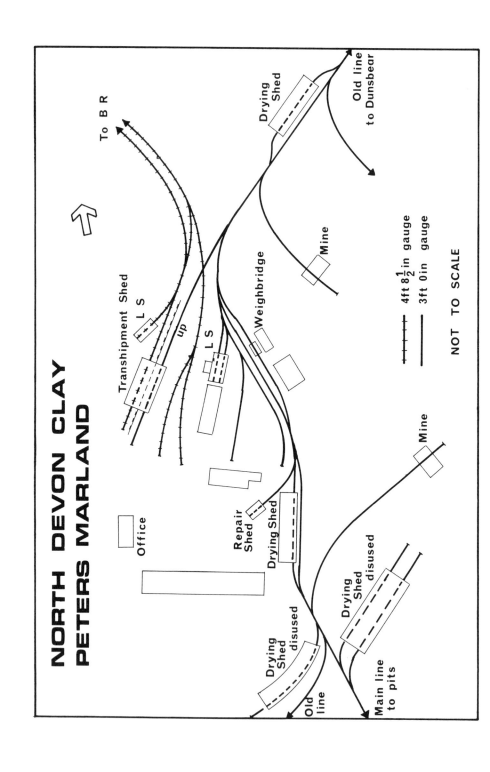

NORTH DEVON CLAY
PETERS MARLAND

To B R

Old line
to Dunsbear

Drying
Shed

Mine

Weighbridge

Transhipment Shed

L S

up

L S

Office

Repair
Shed

Drying Shed

Mine

Drying
Shed
disused

Drying
Shed
disused

Old
line

Main line
to pits

4ft 8½in gauge

3ft 0in gauge

NOT TO SCALE

34 One of the Lee Moor Tramway locomotives has been put on static display at this
location on completion of its external renovation (SX 521556).

Gauge: 4ft 6in

LEE MOOR No.?	0-4-0ST	OC	P	784	1899	(a)

(a) ex Lee Moor Tramway Preservation Society,
Torycombe, 7/1970

NORTH DEVON CLAY CO.LTD.,PETERS MARLAND (f Marland Brick & Clay Works Ltd.)

35 The 3ft 0in gauge Marland Light Railway was opened in 1880 to convey clay from
the workings on Merton and Marland moors to the LSWR at Torrington station.
About 4½ miles of this route were later closed and most of the course used for
the standard gauge North Devon and Cornwall Jct. Light Railway,opened by the SR
on 27/7/1925. Sidings from this line then provided rail access to the processing
works while several miles of narrow gauge remained to bring clay from the
numerous mines to this works. Workmen's passenger services had been operated on
the narrow gauge from Torrington to Marland.
During 1970 a system of internal roadways was built to connect the opencast
workings,which had superseded the mines,to the works. On completion of these
road transport was used,the last clay being transported over the 3ft gauge on
13/11/1970. All remaining narrow gauge track was lifted 11-12/1970. The standard
gauge remains in use at present. The standard gauge loco shed is at SS 503125,
the narrow gauge at SS 504125.

Ref: 'The North Devon & Cornwall Junction Light Railway' by Whetmath & Stuckey;
West Country Handbooks/Oakwood Press, 1963
RW , 1/1960, p

Gauge: 4ft 8½in

	MERSEY	0-4-0ST	OC	BH	1059	1892			
			Reb	C&J		1925	(a)	Scr	/1950
79		0-6-0ST	IC	MW	1049	1888	(b)	Scr	c/1946
	PROGRESS	0-4-0DM		JF	4000001	1945	New		
	PETER	0-4-0DM		JF	22928	1940	(c)		
	-	4wDM		RH	443642	1960	(d)		

(a) ex Lever Bros ,Port Sunlight,Ltd ,Ches,
via C&J, c/1925
(b) ex P.& W.Anderson,contrs,North Devon &
Cornwall Jct.Light Railway construction,
c/1925
(c) ex JF , 5/1950; Whitehead Iron & Steel
Co Ltd ,Newport, Mon until 4/1950

(d) ex M.E.Engineering Ltd , Cricklewood,
London, c1/1975; prev Lec Refrigeration
Ltd , Bognor Regis, Sussex

Gauge: 3ft 0in

1	MARY	0-6-0ST	OC	BH	576	1880	New	Scr	c/1925
2	MARLAND	0-6-0T	OC	WB	566	1883	New	Scr	/1925
3	PETER	0-4-0T	OC	Lewin		1871	(a)	Scr	by/1923
		0-4-0VBT					(b)	Scr	c/1908
11	AVONSIDE	0-6-0ST	OC	AE	1428	1901	New	Scr	c/1925
	(JERSEY I)	0-4-0	OC	FJ	129	1873	(c)		
		Reb	Peters Marland			1910		Scr	10/1949
	(JERSEY II)	0-4-0	OC	FJ	139	1874	(c)		
		Reb	Peters Marland			1915		Scr	3/1952
4	MERTON	0-4-0	OC	FJ	150	1875	(c)		
		Reb	Hodges,Exeter			1914		Scr	10/1949
	FORWARD	4wDM		JF	3900012	1947	New	(2)	
	(ADVANCE)	4wDM		JF	3930037	1949	New	(2)	
	(EFFICIENCY)	4wDM		JF	3930048	1951	New	(4)	

		RH	435398	1959	New	(3)	
	4wDM						
EFFICIENCY	4wDM	RH	446207	1961	New	Scr	/1971
-	4wDM	RH	435393	1959	(d)	(1)	
-	4wDH	RH	518187	1965	New	Scr	/1971

(a) ex ?

(b) ex ? ,South Shields,Co.Durham.

(c) ex Jersey Harbour Committee,St.Helier
    Breakwater,8/1908;rebuilt from 0-4-0ST
(d) ex Cementation Co.Ltd.,via Bungey,
    c7/1965;for spares only.

(1) Dismantled;remains scrapped by/1969

(2) Scr.on site 11/1970 by R.Gorman of
    Exeter.

(3) to Seaton & District Electric
    Tramway Co.,Seaton,c9/1972.

(4) to G.W.Glover, Upton Pyne, near
    Exeter, /1974

PLYMOUTH TAR DISTILLERIES LTD.,CATTEDOWN,PLYMOUTH

36 A tar processing works,with sidings connecting with the BR (ex SR) Cattedown
branch.The locomotive stood in the open at SX 491536.

Gauge: 4ft 8½in

-	4wDM	FH	3057	1946	(a)	(1)

(a) ex SWGB,Weston-super-Mare Gasworks,
    Somerset/1968

(1) to Somerset Railway Museum,Bleadon
    & Uphill Station,Somerset,c1/1971.

J.R.PRATT & SON LTD.,CHARDSTOCK SAND QUARRY,NEAR AXMINSTER

37 A sand quarry,closed 1945,and rail system dismantled.

Gauge: 2ft 0in

-	4wDM	RH	198306	1940	New	(1)

(1) to ? /1945;rebuilt as 4ft 8½in gauge
    4wDM and sold to Pollock Brown &
    Co.Ltd.,Northam,Southampton/1972.

RENWICK,WILTON & DOBSON(FUELS) LTD.,EXMOUTH JUNCTION COAL CONCENTRATION DEPOT,EXETER

38 A depot on the site of the SR Engineers Department Concrete Works at SX 934938,
on the north side of the BR Exeter-Salisbury line east of St.James'Park tunnel.
Operational from 1967.

Gauge: 4ft 8½in

-	0-4-0DM	DC	2269	1949	(a)
		VF	D98	1949	

(a) ex W.Cory & Sons Ltd.,Gallions Jetty,
    Essex,8/1967.

SCATTER ROCK MACADAMS LTD.,BRIDFORD

39 An aerial ropeway connected Christow station on the GWR Teign Valley line with the lower end of the tramway at Stone (SX 825860).A ledge on the hillside took the tramway to the foot of the incline to the quarry (SX 822855). Locos worked the lower section and horses worked the quarry. The quarry was taken over by Roads Reconstruction (1934) Ltd.,and the plant was dismantled in 1953.

Gauge: 2ft 0in

-	4wDM	Jung	(5189?)	(1)
-	4wDM	Dtz		s/s

(1) to Cranmore Depot,Somerset,c/1953.
of Roads Reconstruction (1934) Ltd.

SEATON & DISTRICT ELECTRIC TRAMWAY CO.,SEATON.

40 A company operating a summer passenger service of 'scaled down' tramcars over a 1½ mile line on the trackbed of the BR branch from Seaton to Colyford. The cars were initially battery powered,and then from overhead trolley wire. The diesel locomotive is available for works trains. The depot is at Seaton station site (SY 252901). Services commenced in 1971.

Gauge: 3ft 0in

-	4wDM	RH	435398	1959	(a)

(a) ex North Devon Clay Co.Ltd.,Peters
Marland, c9/1972

C.T.SHEARS,WEST OF ENGLAND TRANSPORT COLLECTION,WINKLEIGH AIRFIELD.

41 A large collection of elderly and preserved buses and commercial vehicles housed in a hangar at SS 615096. It was intended to lay a small narrow gauge railway as part of the museum,but this has not been done.The locomotives have remained stored inside the hangar during their stay here.

Gauge: 2ft 0in

10		4wPM	MR	9104	1942	(a)	(1)
	PENLEE	4wDM	HE	2666	1942	(b)	(1)

(a) ex Exeter City Council, c3/1968
(b) ex Penlee Quarries Ltd.,Cornwall,
8/1967

(1) to M.E.Engineering Ltd.,Cricklewood,
London, 4/1974

SIDMOUTH HARBOUR COMPANY

42 The company was incorporated in 1836 and a woodway of about 3ft 6in gauge was laid from the harbour site at Chit Rocks (SY 121869) to Hook Ebb (SY 155877) where stone was to be quarried. It ran along the esplanade,crossed the River Sid on a timber viaduct and tunnelled through Salcombe Cliff for one third of a mile continuing along the foreshore on timber piles. A steam locomotive was delivered by sea which proved to be too big for the tunnel,but was used for giving rides along the promenade. The company ran out of funds in 1837,and a year later all the equipment had gone. The one foundation stone,the tunnel and many of the piles near Salcombe Mouth remain.

Ref: IRR 55 (8/1974) p282

SOUTH DEVON GRANITE CO.LTD.,NEAR TAVISTOCK

43   A tramway serving quarrying activities,exact location uncertain. Rail system
      closed and dismantled.

Gauge: 2ft 0in

-		4wPM	MR	1080	1918	(a)	(1)

(a) ex Stewart & Partners Ltd , /1928;orig   (1) to Bennet's Sand & Gravel Co ,via
        WDLR 2801   Oswald Bond,dealer,Cardiff, /1935

SOUTH WESTERN GAS BOARD

   Exeter Gas Works (Exeter Gaslight & Coke Co until 1/5/1949)

44   This works on the west bank of the river Exe was established in 1836 by the
      Exeter Commercial Gas Light & Coke Co. which was taken over in 1839 by the
      older Exeter Gaslight & Coke Co. It was served by the Basin Branch railway
      opened in 1867 to serve the Exeter Canal. This in turn connected with both
      the BR (ex GWR) main line and the Teign Valley branch.
      The gasworks loco shed was at SY 921918. Rail traffic to the works ceased in
      1971; works closed and being demolished in 1974.

Gauge: 4ft 8½in

-	0-4-0ST	OC	(HL?)				(a)	s/s
-	0-4-0ST	OC	P	1301	1912	New	Scr	/1947
-	0-4-0ST	OC	AB	737	1893	(b)	(1)	
No.1 LOCO	0-4-0ST	OC	P	2031	1942	New	(3)	
No.2 LOCO	0-4-0ST	OC	P	2074	1946	New	(2)	
No.3	0-4-0DH	HE	6263	1964	New	(4)		
-	4wDM	RH	402809	1956	(c)	(5)		

(a) ex ?   , by 5/1903   (1) Scr on site by E.Pearse & Co Ltd,
(b) ex WD Starcross, via Hodges,Exeter,   Exeter, c/1942
    /1923   (2) Scr on site by Industrial Dismantling
(c) ex Torquay Gasworks, 8/1968   Ltd,Exeter, c2/1965
                                        (3) to Torquay Works, c5/1956;retd 3/1957;
                                            to Dart Valley Railway Co Ltd,
                                            Ashburton, 9/1969
                                        (4) to NCB Coal Products Division,
                                            Derwenthaugh Coke Ovens, Co.Durham,
                                            5/1971
                                        (5) to Small & Lewis Ltd ,scrap merchants,
                                            Gloucester, c6/1971

   Hollacombe Gas Works,Torquay

45   A small works adjacent to,and served by sidings off,the BR (ex GWR) line between
      Torquay and Paignton. The loco stood in the open at SX 898622. The works was
      closed for production in 1968 and much of the plant has been dismantled.

Gauge: 4ft 8½in

-	0-4-0ST	OC	P	2031	1942	(a)	(1)
-	4wDM	RH	402809	1956	New	(2)	

(a) ex Exeter Gasworks, c5/1956   (1) retd to Exeter Gasworks, 3/1957
                                         (2) to Exeter Gasworks, 8/1968

STONEYCOMBE LIME & STONE CO.LTD.,STONEYCOMBE QUARRY,NEAR NEWTON ABBOT

46   Quarries and plant on the south of the BR (ex GWR) main line near Dainton
(SX 862672).An internal rail system served the workings but was replaced by
dumper trucks and dismantled. The quarries remain extensive and active as part of
ECC Quarries Ltd.

Gauge: 2ft 0in

-	0-4-0ST	OC	KS	4161	1921	(a)	s/s
-	4wDM (f PM)		MR	5418	1936	New	(1)

(a) ex F.Munn,dealer,Cardiff,by 8/1932;   (1) to Bungey
orig Cardiff Corporation Waterworks

TEIGN VALLEY GRANITE CO.LTD.,HENNOCK GRANITE QUARRIES,TRUSHAM,NEAR NEWTON ABBOT

47   Quarries (at SX 848808?) with a standard gauge siding connection to the GWR
Teign Valley line. Use of a private locomotive had ceased on the standard gauge
before 1926 and the rail connection was subsequently closed and dismantled.
The quarry remained active as a unit of Roads Reconstruction (1934) Ltd and
later of ARC (South Western) Ltd.

Ref: IRR 49 (8/1973) p90

Gauge: 4ft 8½in

FINETTA	0-4-0ST	OC	AE	1565	1911	New	(1)

(a) to WD Codford,Wilts,c3/1917;later to
Sandford & Conygar Quarries Co,
Somerset

Gauge: narrow

-	4wP	s/s after 7/1926

TEIGNMOUTH QUAY CO.LTD.,TEIGNMOUTH

48   Quays largely used for the import of timber and the export of ball clay. Sidings
serve the quays and connect with the BR (ex GWR) main line. Since the tracks are
inset into the road surface wagons can be moved with a road tractor.The locomotive
listed was a road vehicle convertible to rail use;it is doubtful if rail wheels
were ever fitted.

Gauge: 4ft 8½in

THE ELEPHANT	2-2-0VBT	G S	5644	1923	New	(1)

(1) to A.J.Bolton,New Barnet,Herts,for
preservation, /1963

TIVERTON MUSEUM SOCIETY,BLUNDELLS ROAD,TIVERTON

49   Locomotive preserved on a plinth at SS 959127 on the opposite side of the road
to the former Tiverton station.

Gauge: 4ft 8½in

1442	0-4-2T	IC	Sdn		1935	(a)

(a) Wdn by BR (WR), 5/1964;purchased by Lord
Amory and presented for display 10/1965

50   A branch (from the GWR near Starcross?) to Mamhead Forest area. Line closed and
     dismantled;the site at Mamhead was acquired by the Forestry Commission,which see.

Gauge: 4ft 8½in

| | | 0-4-0ST | OC | AB | 737 | 1893 | (a) | (1) |

(a) ex McAlpine,contrs.   (1) to Hodges,Exeter:to Exeter Gaslight &
                                               Coke Co./1923.

WATTS,BLAKE,BEARNE & CO.LTD.

Preston Clay Pits,near Newton Abbot.

51   Tramway serving clay workings;locomotive haulage replaced by cable haulage and
     dumper trucks c1940.

Gauge: 2ft 0in

| | 4wPM | MR | 1196 | 1918 | (a) | (1) |
| | 4wPM | KC | | | | (1) |

(a) ex WDLR 2917 ,/1920   (1) Sold for scrap/1954.

No.10 Adit,West Golds Mine

52   A tramway serving underground workings opened c1963;the locomotive is used
     underground and cable haulage brings the tubs to unload at surface. There are a
     number of similar adits in the district which do not employ locomotive haulage.
     Owing to underground flooding the locomotive was stored on surface temporarily
     about 9/1970. Location SX 856725.

Gauge: 2ft 6in

| | 4wBE | CE | 5382 |

WESTERN COUNTIES BRICK CO.LTD.,PINHOE BRICKWORKS,EXETER.(Incorporating J.& W.J.Saunders
                                                                        Ltd.)
53   A tramway connected the claypits and brickworks at SX 956944.System closed and
     dismantled,although the brickworks remains active.

Gauge: 2ft 0in

| | 4wPM | L | 7196 | 1935 | New | (1) |
| | 4wPM | L | 30233 | 1946 | New | (2) |

(1) to A.G.Pitts & Co.Highbridge,Somerset.
(2) to E.J.Godwin(Peat Industries)Ltd.,
    Meare,Somerset.

WESTLEIGH STONE & LIME CO.LTD.,BURLESCOMBE

54   Extensive limestone quarries to the north of Westleigh village. A narrow gauge tramway was built by the Bristol & Exeter Railway in 1873 to connect the quarries (ST 064175) with the broad gauge main line at Burlescombe station (ST 072170), about ¾ mile away. This line was operated by the Bristol & Exeter Railway under a 25 year lease. On expiry of this lease in 1898 the line was rebuilt to standard gauge and it's operation taken over by the quarry company. An internal narrow gauge system served the quarries and the crushing plant.
From 1950 road transport has been used exclusively and all rail installations have been removed. The quarries remain active as a unit of ECC Quarries Ltd.

    Ref: 'The Locomotives of the GWR,Part 3' (RCTS) p64

Gauge: 4ft 8½in

CANTREFF		0-6-0ST	IC	MW	1235	1893	(a)	(1)
-		0-6-0ST	OC	P	1717	1926	New	Scr 12/1954

(a) ex Cardiff Corporation Waterworks,   (1) to P ,/1926 (in part exchange for P
    c/1900   1717);resold to Byfield Ironstone
                                                 Co Ltd, Northants, 6/1929

Gauge: 3ft 0in (Bristol & Exeter Railway tramway)

1381	(f 112)	0-4-0WT	OC	B&ER	1873	New	(1)
1382	(f 113)	0-4-0WT	OC	B&ER	1875	New	(2)

                   (1) to Bute Works Supply Co ,Cardiff,
                       3/1899;resold to Manchester
                       Corporation Rivers Department,
                       Davyhulme,Lancs
                 (2) to Bute Works Supply Co ,Cardiff,
                       3/1899

Gauge: 3ft 0in (Quarry system)

-	4wPM	L	3230	1931	New	s/s
GIRL PAT	0-4-0DM	AE	2061	1931	New	Scr 5/1954
-	0-4-0DM	AE	2076	1934	New	Scr 5/1954
-	4wDM	RH	166029	1932	New	(1)
-	4wDM	RH	218023	1943	New	(1)

                 (1) to Cementation Co Ltd ,contrs,
                       Doncaster,Yorks (WR), 5/1954

    ADDENDA: Late information, add:

G.W.GLOVER, ROSE COTTAGE, UPTON PYNE, NEAR EXETER

55   Locomotive purchased and moved here as a relevant exhibit of a collection of farm tractors and agricultural machines.

Gauge: 3ft 0in

-	4wDM	JF 3930048	1951	(a)

(a) ex North Devon Clay Co Ltd , Peters Marland,
    /1974

Non·locomotive systems

BIDEFORD BLACK PIGMENTS LTD.

A A mine at East-the-Water (SS 472263) in carboniferous strata.anthracite was mined in the area in 1824;the latest working latterly obtained paint pigments and fillers. A 2ft 0in gauge tramway ran from the adits to the mill. 1ft 6in gauge was also in use. Production ceased in mid-1960's.

BOVEY POTTERY

B A tramway ran from the claypits across the road to the pottery.closed and dismantled (SX 815771)

BULKAMORE IRON MINE

C A tramway from the mine (SX 649632) dropped by an incline,possibly ropeworked, to the GWR Ashburton branch at SX 756638,crossing the river Dart en route. Production was probably 1874-5;mine and tramway were in situ but disused on the 1885 O.S. map.

FARTHERFORD TRAMWAY

D A tramway constructed in the 1890's(?) to convey building stone. From a small quarry at SX 604946 in the East Okement valley a few yards south of Fartherford Viaduct (LSWR) it ran under the viaduct and climbed steadily up the valley side to a terminus close below Okehampton station (SX 592945).Only the earthworks remain.

FREMENTOR QUARRY

E A shortlived quarry producing a poor quality granite. In 1869 it was connected to Impham Quay on the Tamar by an extremely rickety 2½ mile long horse tramway.

GRAND WESTERN CANAL

F Tramways connected canal basins with quarries at: Westleigh (ST 069176)
Ponds Green (ST 072194)
Whipcott (ST 071184)

HAYTOR GRANITE CO.

Dewerstone Tramway

G A tramway built in 1858 to exploit the granite of the Dewerstone Rock (SX 538639) by providing a connection to the GWR Tavistock branch near SX 530645.The link with the GWR was never made and the line saw little use.Two reversing points and an incline took the tramway up the side of the rock and the route is easily traced.

Haytor Tramway

H A 4ft 3in gauge stoneway which connected quarries at Haytor Rock (SX 754760)with the Stover Canal at Teigngrace,seven miles away.Horse worked,it opened 16/9/1820 and became disused by 1858.Much of the track is still in place on the upper sections.

Ref:'The Haytor Granite Tramway and Stover Canal' by M.C.Ewans, D&C 1964.

HAYTOR IRON MINES LTD.

J   A 1000 ft incline from adit level to the Bovey Tracey road was built about 1920,
thus reducing the length of the journey to Bovey Tracey station by 1½ miles.
Mines closed and dismantled,although the route of the incline can still be seen.

NEW FLORENCE MINING CO. (Florence Mining Co. until 1880)

K   A tramway of narrow gauge connected these mines north of North Molton (at
SS 754322) with an exchange siding on the GWR Devon & Somerset line near South
Molton (SS 729272). The tramway was built in 1874 and in 1877 a branch was built
from SS 746311 to the Croborn Iron mines (SS 739318). Operation of the tramway
probably ceased when the mines were abandoned 6/1894.
The earthworks of the line are easily traced for much of its length.

Ref: 'Days of Renown' by J.N.Slader; West Country Publications,1965.

ODAMS CHEMICAL MANURE CO.

L   A ¼ mile siding from the LSWR Exmouth branch ran alongside the river Clyst to
the works at SX 976880. 'Motive power' was by block and tackle attached to steel
posts along the track,although LSWR 'O2' 0-4-4T's were permitted over the siding.
Factory closed 1938

PLYMOUTH & DARTMOOR RAILWAY

M   Incorporated 2/7/1819 and opened 26/9/1823 this horse drawn railway ran from
Prince Rock and Sutton Harbour (Plymouth) to Princetown via Roborough,Dousland
and the Fogintor Quarries.Branches ran to Cann Quarry and Plympton and the later
Lee Moor Tramway branched from the former branch.
The GWR Princetown branch (opened 1883) was built over part of the upper end
of the line but some traffic continued until 1900 on the lower section.The rails
above Marsh Mills,not used by the Lee Moor tramway,were lifted in 1916. All the
line was of the 4ft 6in gauge. A good deal of the route can still be traced.

Ref: 'The Plymouth & Dartmoor Railway' by H.G.Kendall;Oakwood Press

PLYMOUTH BREAKWATER RAILWAY

N   A 3ft 6in gauge plateway opened 8/1812 ran from the quarry at Oreston to the quay.
At the quay loaded wagons were run onto the deck of a vessel,sailed to the
Breakwater (SX 471503) and tipped,initially from the stern of the vessel,later
after being run out onto the breakwater. Construction continued until c1845.

RATTLEBROOK TRAMWAY

P   A 4ft 8½in gauge line built in 1879 by the West of England Compressed Peat Co.
This company failed in 1880,and the line passed through many hands,not all known,
until lifted in 1931. It connected with the LSWR at Bridestowe (SX 522872)and
climbed over 1000 ft up onto the moor. There was a reversing point at SX 546887,
and the terminus was the works at SX 560871.
A petrol trolley is believed to have been used in the lifting.

SILVERTON TRAMWAY

Q   A quarter mile standard gauge siding from the GWR main line at Silverton to
    paper mills at SS 978011. It was worked by horse and later road tractors and
    went out of use in the mid-1960's.

TAVISTOCK CANAL CO.

R   In 1846 the canal's Mill Hill branch was relaid as a tramway to serve the slate
    quarries at Mill Hill (SX 453747) but traffic did not materialise and the line
    was disused by 1860. Most of the route can be followed still.

    Also the canal used a platerail,later edgerail,incline to convey ores and goods
    between the canal basin at SX 444701 and Morwellham Quay below. This was in use
    between 1817 and 1873 and was the longest canal incline in southern England.

WAR DEPARTMENT,OKEHAMPTON RANGES

S   A 1ft 6in gauge target railway laid with very heavy section rail. Location
    SX 603898,much of the route being in a shallow cutting.

WESTERN COUNTIES BRICK CO.LTD.,STEER POINT BRICKWORKS.

T   A 1ft 6in gauge tramway was used until 1953-4 to convey shale from the pit to
    the works at SX 546504 via a double track cable incline commencing in a tunnel
    under the road. At an earlier date a line ran from the works to a quay on
    Cofflete Creek.

WHEAL FRIENDSHIP

U   Workings at SX 502794 (near Mary Tavy) commenced before 1790. In 1826 a 3ft gauge
    plateway was installed in the inclined adit. The mine closed in 1873 and plant
    was sold. From 1881 to 1900 it was worked again as Devon Friendship and about
    700 fathoms of tramway connected Bennetts shaft to,and served,the dressing floor.

ZEAL TOR TRAMWAY

V   The tramway was constructed as a woodway in 1847 to convey peat from Redlake
    Mires. In 1850 the partnership in lved was dissolved. From 1877 the Brent Moor
    Clay works used part of the line but after a few years they too failed.
    The tramway ran from Shipley Bridge (SX 680629)(North of South Brent),where the
    remains of the clay works on the site of a former naptha works can be seen,to
    Redlake (SX 645664). Most of the route can be traced by the stone sleeper blocks
    in the moor.

Contractors lines

P. & W. ANDERSON LTD.

C1   Construction of the North Devon & Cornwall Light Railway from Torrington to Halwill, 1923-5.

Gauge: 4ft 8½in

No.186	BIRKENHEAD	0-4-0ST	OC	HC	650	1903	(a)	s/c
79		0-6-0ST	IC	MW	1049	1888	(b)	(1)
57		0-6-0ST	IC	MW	1153	1890	(c0	s/s

(a) (ex L.P.Nott, Birkenhead ?)
(b) orig T.A.Walker, MSC contract, ARDWICK; ex Easton, Gibb & Son Ltd , Rosyth Dockyard contract
(c) ex Ministry of Munitions, Avonmouth Factory

(1) to North Devon Clay Co Ltd , Peters Marland, c /1925

Gauge: 3ft 0in

No.36	BUNTY	0-4-0ST	OC	WB	1480	1896	(a)	s/s
No.51	ALSTON	0-4-0WT	OC	WB	1434	1894	(b)	s/s
No.52	GYP	0-4-0T	OC	AB	761	1895	(c)	(1)

(a) (ex John Best, Nidd Valley contract, Yorks ?)
(b) ex   ?
(c) ex Morrison & Mason

(1) to Abergavenny Water Works,

Gauge: 2ft 0in

| | WESTERN LEA | 0-6-0WT | OC | HC | 1314 | 1918 | (a) | (1) |

(a) ex Nott, Brodie & Co , Avonmouth, Glos   (1) to Meeth (North Devon) Clay Co Ltd , c /1925

BRANSON & MURRAY

C2   Construction of Plymouth Defence Works for H.M.Government, c /1865; contract later taken over by H.M.Government.

Gauge: 4ft 8½in

| | | 0-4-0T | OC | FJ | 46 | 1865 | New | (1) |

(1) to H.M.Government, Plymouth

THOMAS BRASSEY & OGILVIE

C3   Construction of the North Devon Railway, from Crediton to Bideford, 1851-4.

Gauge: 7ft 0¼in

| | VENUS | 2-4-0 | | IC | Stothert & Slaughter | 1844 | (a) | (1) |

(a) ex Midland Railway, 469 , 3/1863; orig Bristol & Gloucester Railway, 2

(1) to Thomas Brassey, operation of the North Devon Railway, /1854

DEVON COUNTY COUNCIL, ROADS DEPARTMENT, NORTHERN DIVISION, BIDEFORD

C4   Locomotives used on road widening works, including the Barnstaple- Bideford road at Instow and the Barnstaple- Ilfracombe road at Knowle. Served by a plant depot at Nutaberry, Bideford.

Gauge: 2ft 0in

No.59	BUNTY		0-4-0ST	OC	KS	4265	1922	(a)	(1)
No.60	MAID OF SKER		0-4-0ST	OC	KS	4251	1922	(b)	(1)
No.73	ROSE OF THE TORRIDGE		0-4-0ST	OC	KS	4258	1922	(b)	(1)

(a) ex Wilminstone Quarry   (1) to A.Waddington & Son , Teignhead,
(b) ex Beacon Down Quarry   /1934

JAMES & JOHN DICKSON

C5   Construction of the GWR Exeter- Christow line, 1894-1903

Gauge: 4ft 8½in

| | CHAGFORD | 0-4-0ST | OC | MW | 1087 | 1889 | (a) | (1) |
| | LONGDOWN | 0-6-0T | IC | RS | 2383 | 1880 | (b) | (2) |

(a) ex J.E.Billups, Newbury, Berks ,   (1) to Topham, Jones & Railton Ltd , Kings
    LAMBOURNE   Dock, Swansea, 35 , c /1903
(b) ex W.Jackson, Freshwater, Yarmouth &   (2) to   ?   , Canada Dock construction,
    Newport Railway construction, IoW   Liverpool

A.E.FARR LTD.

C6   Construction of roads and other works at Countess Weir Sewage Works, including replacement of the narrow gauge railway, for Exeter City Council, 1962.

Gauge: 2ft 0in

| - | | 4wDM | | MR | 5246 | 1930 | (a) | s/s |

(a) ex Westbury Depot, Wilts

HOWARD FARROW LTD.

C7   Construction of new sidings for the GWR at Exeter St. Davids, 1943.

Gauge: 4ft 8½in

| 366 | TRYM | 0-4-0ST | OC | HE | 287 | 1883 | (a) | (1) |

(a) ex Hendon Depot, Middx   (1) to Hendon Depot, Middx

SIR JOHN JACKSON LTD. (Sir John Jackson until /1898)

C8   Construction of extensions at Devonport Dockyard, Keyham, 1896-1907.

Gauge: 4ft 8½in

148	WESTMINSTER	0-6-0T	IC	SS	3478	1888	(a)	(1)
	DEVONPORT	0-6-0ST	IC	MW	951	1885	(b)	(1)
	LORD ROBERTS	0-4-0ST	OC	MW	1018	1887	(c)	s/s
	TORCROSS	0-4-0ST	OC	MW	1036	1887	(d)	(2)
	TYNE	0-4-0ST	OC	MW	1051	1888	(e)	s/s
	CLYDE	0-4-0ST	OC	MW	714	1879	(f)	s/s
	LORD NELSON	0-4-0ST	OC	MW	1090	1888	(g)	s/s
	MOUNT EDGECUMBE	0-4-0ST	OC	MW	1342	1897	(c)	s/s
	MIDDLESBROUGH	0-4-0ST	OC	MW	Reb	1883,	Lennox	Lange;
					Reb	1903		(3)
	KATHLEEN	0-4-0ST	OC	AB	867	1900	New	s/s
	VICTORIA	0-4-0ST	OC	AB	887	1900	New	(4)
	KING EDWARD VII	0-4-0ST	OC	AB	888	1901	New	(5)
	DOVER	0-4-0ST	OC	AB	891	1901	New	(1)
	ETHEL	0-4-0ST	OC	AB	853	1900	(h)	s/s
	HAMOAZE	0-4-0ST	OC	Barclays	229	1876	(j)	s/s
	GLASGOW	0-4-0ST	OC	AB	185	1877	(j)	(6)

(a) ex T.A.Walker, MSC contract, Lancs ,
    OPENSHAW
(b) ex T.A.Walker, MSC contract, Lancs ,
    ACCRINGTON
(c) ex Pauling & Co Ltd , Westbury contract,
    Wilts
(d)ex T.A.Walker, MSC contract, Lancs ,
    BARHAM or ex Cochran & Co (Annan) Ltd
    Annan, Dumfries
(e) ex T.A.Walker, MSC contract, Lancs ,
    CANTERBURY
(f) orig T.A.Walker, Deal, Kent, MARTIN,
    also with Sir John Jackson at Warrington,
    Lancs
(g) ex T.A.Walker, MSC contract, Lancs ,
    CADISHEAD
(h) ex ? , /1907 (New to Sir John Jackson,
    Westminster)
(j) ex ? , /1907

(1) to Grays Depot, Essex
(2) if ex Walker;then:- to Cochran & Co
    (Annan) Ltd , Annan, Dumfries
    if ex Cochran;then:- to RAF Kidbrooke
    London, 121
(3) to H.M. Dockyard, Devonport, 3
(4) to Thos W Ward Ltd , Inverkeithing,
    Fife, JJ 711
(5) to Lever Bros , Port Sunlight, Cheshire,
    KING EDWARD VII
(6) to Ministry of Munitions, Wiltshire

JOHN MACKAY

C9   Contract at Horrabridge, 1883

Gauge: 4ft 8½in

	ZULU	0-4-0ST	OC	MW	855	1882	New	(1)

(1) later Patent Shaft & Axletree Co Ltd ,
    Wednesbury, Staffs

MOUSLEY & LOVATT

C10   Construction of the LSWR Budleigh Salterton- Exmouth line, 1901-3

Gauge: 4ft 8½in

5		0-6-0ST	IC	HE	152	1876	(a)	(1)

(a) ex St Albans contract between 2/1901 and
    8/1902 (acquired by Mousley & Lovatt
    from John Gibb, c /1883)

(1) to Salford Dock extension contract,
    Lancs by 7/1903; later sold to
    Nottingham Corporation Electricity Dept.

JAMES NUTTALL

Construction of the Lynton and Barnstaple Railway, 1895-8

Gauge: 1ft 11½in

C11	EXCELSIOR	0-4-2T	OC	WB	970	1888	(a)	(1)
	SLAVE	0-4-0ST	OC	?				s/s
	-	0-4-0ST	OC	AB	703	1893	(b)	(2)

(a) ex C.J.Naylor, Kerry Tramway,   (1) to F.J.Barnes & Co , Easton, Dorset
    Montgomeryshire   (2) to (Ritchie Hart & Co, by 5/1899 ?)
(b) ex Fergus Reclamation Co, Ennis,
    Co.Clare, Ireland

It is possible that a 3ft 0in gauge locomotive WINNIE was also used in this contract.

S.PEARSON & SON LTD.

C12   Doubling of the Kingsbridge- Ivybridge section of the GWR, 1890-3

Gauge: 7ft 0¼in

2172	OWL	0-4-0WT	IC	AE	900	1873	(a)	(1)
2174	GOAT	0-4-0WT	IC	AE	901	1873	(a)	(1)

(a) ex GWR , 11/1890   (1) resold to GWR , 6/1893; later rebuilt
                                   to 4ft 8½in gauge

PETHICK BROS. LTD.

C13   Construction of the Devonport section of the Plymouth, Devonport & South
       Western Junction Railway, c /1890 (see also Robert T.Relf & Son).

Gauge: 4ft 8½in

	-	0-4-0ST	OC	HE	365	1885	(a)	(1)

(a) ex Holme & King, Brentwood, Essex,   (1) to John Strachan, Yorks, WR, /1893
    PHYLLIS

W.J.PICKERING

C14   Contract at Barnstaple Junction

Gauge: 4ft 8½in

	FORTESCUE	0-6-0ST	IC	HE	3	1865	New	(1)

(1) to J.Aird & Co , Nottingham

PITTRAIL LTD.

C15 Lifting of the BR Thorverton - Westexe Halt and Tiverton- Morebath Junction
lines, 9/1964- 1/1965

Gauge: 4ft 8½in

-	4wDM				(a)	s/s by 12/1964
-	2-2-0PM				(b)	s/s /1965
W.D. No.1	0-4-0DM	HE	1840	1936	(c)	s/s

(a) converted from Austin 'Champ'
(b) converted from Morris car
(c) ex WD, Bicester, c /1962

ROBERT T. RELF

C16 Construction of the LSWR Okehampton - Lydford line, 1872-4

Gauge: 4ft 8½in

LYDFORD	0-4-0ST	OC	MW	379	1872	New	(1)
LADY PORTSMOUTH	0-6-0ST	IC	MW	50	1862	(a)	(2)

(a) ex J.T.Leather, Waterloo Main Colliery, (1) to LSWR, 457, ST MICHAEL, 3/1883
    Leeds, 2/1872   (2) to LSWR, 392, LADY PORTSMOUTH, 12/1879

C17 Construction of the LSWR Meldon Junction (Okehampton)- Holsworthy line, 1876-9.

Gauge: 4ft 8½in

PIONEER	0-4-0ST	OC	MW	594	1876	New	(1)
JESSIE	0-4-0ST	OC	MW	628	1876	New	(2)

(1) to LSWR, 407 , 9/1881
(2) to LSWR, 408 , 9/1881

ROBERT T. RELF AND SON

C18 PD&SWJR Lydford - Devonport line construction, 1887-1890 (see also Pethick
Bros Ltd)

Gauge: 4ft 8½in

3		0-6-0ST	IC	MW	s/s

At least one other locomotive used on this contract

C19 Unknown contract, 1893.

Gauge: 4ft 8½in

ST MICHAEL	0-4-0ST	OC	MW	379	1872	(a)	s/s

(a) ex LSWR, 457 , 6/1893

J.L.REED

C20   Construction of the Devon & Somerset Railway from Norton Fitzwarren to Barnstaple, 1864-1873.

Gauge: 4ft 8½in

-	0-6-0	T	FW			(1)
-	0-6-0	T	FW			(1)
-	0-6-0	T	FW			(1)
-	4wT	G	AP	611	1870	(1)

(1) for sale, 9/1873

ROBERT SHARPE AND SONS

C21   Contract in North Devon

Gauge: 4ft 8½in

No.11	0-4-0T	OC	FJ	47	1865	New	(1)

(1) to Bolckow Vaughan & Co, Byers Green,
Co.Durham (by 1878?)

STAVERTON BUILDERS LTD.

C22   Construction of East Yelland Power Station for the British Electricity Authority, 1950 -1955.

Gauge: 4ft 8½in

STAVERTON	0-6-0ST	OC	AB	1844	1924	(a)	s/s

(a) ex Fleming Adnitt Ltd , Wath-Elsecar Screens,
Yorks, WR, FORTH

TAYLOR, WOODROW & CO. LTD.

C23   Construction of East Yelland Power Station for the British Electricity Authority, 1950-2.

Gauge: 4ft 8½in

SL 2	0-4-0T	OC	9E		1908	(a)	(1)

(a) ex BR (SR), 101, 10/1949   (1) to ? , 8/1952

A.WADDINGTON & SON

C24   Construction of the Teignhead Reservoir for Torquay Corporation, 1934-40.

Gauge: 2ft 0in

MAID OF SKER	0-4-0ST	OC	KS	4251	1922	(a)	(1)
ROSE OF THE TORRIDGE	0-4-0ST	OC	KS	4258	1922	(a)	(1)
-	0-4-0ST	OC	KS	4265	1922	(a)	s/s

(a) ex Devon County Council, Bideford   (1) to Stonebridge Park contract, London,
    Depot, /1934   by 3/1936

GEORGE WIMPEY & CO. LTD.

C25   Construction of the Exeter- Plymouth road at Chudleigh, 1922-4.

Gauge: 2ft 0in

KIDBROOKE	0-4-0ST	OC	WB	2043	1918	(a)	(1)

(a) ex WD, Kidbrooke, London, /1922   (1) to Newhaven contract, Sussex.

Unknown Contractor

C26   Construction of the South Devon Railway, 1844-8

Gauge: ?

–	0-4-2	Charles Tayleur, Vulcan Foundry	201	1844	New s/s

SOMERSET

MINEHEAD
BRIDGWATER
FROME
TAUNTON
YEOVIL

27
C4
C10
D
22
J
C5
24
21
41
53/35
10
C3
C9
C6
C7
48
G
55
54
43
C2
L
13
C1
47
K

Unknown Locations
3 17 30

0 4 8 12 16
MILES

Somerset

Locomotive worked systems

A.R.C.(SOUTHERN) LTD., NEW FROME QUARRY, FROME (f. Roads Reconstruction (1934) Ltd.)

1   This company has worked a number of quarries to the north-west of Frome, at one time using the nominal operating company of the New Frome Quarry Co. Some workings and a 2ft 3in gauge railway were taken over in the early 1930's from the Somerset Quarry Co Ltd (which see). The quarries were served by a 2ft0in gauge tramway which was superceded by a 4ft8½in gauge line in 1943 and lifted in 1945. This standard gauge line was some two miles long and connected Whatley Quarry (ST 731479) with the GWR (later BR) Frome - Radstock line near Hapsford. Offices, workshops and two locomotive sheds (at ST 756491 and at ST 759494) were near Hapsford Quarry. This line passed through a short tunnel which was replaced c/1966 by a new larger bore alongside. In 1973-4 an entirely new, shorter link from Whatley Quarry to new exchange sidings with the BR at ST 759498 was built. This includes two long tunnels and a viaduct which passes over the old alignment. The old line from the junction west of Great Elm level crossing,via Hapsford,to the old BR exchange sidings was then lifted, c11/1974

Gauge: 4ft8½in

154	MEDWAY	0-4-0ST	OC	AB	969	1903	(a)	(7)
292	NIDD	4wVBT	VCG	S	6090	1925	(b)	Scr c4/1969
758		0-4-0ST	OC	KS	3112	1918	(c)	(2)
784	1	0-4-0ST	OC	VF	798	1876	(d)	Scr 8/1949
789	2	4wVBT	VCG	S	9374	1947	New	(5)
794	3	4wVBT	VCG	S	9386	1948	New	(4)
153		4wVBT	VCG	S	9387	1948	New	(6)
1262		0-4-0DM		JF	19645	1932	(e)	(1)
2162	1	4wVBT	VCG	S	9391	1949	(f)	(3)
2166	2	4wDH		TH/S	133V*	1963	New	
2317		4wDH		TH/S	136C	1964	New	
		4wBrakeTender		TH/S	149C	1965	New	(8)
	3	4wDH		TH	152V	1965	New	
	-	4wDH		TH	200V	1968	New	

* The loco is officially 133C, i.e. a rebuild, but carries plates as shown.

(a) ex APCM Burham Works, Kent, via Cohen, c/1943
(b) ex Cranmore Depot, 9/1944
(c) ex Vobster Quarry
(d) ex Sandford Quarry, /1946
(e) ex Cranmore Depot
(f) ex Sandford Quarry, 9/1964

(1) to Sandford Quarry
(2) to Vobster Quarry, c/1949
(3) to TH, Kilnhurst, Yorks WR, 1/1965
(4) Scr on site by Bidwell, Clandown, Radstock, 6/1967
(5) to Vobster Quarry, /1963; ret 8/1965; then to Somerset Railway Museum,10/1971
(6) to Welsh Mill Childrens Adventure Playground, Frome U.D.C., 11/1971
(7) Dism /1956; frame & tank retained as a water carrier until scr c11/1974
(8) Scr c/1969 after collision damage

2

Gauge: 2ft0in

41		0-4-2ST	OC	KS	3065	1918	(a)	(1)
-		0-4-0T	OC	AE	2072	1933	(b)	(2)
-		4wDM		RH	198313	1940	New	(3)
-		4wDM		RH	200507	1940	New	(4)

(a) ex Air Ministry, Eastleigh, Hants, per Sussex Trading Co Ltd, c/1920; to Cranmore Depot by 4/1924; ex Tytherington Quarry, Glos,after 7/1933
(b) ex Pugsley, c11/1941; f Durham County Water Board, 84 AUKLAND

(1) to Cranmore Depot, c /1948
(2) to Cranmore Depot
(3) to Vobster Quarry
(4) to Emborough Quarry

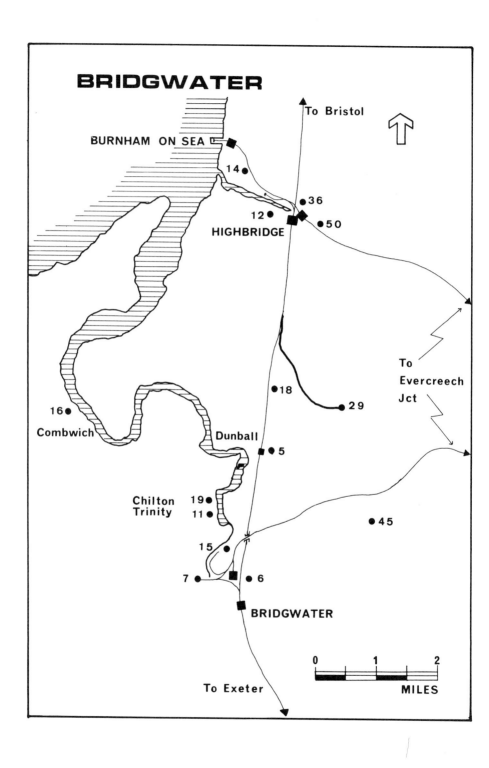

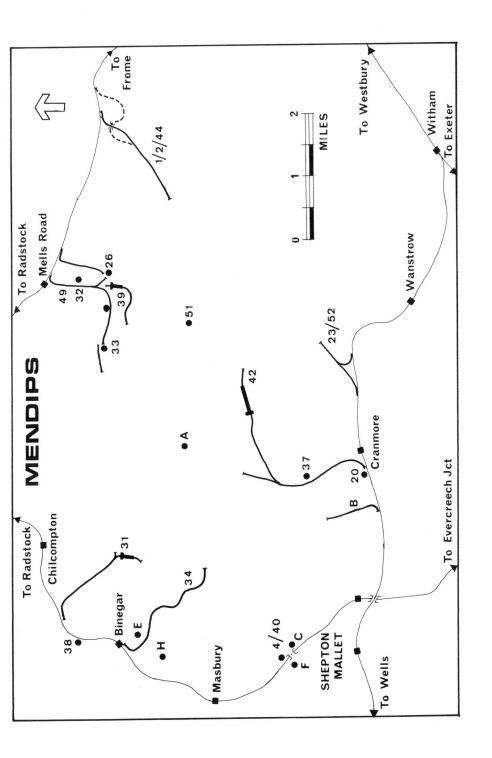

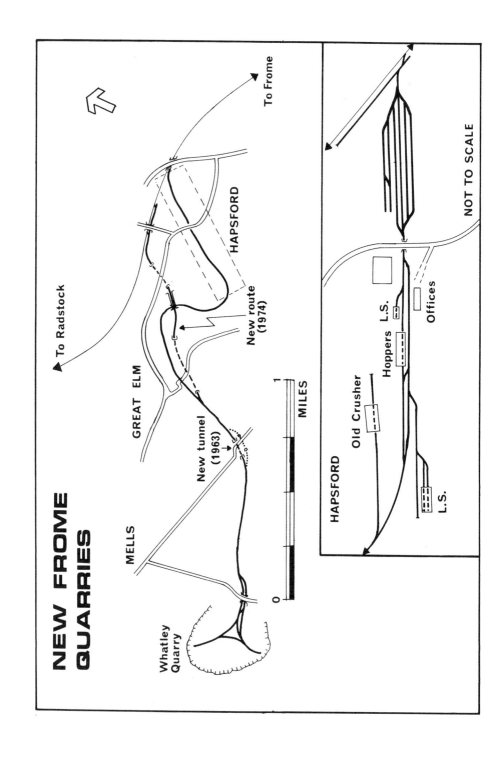

NEW FROME QUARRIES

To Radstock

To Frome

MELLS

GREAT ELM

HAPSFORD

Whatley Quarry

New tunnel (1963)

New route (1974)

MILES

0   1

HAPSFORD

Old Crusher

Hoppers   L.S.

Offices

L.S.

NOT TO SCALE

BARHAM BROS. LTD.,BRICK MANUFACTURERS, BRIDGWATER

3   A tramway serving a brickworks,location uncertain.

Gauge: 2ft 0in

-	4wPM	L	7437	1936	New	s/s
-	4wPM	L	33558	1949	New	s/s

W.B.BEAUCHAMP, WINDSOR HILL GRANITE QUARRY, NEAR SHEPTON MALLET

4   This quarry is known to have had loco(s) on a narrow gauge system by 1889.
     Quarry closed,later possibly owned by Westbury Iron Co. Reopened by Roads
     Reconstruction Ltd,which see.

Gauge: 2ft 0in

TERRIER	0-4-0ST	OC	WB	300	1880	New	s/s

JOHN BOARD & CO.LTD., PORTLAND CEMENT & LIME WORKS, DUNBALL

5   The tramway connected the quarries (ST 325415) with the works (ST 317410). The
     quarries closed and the rail system was closed and lifted in 1954.

Gauge: 2ft 0in

-	0-4-0ST	OC	KS	2390	1915	(a)	Scr c /1937
MEADOWHEAD	0-4-0ST	OC	KS	3102	1917	(b)	(1)
-	4wDM		RH	175418	1936	New	(2)
-	4wPM		L	6299	1935	New	(3)
-	4wPM		L	10498	1938	New	(4)
-	4wPM		L	26366	1944	New	(4)

(a) ex Balfour,Beatty & Co Ltd ,contrs ,   (1) Sold for scrap, c /1934
    Ripon,Yorks, by 2/1929   (2) to Greenwoods Tileries Ltd ,Barrow
(b) ex Air Ministry,Kidbrooke,Kent,by   Haven,Lincs , via Fred Watkins
    7/1924   (Boilers) Ltd ,Coleford,Glos ,/1954
                                               (3) to Trollope & Colls Ltd ,Northumberland
                                               (4) to Eclipse Peat Co Ltd ,Ashcott

BRITISH CELLOPHANE LTD.,BRIDGWATER

6   Standard gauge sidings serve the works on the east side of the BR (ex GWR)
     main line.The loco shed is at ST 310384. Shunting was performed by a BR loco
     from 8/1961 until 7/1969.

Gauge: 4ft 8½in

-	0-4-0ST	OC	P	1904	1936	New	(2)
DEVON	0-4-0ST	OC	AB	1286	1914	(a)	(1)
D2133	0-6-0DM		Sdn		1960	(b)	

(a) ex Abelson & Co (Engineers) Ltd ,   (1) ret to Abelson & Co (Engineers) Ltd ,
    Sheldon,Birmingham, /1950   Sheldon,Birmingham, 4/1951
(b) ex BR (WR),Bristol, D2133, 7/1969   (2) Scr on site, c12/1962

BRITISH RAILWAYS

Docks Department,Bridgwater (G.W.R. until 1/1/1948)

7   Locomotives used to shunt rail traffic in the docks area (ST 295375).

     Ref: 'Locomotives of the G.W.R.,Part 11' (RCTS)

Gauge: 4ft 8½in

15	4wPM	MR	2138	1923	(a)	(1)
23	4wPM	MR	3731	1925	New	(2)

(a) ex Wednesbury Goods Yard, Staffs, /1932 (1) to Swindon Works,Wilts,2/1951;Scr /1951
(2) to Swindon Works,Wilts; Scr c /1960

Engineers Department, Taunton (G.W.R. until 1/1/1948)

8   Standard gauge sidings serve the depot on the north side of the BR (ex GWR) main line at the east end of Taunton station. From c/1965 no departmental locomotive has been stationed here (ST 232258)

Ref: ' Locomotives of the G.W.R.,Part 11' (RCTS)

Gauge: 4ft 8½in

24	4wPM	MR	3821	1926	New	(1)
DS1169	4wDM	RH	237923	1946	(a)	(2)

(a) ex Broad Clyst Sleeper Depot,Devon, (1) to Swindon Works, Wilts ;Scr c /1960
  c /1964   (2) to Yeovil P.Way Yard, c /1965

Permanent Way Yard, Taunton

9   Sidings on the south of the Exeter main line west of Taunton station (ST 210257) which are used for the assembly and loading onto wagons of pre-assembled track. The yard has been used for this purpose since c /1960.

Gauge: 4ft 8½in

PWM 652	0-6-ODE	RH	431759	1959	New

Permanent Way Yard, Yeovil

10   A yard on the north side of the Salisbury line at the eastern end of Yeovil Junction station (ST 572142). A departmental locomotive has been allocated here from c /1965 until 1973.

Gauge: 4ft 8½in

DS1169	4wDM	RH	237923	1946	(a)	(1)

(a) ex Taunton Engineers Dept , c /1965   (1) Wdn 3/1972; to Cohen ,Cransley Depot, Northants, 6/1973

JOHN BROWNE & CO.(BRIDGWATER) LTD.,CHILTON TRINITY TILEWORKS, BRIDGWATER (Somerset Trading Co until /1951; John Browne & Co until /1949)

11   The tramway served the works at ST 299392. The works closed c /1966; the rail system has been dismantled and the location is now occupied by the Chilton Development & Trading Co Ltd.

Gauge: 2ft 0in

-	4wPM	MR	314	1917	(a)	Scr c /1962
-	4wPM	MR			(b)	Scr c /1957
-	4wDM	MR			(c)	s/s c /1969
-	4wDM	MR	5082	1930	(d)	s/s c /1969

(a) ex WDLR , 1715
(b) ex WDLR
(c) ex   ?
(d) ex Kempson & Phillips,contrs,Isleworth,
    Middx

N.D.BUNCOMBE,HUNTSPILL ROAD GARAGE,HIGHBRIDGE,SOMERSET

12   A locomotive brought to this location for preservation,and stored awaiting renovation.

Gauge: 4ft 8½in

WHITEHEAD	0-4-0ST	OC	P	1163	1908	(a) (1)

(a) ex Whitehead Hill & Co.,Oakfield   (1) to Great Western Society Ltd.,Taunton
    Wireworks,Cwmbran,Mon.,2/1967   Depot, /1971.

BUTLINS LTD.,MINEHEAD HOLIDAY CAMP,

13   Two locomotives restored externally and on display in the holiday camp at SS 984464 from 1964 onwards.

Gauge: 4ft 8½in

LMS	6229	DUCHESS OF HAMILTON	4-6-2	4C	Crewe	1938	(a)	(1)
	32678		0-6-0T	1C	Bton	1880	(b)	(2)

(a) ex BR(LMR) 4/1964 after repainting in   (1) to BRE Swindon, 13/3/1975, for
    LMS livery at Crewe Works.   renovation prior to exhibition at the
(b) ex BR(SR) 7/1964 after repainting in   National Railway Collection, York
    LBSCR livery at Eastleigh Works.   (2) to West Somerset Railway Co , Williton,
                                   4/1975

COLTHURST SYMONS & CO.LTD.

Burnham-on-Sea Brickworks

14   A tramway serving the works at ST 309479. The rail system was replaced c1961; works since closed.   -

Gauge: 2ft 0in

-	4wPM	L			s/s	
-	4wPM	FH	2048	1937	New	(1)
-	4wPM	FH	2326	1940	(a)	(2)
-	4wPM	FH	1987	1936	(b)	s/s c/1964

(a) ex Dunball Brickworks   (1) Derelict 7/1959; s/s c/1964
(b) ex Dunball Brickworks, 9/1959   (2) Derelict 1/1966; s/s /1966

Castlefield Brickworks,Bridgwater

15   Rail traffic on the tramway ceased 1959,and the track was lifted c1960

Gauge: 1ft 8in

-	4wDM	FH	2798	1944	(a)	Scr c/1960
-	4wPM	FH	2115	1938	(b)	Scr 7/1959

(a) ex FH, 8/1947;prev. MoS
(b) ex Crossway Brickworks, c/1959

Combwich Brickworks,near Bridgwater

16   Tramway serving the works(at ST 260420?). Works closed;demolished 1967

Gauge: 1ft 8in

-	4wDM	FH	3061	1946	New	(1)

                (1) to W.Thomas & Co.Ltd.,Poole Siding
                     Brickworks,Wellington,c/1966.

Crossway Brickworks, near Bridgwater

17 Tramway closed and most of the track lifted by 9/1959

Gauge: 1ft 8in

–	4wPM	FH	2115	1938	New	(1)

(1) to Castlefield Brickworks, c/1959

Dunball Brickworks, near Bridgwater

18 Tramway closed and lifted.

Gauge: 2ft 0in

–	4wPM	L				s/s
–	4wPM	FH	1987	1936	New	(2)
–	4wPM	FH	2326	1940	New	(1)

(1) to Burnham-on-Sea Brickworks
(2) to Burnham-on-Sea Brickworks, 9/1959

Saltlands Tileworks, Chilton Trinity, near Bridgwater (William Thomas & Co.Ltd. until c1962)

19 A tramway operated by horses until 1941 when locomotives were introduced. Rail system closed and replaced by road transport 1960. Works closed 1963. Location (ST 302391?)

Gauge: 1ft 8in

–	4wPM	Austro-Daimler			(a)	(1)
–	4wPM	L	5318	1934	(b)	(2)
–	4wPM	FH	3424	c1950	New	(3)

(a) ex F.Watkins (Boilers)Ltd.,Coleford Glos.,c/1941
(b) ex L;f. Birkenhead Gas Co.Ltd.,Ches.

(1) Scr c/1950 but chassis retained as a mobile refuge for workmen
(2) to Poole Siding Works,Wellington,c/1946
(3) to R.P.Morris,Longfield,Kent,for preservation,/1969

Uncertain Locations

The FH locomotives listed above were New to the company,but may have been at other works than the one initially listed
L records quote the following locomotives to Colthurst Symons,but it is not known to which of the above,or other,locations they were delivered. They presumably include the unidentified ones listed above.

Gauge: narrow

–	4wPM	L	6343	1935	New	s/s

Gauge: 1ft 8in

–	4wPM	L	6732	1935	New	s/s
–	4wPM	L	7578	1936	New	s/s
–	4wPM	L	8575	1936	New	s/s

CRANMORE RAILWAY CO. LTD., CRANMORE, SHEPTON MALLET

20   The operating company for the East Somerset Railway preservation project of the Shepherd Railway Preservation Trust. A locomotive shed and other facilities have been built adjacent to Cranmore station (ST 664429) on the BR (ex GWR) Witham - Wells linc. Work commenced on the buildings in 1973 and the project was opened to the public from 1/8/1974

Ref: RM No.882 (10/1974) , p.499

Gauge: 4ft 8½in

68005		0-6-0ST	IC	RSH	7169	1944	(a)
-		0-4-0CT	OC	D	4101	1901	(b)
	LORD FISHER	0-4-0ST	OC	AB	1398	1915	(c)
	GLENFIELD	0-4-0ST	OC	AB	1719	1920	(c)
47493		0-6-0T	IC	VF	4195	1927	(c)
928	STOWE	4-4-0	3C	Elh		1934	(d)
75029	THE GREEN KNIGHT	4-6-0	OC	Sdn		1959	(d)
92203	BLACK PRINCE	2-10-0	OC	Sdn		1959	(d)

(a) ex Johnsons(Chopwell) Ltd ,Co.Durham, 8/1973
(b) ex British Steel Corporation, Shelton Works,
    Staffs, 9/1973
(c) ex Somerset & Dorset Railway Circle,
    Radstock Depot, 11/1973
(d) ex BR ,Eastleigh Depot, Hants, 11/1973

FISONS LTD., AGRO-CHEMICAL DIVISION, ASHCOTT (Cambridge Division until /1970; f Eclipse
                                                   Peat Co. Ltd.)

21   Extensive peat workings on Shapwick and Meare Heaths. Processing works exist or have existed at the following locations,each with its own tramway system:
Broomfield Works, Ashcott (Head office)   (ST 454406 and ST 451406)
Great Plain Works, Ashcott   (ST 442402)
Shapwick Works
Pools Heath site,Westhay   (ST 421424)
Adjacent to Great Plain Works the narrow gauge crossed the BR (ex S&DJR) line on a level crossing laid under an agreement of 11/1922. This crossing was the site of a collision between narrow and standard gauge locos on 26/8/1949.

Gauge: 2ft 0in

	4wPM	Eclipse			New	s/s	
-	4wDM	Eclipse			New	(2)	
-	4wDM	Eclipse					
-	4wDM	Eclipse					
-	4wPM	MH	A125	1925	(a)	Scr c /1966	
-	4wDM	MR	4604	1932	(b)	Scr c /1966	
-	4wPM	MR			(1)		
-	4wDM	RH	222097	1944	(c)	s/s c /1969	
-	4wDM(f.PM)	L	10498	1938	(d)		
-	4wDM(f.PM)	L	26366	1944	(d)		
-	4wDM(f.PM)	L	34758	1949	New		
-	4wDM(f.PM)	L	38296	1952	New	(3)	
-	4wDM(f.PM)	L	42494	1956	New		
-	4wDM	L	50888	1959	New		
-	4wDM	LB	51989	1960	New		
-	4wDM	LB	53726	1963	New(j)		
-	4wPM	L	37170	1951	(e)		
-	4wDM	LB	55070	1966	New		
-	4wPM	L	40009	1954	(f)	(4)	
-	4wDM	L	42319	1956	(g)		
-	4wPM	L	37658	1952	(h)		

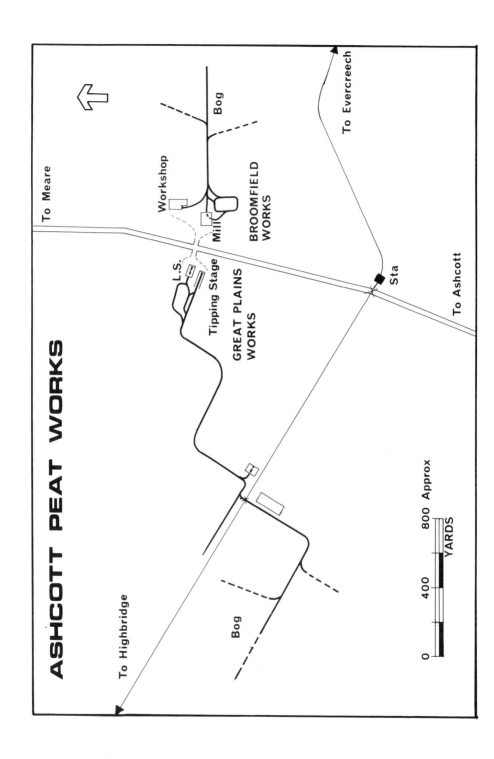

(a) ex contractors,Avonmouth Docks
(b) ex McAlpine
(c) ex Wm Cory & Son Ltd.,Longreach,Kent
(d) ex John Board & Co.Ltd.,Dunball
(e) ex White Moss Peat Works,Alsager,
    Ches.,c/1965
(f) ex R.P.Morris,Longfield,Kent,6/1970
(g) ex Fina Peat Products Ltd.,Wilmslow,
    Ches.,c6/1970
(h) ex R.P.Morris,Longfield,Kent,6/1970;
    f. Edward Comise Ltd.,Scotland.
(j) to Fina Peat Products Ltd.,Wilmslow,
    Ches.,/1965;returned 12/1970

(1) Scr after accident,/1949
(2) to White Moss Peat Works,Alsager,
    Ches.,c/1962
(3) to White Moss Peat Works,Alsager,
    Ches.,c/1966
(4) to Fina Peat Products Ltd.,Wilmslow,
    Ches.,2/1971

FOSTER YEOMAN (DULCOTE) LTD.

Dulcote Quarry,near Wells.

22 Extensive roadstone quarries on the north of the BR(ex GWR) Wells-Witham line
at ST 573440. Short,numerous,narrow gauge lines connected the quarry with a
standard gauge siding.Narrow gauge tramway ceased operation in 3/1955 and has
been lifted;the quarry remains active using road transport.

Gauge: 2ft 0in

| | | 4wDM | RH | 237909 | 1946 | New | (1) |

(1) Dsm by /1959;scr c/1962.

Merehead Stone Terminal,Cranmore

23 A modern rail installation,opened 1971. A new line from the BR Wells-Witham
line was laid to run north to the mechanised loading installation at ST 693438,
serving the extensive quarries to the north of this point.Initially all rail
traffic was moved by the BR locos. In a second stage another new line was laid
to form a triangular connection with the BR line,and locomotives purchased to
move stock in the terminal area.

Gauge: 4ft 8½in

3002		0-6-0DE	Derby	1952	(a)
3003		0-6-0DE	Derby	1952	(b)
33		0-6-0DE	Derby	1954	(c)

(a) ex BR , 12/1972
(b) ex BR , 5/1973
(c) ex BRE Derby , 2/1975, f BR 08 032 (ex D 3044)

E.J.GODWIN (PEAT INDUSTRIES)LTD.,WESTHAY PEAT WORKS,WESTHAY

24 A tramway connecting several peat diggings to the works at ST 418425. Use of the
rail system had ceased and the locos were stored by 1966.

Gauge: 2ft 0in

| | | 4wDM (f.PM) | MR | | | (a) |
| | | 4wPM | L | 30233 | 1946 | (b) |

(a) ex ? , c/1952
(b) ex Western Counties Brick Co.Ltd.,
    Exeter,Devon.

GREAT WESTERN SOCIETY LTD.,TAUNTON

25   Locomotives and rolling stock are kept in part of the yard of the former MPD at the south west end of Taunton station (ST 226254) while their restoration is in hand. The group commenced on this site in 1970.

Gauge: 4ft 8½in

2	PONTYBEREM	0-6-0ST	OC	AE	1421	1900	(a)
5572		2-6-2T	OC	Sdn		1929	(b)
1163	WHITEHEAD	0-4-0ST	OC	P	1163	1908	(c)

(a) ex NCB East Wales Area,Penrikyber
    Coll.,8/1970
(b) ex Woodham Bros.,Barry,9/1971
(c) ex G.D.Buncombe,Highbridge,/1971

MELLS QUARRY CO.,BILBOA QUARRY,MELLS

26   A quarry at ST 715495 served by a 4ft 8½in gauge line from the GWR Frome-Radstock line near Mells Road. This line,the Bilboa Railway,was laid under an agreement dated 10/1925. The quarry was taken over by Roads Reconstruction (1934) Ltd. in 1934,when a connection was laid in from the Newbury Railway and the original line was closed. Mells Quarry Co. had its own locomotive,believed to have been an 0-4-0, s/s.

MENDIP DISTRICT COUNCIL,WELSHMILL ADVENTURE PLAYGROUND,FROME (Frome U.D.C. until
                                                                                               1/4/1974)

27   The locomotive is on view in this park at ST 778486.

Gauge: 4ft 8½in

ARC		4wVBT	VCG	S	9387	1948	(a)

(a) ex ARC(Southern)Ltd.,New Frome Quarry,
    11/1971.

MINISTRY OF DEFENCE

    Army Department,Norton Fitzwarren Depot. (War Department until 1/4/1964)

28   Opened c1942 as a US Army stores.Taken over by the WD in 1946 to become No.3 Supply Reserve Depot. The main depot closed in 1966 and has become an industrial trading estate,but a small section is still in Army use,without normal rail traffic. The depot was served by sidings on the north of the BR(ex GWR) Taunton-Norton Fitzwarren line,with a loco shed at ST 204257

Gauge: 4ft 8½in

    Worked by standard MoD(AD) diesel locomotives.

Royal Ordnance Factory, Puriton

29 A chemical and explosives factory opened c1940. Served by a standard gauge branch from the BR (ex GWR) Taunton-Bristol line near W,Huntspill (ST 318437),and by an internal narrow gauge line. During 1971-3 the construction of the M5 motorway necessitated the rebuilding of the standard gauge line on a new alignment with more severe gradients on either side of the viaduct over the motorway;this in turn has resulted in the introduction of more powerful locomotives.

Gauge: 4ft 8½in

		WELLINGTON	0-4-0ST	OC	AB	2082	1940	(a) (1)
	No.2		0-4-0DM		AB	349	1941	New (2)
		_	0-4-0DM		AB	352	1941	New (3)
	2	(f. 1)	0-4-0DM		JF	22986	1942	New (4)
3213	2		0-4-0DM		JF	4210082	1953	New (5)
4764	3		0-4-0DM		JF	4210126	1957	New
6320		BRIDGWATER No.1	0-4-0DM		AB	578	1972	New
6321		BRIDGWATER No.2	0-4-0DM		AB	579	1972	New

(a) ex ROF Chorley,Lancs

(1) to ? ;resold to NCB Ellistown Coll., Leics./1948
(2) to Abelson,Sheldon,Birmingham,5/1957; resold to Haunchwood Brick & Tile Co.Ltd.,Warwicks,4/1959
(3) to ROF Birtley,Co.Durham, by/1966
(4) to Birds Commercial Motors Ltd.,Long Marston,Warwicks,/1966
(5) to Coopers (Metals)Ltd.,scrap merchants, Swindon,Wilts, c2/1973

Gauge: 2ft 6in

_	4wBE	GB	1698	1940	New
_	4wBE	GB	1699	1940	New
_	4wBE	GB	1877	1943	New

MINISTRY OF MUNITIONS, BRIDGWATER FACTORY

30 A First World War factory,long closed. Location uncertain.

Gauge: 4ft 8½in

_	2-2-0T	OC	9E		1906	(a) s/s

(a) ex LSWR '738', 3/1917

MOOREWOOD COLLIERY CO.LTD.,MOOREWOOD COLLIERY,OAKHILL

31 Colliery at ST 642495 originally sunk c1860,closed by 1873. Reopened from 1909, and a tramway was built 1913-14 to transport its output to a siding on the S&DJR. From the colliery the line rose via a rope worked incline,and the locomotives were used on the more level section from the head of the incline to the S&DJR. Tramway replaced by lorries sometime between 1925-30. Colliery closed 12/1932.

Ref: 'The History of the Somerset Coalfield'by C.G.Down & A.J.Warrington; D&C.

Gauge: 2ft 0in

_	0-6-0ST	OC	P	1412	1915	New	(1)
_	0-4-0ST	OC	WB	1725	1903	(a)	s/s /1933
_	0-6-0WT	OC	HC	1298	1917	(b)	(1)

(a) ex New Westbury Iron Co.Ltd.,Wilts   (1) to Stanley Engineering Co.Ltd.,Bath,
(b) built for WDLR;purchased per a dealer,   7/1933;resold to Sutton Sand Co.,
      c7/1922.   Kildare,Ireland, 6/1934

NEW MELLS COLLIERY CO.LTD.,MELLS COLLIERY,NEAR FROME (Mells Coal Industry Ltd.until

5/8/1937;Horner Trustees until 15/1/1934;Mells Collieries Ltd. until 23/8/1930)

32   A colliery at ST 713505 which had closed by 1881 and was reopened c1909.It
      finally closed 30/10/1943.It was served by sidings off the Newbury Railway and
      these were shunted by the Newbury Railway locomotive(until1927?). See under
      John Wainwright & Co.Ltd. and Westbury Iron Co.Ltd. also.

      Ref: 'The History of the Somerset Coalfield' by C.G.Down & A.J.Warrington;D&C.

Gauge: 4ft 8½in

–		(0-4-0ST	OC	HE?)			(a)	s/s
820		0-6-0T	OC	CF	1161	1898	(b)	(1)

(a) possibly ex Newbury Collieries Ltd.,   (1) to Cohen,London,for scrap,2/1945
      c8/1927
(b) ex GWR,Swindon,'820', 3/1931.

NEWBURY COLLIERIES LTD.,NEWBURY COLLIERY,NEAR FROME.(Llwydcoed Collieries Ltd. by 4/

1912;Newbury Collieries Ltd. by 1917)

33   Colliery at ST 696497 at the end of the Newbury Railway (q.v). A narrow gauge
      line ran on from here to Mackintosh Colliery also.a locomotive was shedded
      here by 1910,presumably being purchased from John Wainwright by Llwydcoed
      Collieries Ltd. The colliery closed 8/1927 and the loco was possibly sold to
      either Mendip Mountain Quarries Ltd. or Mells Collieries Ltd. by this date.

      Ref: 'The History of the Somerset Coalfield' by C.G.Down & A.J.Warrington;D&C.

OAKHILL BREWERY CO.LTD.,OAKHILL

34   The company was founded 1889 to take over the old brewery established in 1767.
      A narrow gauge line opened in 1904 which connected the brewery with the S&DJR
      line at Binegar station (ST 615493). The line had closed by 1921 when the track
      was lifted. A fire in 1925 partly destroyed the works.

Gauge: 2ft 6in

MENDIP	0-4-0ST	OC	WB	1701	1903	New	(1)
OAKHILL	0-4-0ST	OC	P	1021	1904	New	(2)

                          (1) to N.Hingley,Netherton,Staffs,via
                                Pugsley,Stoke Gifford,/1920
                          (2) to B.P.C.M.Ltd.,Penarth Works,Glam.

PETTERS LTD., WESTLAND WORKS, YEOVIL

35   Locos used on the sidings serving the works of this diesel and oil engine manufacturer. The works and aerodrome site was sold in 7/1935 to the then newly formed Westland Aircraft Ltd (which see). The business was sold to Brush Electrical Engineering Co Ltd as from 1/1/1939.

Gauge: 4ft 8½in

EVA	0-4-0ST	OC	MW	213	1866		
		Reb	MW	736	1879		
		& Reb	P.Baker,Cardiff			(a)	(1)
ACE	0-4-0DM		JF	19425	1931	New	(2)

(a) ex Dixon & Cardus Ltd ,Northam,Hants ,   (1) to ?   ,for scrap, /1935
    /1920   (2) to Brush Electrical Engineering Co Ltd ,
                                        Loughborough,Leics

A.G.PITTS & CO.,HIGHBRIDGE STATION BRICKWORKS (Branch of Western Counties Brick Co.Ltd.)

36   A narrow gauge system served the brickworks. The works closed for production c /1957 and the tramway was lifted.

Gauge: 2ft 0in

-	4wPM	L	7196	1935	(a)	Scr c /1954
-	4wPM	L		1953	New	Scr c /1961

(a) ex J & J W Saunders, Pinhoe Brickworks,
    Exeter,Devon.

ROADS RECONSTRUCTION (1934) LTD

The company was formed from Roads Reconstruction Ltd and a number of smaller roadstone quarrying concerns. The majority of the quarries were nominally operated by subsidiary companies,details given where known. At a later stage the group has become part of the Amalgamated Roadstone Corporation Ltd and subsequently the Amey Roadstone Corporation Ltd.,which see for extant locations.

Cranmore Depot (Roads Reconstruction Ltd until 17/2/1934)

37   A plant depot on the site of the former Waterlip Quarry of the Mendip Granite and Asphalt Co Ltd (ST 660445). A standard gauge line ran for about a mile to the works and connection with the GWR Wells - Witham line at ST 666430 on the route of an earlier horse worked narrow gauge line. Locomotives were stored and repaired at this depot.

Gauge: 4ft 8½in

154	4wVBT	VCG S	6090	1925	(a)	(1)
1700	0-4-0PM	MW	1954	1918	(b)	(2)
-	0-4-0DM	JF	19645	1932	(c)	(3)

(a) ex S , 3/1927   (1) to New Frome Quarry, 9/1944
(b) ex ROD , 1700   (2) to Vobster Quarry, c /1927
(c) ex Sandford Quarry; to New Frome Quarry;(3) to ICI, Winnington Works, Ches ,via
      ex Sandford Quarry, /1943   Abelson,Sheldon,Birmingham, 1/1946

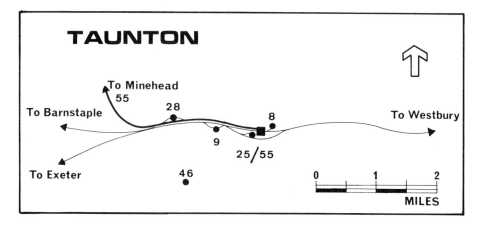

TAUNTON

To Minehead
55
28
To Barnstaple
To Westbury
8
9
25/55
To Exeter
46

0   1   2
MILES

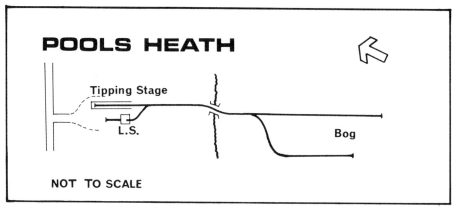

POOLS HEATH

Tipping Stage

L.S.

Bog

NOT TO SCALE

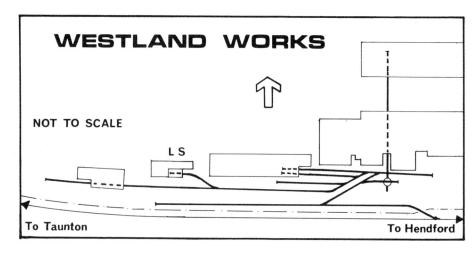

WESTLAND WORKS

NOT TO SCALE

L S

To Taunton

To Hendford

Gauge: 2ft 0in

GAMECOCK	0-4-0ST	OC	P	1030	1904	(a)	Scr	c /1927
(157)	0-4-2ST	OC	KS	856	1904	(b)	Scr	/1951
(41)	0-4-2ST	OC	KS	3065	1918	(c)	s/s	c /1951
-	0-4-0T	(AE?)				(d)	s/s	
-	0-4-0T	(AE?)				(d)	s/s	
-	0-6-0DM	Dtz	88153			(e)	s/s	c /1950
3	0-4-0WT	OC	AB	1855	1931	(g)	Scr	/1959
-	0-4-0T	OC	AE	2072	1933	(f)	(1)	
-	0-4-0T	OC	AE	2073	1933	(g)	(1)	
D1	0-4-0DM	KS	4427	1929		(h)	s/s	c /1957
-	4wDM	Crossley				(h)	s/s	c /1955
-	4wPM	MR	400	1917		(h)	s/s	c /1955
-	4wPM	MR	587	1917		(h)	s/s	c /1955
D9 151	4wDM	Jung	5189			(j)	s/s	c /1955

(a) ex Somerset Basalt Quarry Co Ltd
(b) ex Air Ministry, Winchester, Hants , by
    4/1924; to Sandford Quarry by 1/1927;
    ret by 3/1931
(c) ex New Frome Quarry by 4/1924; to
    Tytherington Quarry, Glos , by 12/1928;
    ex New Frome Quarry, c /1948
(d) ex Sandford Quarry, Banwell
(e) ex Sandford Quarry, Banwell, c /1942
(f) ex New Frome Quarry
(g) ex Grovesend Quarry, Glos , 4/1949
(h) ex Black Rock Quarries Ltd
(j) ex (Scatter Rock Macadams Ltd?), c /1953

(1) to ? ,India, via Oswald Bond,dealer,
    Cardiff, c /1951

Emborough Quarry (Emborough Stone Co.(1928) Ltd. until 17/2/1934)

38   A quarry on the west of the BR (ex S&DJR) line at ST 620505 approx. Opened
c/1901 on the site of an earlier brick and tile works. Operated by the
Emborough Stone Co as a branch of Roads Reconstruction (1934) Ltd. Shunting on
the standard gauge was later performed by winch. The narrow gauge system was
replaced by road transport in 12/1955 and track lifted. Standard gauge traffic
ceased by 21/6/1965 and track lifted.

Gauge: 4ft 8½in

-	4wPM	Schneider	c1916	(a)	Scr	c /1951

(a) ex Windsor Hill Quarry, c /1944

Gauge: 2ft 0in

-	4wPM	L	4120	1931	New	s/s	
548	4wDM	RH	164329	1931	(a)	(1)	
549	4wDM	RH	164331	1931	(a)	(1)	
701	4wDM	RH	198313	1940	(b)	s/s	/1961
700	4wDM	RH	200507	1940	(c)	s/s	/1961
844 D10	4wDM	RH	213860	1942	New	s/s	/1961
845 D11	4wDM	RH	213861	1942	New	s/s	/1961

(a) ex Mears Bros , contrs,
(b) ex Vobster Quarry, /1951
(c) ex New Frome Quarry

(1) to Vobster Quarry

Vobster Quarry, Mells Road (Roads Reconstruction Ltd until 17/2/1934 ; Mendip

39   Mountain Quarries Ltd until c/1918; prev John Wainwright & Co Ltd , q.v)

A quarry served by standard gauge sidings with a loco shed at ST 705496. A branch about 1½ miles long connected these installations with the BR (ex GWR) line near Mells Road station. This branch, the Newbury Railway, served also other industrial locations and was formerly operated by the Mells Siding Committee of John Wainwright & Co Ltd (who see for earlier history). The quarry was operated by the Vobster Quarry Co as a branch of Roads Reconstruction (1934) Ltd. A narrow gauge line was operated in the quarry. This was replaced by conveyors and dumpers c/1949 and the track was lifted c/1951. Standard gauge rail traffic ceased 1965 and the quarry was closed c/1966.

Gauge: 4ft 8½in

		0-6-0ST	OC				(a)	Sold for scrap
292	NIDD	0-4-0ST	OC	KS	3112	1918	(b)	(2)
385	(MILDRED)	0-6-0ST	OC	AE	1763	1917	(c)	Scr 2/1959
386		0-6-0ST	OC	HCR	153	1874	(d)	s/s
1700		0-4-0VBT	VCG	S	6219	c1927		
	Reb from	0-4-0PM	MW		1954	1918	(e)	(1)
752	SENTINEL	4wVBT	VCG	S	9398	1950	(f)	(3)
784	1	4wVBT	VCG	S	9374	1947	(g)	(4)
–		4wBE	EE		712	1927	New	s/s
–		4wBE	EE		713	1927	New	s/s
–		4wBE	EE		714	1927	New	s/s
–		4wBE	EE		715	1927	New	s/s
–		4wBE	EE		716	1927	New	s/s

(a) possibly ex John Wainwright & Co Ltd
(b) ex Conygar Quarry
(c) ex Inland Waterways & Docks,Purfleet,
    Essex, No.33 MILDRED, by 6/1920
(d) probably ex John Wainwright & Co Ltd ,
    c /1918
(e) ex Cranmore Depot, c /1927
(f) ex S , 5/1953
(g) ex New Frome Quarry, /1963

(1) to Sandford Quarry
(2) to New Frome Quarry; ret c /1949;
    Scr by (Usher of Trowbridge ?), /1955
(3) to TH , Kilnhurst, Yorks WR, 1/1965
(4) ret to New Frome Quarry, 8/1965

Gauge: 2ft 0in

190	D8	0-4-0DM	Dtz	9898	1931	(a)	Scr c /1954
548		4wDM	RH	164329	1931	(b)	(1)
549	D3	4wDM	RH	164331	1931	(b)	s/s c /1953
675		4wDM	RH	182145	1936	(c)	(2)
701	D6	4wDM	RH	198313	1940	(d)	(3)
–		4wDM				(e)	Scr c /1955

(a) ex Grovesend Quarry, Glos , c /1948
(b) ex Emborough Quarry
(c) ex Borough of Slough,Bucks , /1939
(d) ex New Frome Quarry
(e) ex ? (carried identity 'Locofax
    Comessa, Strasbourg 6295'(dealer?))

(1) to Pugsley, Stoke Gifford
(2) to Devizes Brick & Tile Co Ltd ,Wilts,
    c /1953
(3) to Emborough Quarry, /1951

Windsor Hill Quarry, near Shepton Mallet

40   A reopening of the quarry originally operated by W.B.Beauchamp, served by
standard gauge sidings on the east side of the LMS (ex S&DJR) line at ST 613454.
Quarry closed c /1942.

Gauge: 4ft 8½in

		4wPM	Schneider	c1916	(a)	(1)

(a) ex ROD   (1) to Emborough Quarry, c /1944

SHAPWICK PEAT WORKINGS

41   A line served diggings to the south-west of Shapwick station on the BR (ex
S&DJR) Highbridge - Evercreech line. It was used to carry bags of milled peat
from a mobile peat mill at the workings to a storage shed at ST 422411. The
identity of the operating company is not known. The system was in use c /1960;
later closed and lifted.

Gauge: 2ft 0in

		4wDM	MR		s/s

SOMERSET BASALT QUARRY CO., DOWNHEAD QUARRY

42   A quarry at ST 685461 producing andesite from c/1905. Stone was at first moved
by a horse worked tramway to a crushing plant near Downhead village (ST 690460).
The locomotive worked line was built c/1907 as an extension of the narrow gauge
line from Cranmore (on the GWR Wells- Witham line) to Waterlip Quarry (ST 660445)
At Long Cross (ST 659452) a branch diverged to serve Moon's Hill Quarry. The
Downhead line continued to a total of about 4 miles, crossing the Wells -Frome
turnpike road at ST 673458, the final ¾ mile being a double track rope worked
incline powered by a Brown & May stationary engine just east of the Frome road.
The quarry was closed c/1925 and the track north of Waterlip was lifted. The
Cranmore- Waterlip line was always horse worked, due to a low bridge, until this
time when it was rebuilt as a loco worked standard gauge route. The locomotive
was shedded at Waterlip.

Ref: 'Journal of Industrial Archeology, Vol 8 (1971), p420', Robin Atthill

Gauge: 2ft 0in

GAMECOCK		0-4-0ST	OC	P	1030	1904	New	(1)

(1) to Roads Reconstruction Ltd , c /1925;
Scr c /1927

SOMERSET MINERAL SYNDICATE LTD., COLTON MINE

43   A syndicate formed in 1907 to work iron mines in the area of the West Somerset
Mineral Railway (q.v.) which was reopened. The narrow gauge tramway was built
from the head of the incline at Brendon Hill (ST 023374) eastwards alongside the
road for 1¾ miles and then down a 600 yard incline to Colton Adit (ST 050351).
Here it connected with the 1ft 4in gauge lines used in the adit.
At Timwood adit (ST 033353) 1ft 4in gauge lines were also used, but connected
directly with the West Somerset Mineral Railway. The mines and tramways were
closed and dismantled in 1910.

Ref: 'The West Somerset Mineral Railway' by Roger Sellick; D&C , 1970
     'The Narrow Gauge No.34' (NGRS)

Gauge: 2ft 0in

		0-4-0T	OC	(KS?)			(a)	(1)
		0-4-0WT	IC	WB			(a)	(1)

(a) ex ?   (1) Sold for scrap, /1910

SOMERSET QUARRY CO.LTD., FROME

44   A company working quarries in the Vallis Vale area. The company was taken over by
        Roads Reconstruction Ltd in the early 1930's and the quarries and tramway were
        incorporated into the New Frome Quarry system.

Gauge: 2ft 3in

MIDGE	0-4-0ST	OC	KS	1017	1907	New	s/s
WREN	0-4-0ST	OC	KS	1188	1910	New	s/s

SOMERSET RIVER AUTHORITY,BRADNEY DEPOT,NEAR PURITON (f Somerset Rivers Catchment Board)

45   A plant depot where the locos were based when not in use on temporary riverbank
        sites.

Gauge: 2ft 0in

-	4wDM	RH	168832	1933	New	(1)
-	4wDM	MR	9976	1954	New	s/s c /1971

                        (1) to ? , dealer,Singapore, per C.S.Pratt,
                        Bristol, /1971

TAUNTON BRICK & TILE CO. LTD., BISHOPS HULL BRICKWORKS, TAUNTON

46   Locomotive known to have been supplied to the company,presumed to have been used
        on a tramway at the above works (ST 207240 ?). Rail system no longer exists.

Gauge: 2ft 0in

-	4wPM	L	9716	1937	New	s/s

WILLIAM THOMAS & CO.LTD., POOLE SIDING BRICK & TILE WORKS, WELLINGTON

47   A tramway connected clay pits with the brickworks (ST 150218) on the south of
        the BR (ex GWR) main line east of Wellington station. The tramway was opened
        by 1938, and ceased operation in 1967.

Gauge: 2ft 0in

-	4wDM	RH	192884	1938	New	Scr c /1966
-	4wPM	L	5318	1934	(a)	Scr c /1966
-	4wDM	FH	3061	1946	(b)	Scr /1968

(a) ex Saltlands Tileworks,Bridgwater, c /1946
(b) ex Colthurst,Symons & Co Ltd ,
    Combwich Brickworks, c /1966

UNIGATE FOODS LTD., CHARD JUNCTION DARIES (f United Daries Ltd., prev Wilts United

Dairies Ltd.)

48   A large centralised dairy on the south side of Chard Junction station (ST 341047)
        served by a number of standard gauge sidings used to load bulk milk tank wagons.

Gauge: 4ft 8½in

-	4wDM	RH	183062	1937	New	(1)
No.12	0-4-0DM	RH	304470	1951	(a)

(a) ex British Gas Corporation, Windsor Street   (1) to West Somerset Railway Co Ltd ,
    Gasworks,Birmingham, c8/1974   Minehead, c1/1976

JOHN WAINWRIGHT & CO. LTD., NEWBURY RAILWAY, MELLS (Westbury Iron Co Ltd until 2/1904)

49   A line about 1½ miles long from the GWR Frome - Radstock line near Mells Road
station serving Mells Colliery, Vobster Quarry and Newbury Colliery (ST 695497).
From the latter a narrow gauge line continued to Mackintosh Colliery. The line
was constructed about 1857 to the 7ft 0¼in gauge and later converted to
4ft 8½in gauge. Haulage was by horse before the introduction of locomotives.
About 1918 the line passed to Mendip Mountain Quarries, later the Roads
Reconstruction group, who in c/1934 installed a new branch to the Bilboa Quarry.
See under Roads Reconstruction Ltd for other details.

    Ref: 'The History of the Somerset Coalfield' by C.G.Down & A.J.Warrington; D&C

Gauge: 4ft 8½in

-	0-6-0ST	OC	HCR	153	1874	New	(1)

               (1) to Mendip Mountain Quarries Ltd ,c /1918

Also two other locomotives believed purchased c/1908-10 from John Aird & Sons,Avonmouth
Dock contract,Bristol. One loco (scrapped?) after a collision;the other possibly to
Llwydcoed Collieries Ltd.,Newbury Colliery (with the premises) by 4/1912.

WAR DEPARTMENT, HIGHBRIDGE DEPOT

50   A depot at ST 327467 on the north of the BR (ex S&DJR) line near their
Highbridge Works. Opened c/1942 as a US Army Ordnance Depot; later handed over
to the WD and subsequently closed and track lifted by 1957

Gauge: 4ft 8½in

    Worked by standard WD locomotives.

WESTERN TRINIDAD LAKE ASPHALT CO. LTD.

Barn Close Quarry, Leigh-on-Mendip

51   Tramway served a roadstone quarry. The rail system was closed and dismantled
and the quarry was later taken over by Perry & Perry Ltd.

Gauge: 2ft 0in

-	4wPM	MR	5362	1932	New	(1)

               (1) to Merehead Quarry

Merehead Quarry, East Cranmore

52   A roadstone quarry at ST 697443 served by a narrow gauge line. Tramway closed
and lifted;the quarry site was later taken over and greatly extended by Foster
Yeoman Ltd. (q.v.)

Gauge: 2ft 0in

-	4wPM	MR	5362	1932	(a)	s/s

(a) ex Barn Close Quarry

WESTLAND AIRCRAFT LTD., YEOVIL

53   Company formed 4/7/1935 to acquire from Petters Ltd (which see) the Westland
Aircraft Works (ST 542154) and 73 acre aerodrome. Acquired freehold land and
buildings from Petters Ltd in 7/1938. The locomotive was used to shunt the
rail sidings on the north side of the BR (ex GWR) Yeovil Town - Taunton line.
Rail traffic ceased c4/1967 and sidings lifted.

Gauge: 4ft 8½in

		4wPM	H			
		Reb		1942		Scr c4/1967

WEST SOMERSET MINERAL RAILWAY (Line leased to and operated by A.R.Angus Ltd from

12/1911 for experimental work only; Somerset Mineral Syndicate Ltd , 3/1907 - 3/1910;
Ebbw Vale Steel Iron & Coal Co Ltd from 1869; Ebbw Vale Co Ltd from 16/6/1864; Brendon
Hills Iron Ore Co from 29/9/1859)

54   A line from Watchet Quay to Comberow (7½ miles) for mineral and passenger
traffic. From Comberow a half mile long self acting incline brought mineral
traffic down from Raleighs Cross and Colton MInes and from a four mile extension
to Gupworthy. Fare paying passengers were not carried above Comberow. Loco
facilities on the lower section were at Watchet (ST 067433) and on the upper
section at Brendon Hill (ST 024343).
Opened for goods 28/9/1859 and passengers 4/9/1865. Closed 7/11/1898. Reopened
for mineral traffic Watchet- Brendon 4/7/1907, closed 1909. The line was
finally used for experiments in Automatic Train Control, 1912-14. The track was
lifted in 1917 and the land sold 1924.

Ref: 'The West Somerset Mineral Railway' by Roger Sellick; D&C 1970.

Gauge: 4ft 8½in

-	0-4-0ST	OC	N	370	1856 New	(1)
-	0-4-0ST	OC	N		1857 New	(2)
ROWCLIFFE	0-6-0ST	IC	SS	995	1857 (a)	(3)
-	0-4-0ST	OC	N		(1861?)(b)	(3)
PONTYPOOL	0-6-0ST	IC	SS	1677	1866 New	(4)
ESPERANZA	0-6-0ST	IC	SS	2262	1872 (c)	(5)
WHITFIELD	0-6-0ST	IC	SS	(1011	1857?)(d)	(6)
-	0-4-0ST	OC	N		(e)	(7)
-	4-4-0T	OC	BP	1881	1879 (f)	(8)
212	2-4-0	IC	BP	248	1861 (g)	(9)
213	2-4-0	IC	BP	249	1861 (g)	(9)

(a) either New or ex Ebbw Vale works,c8/1857   (1) to Ebbw Vale works for scrap,(/1897?)
(b) ex Ebbw Vale works, (/1865?)   (2) to ? (for scrap?) after collision,
(c) ex Ebbw Vale works, (/1894?)   8/1857
(d) ex Ebbw Vale works, /1895   (3) to Ebbw Vale works, /1883
(e) ex Ebbw Vale works, 12/1896   (4) to Ebbw Vale works, 8/1/1899
(f) ex Metropolitan Railway, 37 ,per   (5)(ret to Ebbw Vale works, /1894?)
     A.King & Co , 6/1907   (6) ret to Ebbw Vale works, /1895
(g) ex GWR , 17/12/1911   (7) to ? ,Newport,Mon ,for scrap, c /1900
                                         (8) to(Bute Works Supply Co ?),24/7/1910
                                         (9) to Bute Works Supply Co (transferred
                                            to GWR Taunton, 4/11/1917); to
                                            Cambrian Railways, 3/1921

55 The BR (ex GWR) Taunton - Minehead line was opened Norton Fitzwarren - Watchet 31/3/1862 and Watchet - Minehead 16/7/1874, was converted from /ft 0¼in to 4ft 8½in gauge in 10/1882 and closed by BR in 1/1971. The line has since been purchased by Somerset County Council and leased to the West Somerset Railway Co for operation under a Light Railway Order. It is intended to operate steam trains in summer on the Minehead - Blue Anchor section (services recommenced 28/3/1976) and diesel services Minehead - Taunton. Stock is/has been stabled at Taunton (ST 226254), Norton Fitzwarren (ST 204257), Bishop's Lydeard (ST 165289), Williton (ST 085417) and Minehead (SS 976462). The Somerset & Dorset Railway Museum Trust intend that their stock shall eventually be displayed at a museum site at Washford.

Gauge: 4ft8½in

	VULCAN	0-6-0ST	OC	WB	2994	1950	(a)
2996	VICTOR	0-6-0ST	OC	WB	2996	1950	(a)
W50413		4w-4wDMR		Park Royal		1957	(b)
W50414		4w-4wDMR		Park Royal		1957	(b)
32678		0-6-0T	IC	Bton		1880	(c)
53808		2-8-0	OC	RS	3894	1925	(d)
S3	PORTBURY	0-6-0ST	OC	AE	1764	1917	(d)
S9	HENBURY	0-6-0ST	OC	P	1940	1937	(d)
	ISABEL	0-6-0ST	OC	HL	3437	1919	(d)
24		4wDM		RH	210479	1941	(d)
	-	0-4-0ST	OC	P	1788	1929	(d)
No.1		0-4-0F	OC	WB	2473	1932	(d)
900855		4wPMR		Wkm	6967		(d)
7017		B-B. DH		BP	7911	1962	(e)
4561		2-6-2T	OC	Sdn	-	1924	(f)
5521		2-6-2T	OC	Sdn	-	1927	(f)
5542		2-6-2T	OC	Sdn	-	1928	(f)
	-	4wDM		RH	183062	1937	(g)
6412		0-6-0PT	IC	Sdn	-	1934	(h)

(a) ex British Leyland UK Ltd, Longbridge, Birmingham, 11/1973
(b) ex BR , c12/1973
(c) ex Butlins Ltd, Minehead Holiday Camp, 4/1975
(d) ex Somerset & Dorset Railway Museum Trust, Radstock, Avon, various dates from
     5/1975 to 3/1976
(e) ex BR, 7/1975
(f) ex Woodham Bros., Barry Dock, 10/1975
(g) ex Unigate Foods Ltd, Chard Junction Dairies, c3/1976
(h) ex Dart Valley Railway Co Ltd, Torbay Steam Railway, Devon, 3/1976

Non-locomotive systems

COOKS WOOD QUARRY,HOLCOMBE,NEAR RADSTOCK

A   A narrow gauge tramway served these quarries (ST 670478).There was also a
     1ft 6in gauge line serving underground workings part of which was still in situ,
     disused,in 1970

DOULTING STONEWORKS

B   A lengthy narrow gauge tramway connected Chelynch Quarries (ST 650438) to the
     stone works alongside the GWR Wells-Witham branch at ST 653425.Tramway closed
     and removed.

DOWNSIDE QUARRY

C   A standard gauge branch of the S&DJR at Windsor Hill served these quarries at
     ST 617449. Quarries and railway closed.

EVERCREECH QUARRY,LEIGHTON LANE,EVERCREECH

D   A narrow gauge tramway ¼ mile long connected the quarry with a works beside
     the S&DJR Evercreech station (ST 644386).Closed and removed.

GURNEYSLADE BOTTOM QUARRY

E   A narrow gauge tramway,removed after 1929,served these quarries at ST 627494

HAM WOOD QUARRY,WINDSOR HILL

F   A 2ft 0in gauge incline and tramway (closed) connected the quarry at ST 610452
     with a works alongside the S&DJR.Standard gauge sidings and some 2ft 0in gauge
     track and wagons still here in 1971

PARK QUARRY,LANGPORT,NEAR TAUNTON

G   A narrow gauge tramway ran from the quarry at ST 412258 to limekilns at ST 415258
     Quarry and tramway closed and dismantled.

ROWMEAD TRAMWAY,BINEGAR

H   A 1¼ mile narrow gauge tramway from quarries in Binegar Bottom to the main
     Shepton Mallet road at ST 621483,which possibly continued to the S&DJR at
     ST 613490.Closed and lifted

ST.CUTHBERTS LEAD WORKS,PRIDDY,CHEWTON MENDIP

J   A lengthy tramway from the mines (ST 549516) to the works at ST 545505. Gauge
     around 2ft. Closed in 1908 and lifted.

SOUTH WEST MINING SYNDICATE, EXMOOR MINE

K   A haematite working at SS 761378, known also as Blue Gate Mine, commenced in 1853 and reopened in 1910 by this syndicate, but abandoned in 1913. A $\frac{1}{4}$ mile narrow gauge tramway ran from the shafts to the road. Remains lifted.

TREBOROUGH SLATE QUARRY

L   A narrow gauge tramway connected the large quarry at ST 015367 through a tunnel under the road to extensive dumps and a further quarry. In operation in 1896; closed and lifted.

Contractors lines

THOMAS BRASSEY

C1   Contract for ballasting on the Taunton- Barnstaple section of the Bristol &
Exeter Railway, c /1873.

Gauge: 7ft 0¼in

VENUS	2-4-0	IC	Stothert & Slaughter	1844	(a)	s/s
DEFIANCE	0-6-0	IC	Stothert & Slaughter	1845	(a)	s/s

(a) ex LSWR, c /1867

FURNISS & BUXTON

C2   Construction of the Minehead and Watchet railway, -1874.

Gauge:(7ft 0¼in?)

              0-6-0T   ?   (1)

(1) for sale, 8/1874

HUTCHINSON & RITSON

C3   Construction of the Yeovil branch of the Bristol & Exeter Railway.

Gauge: 7ft 0¼in

	0-4-0WT	OC	W.B.Adams,Bow	1848		
	Reb	B&ER	/1856		(a)	s/s

(a) ex Bristol & Exeter Railway, FAIRFIELD, 6/1856; originally combined engine and
carriage

LOGAN & HEMINGWAY

C4   Construction of the Frome avoiding line (Clink Road Jct- Blatchbridge Jct) for
the GWR, 1931-4

Gauge: 4ft 8½in

3	0-6-0ST	IC	MW	1966	1918	(a)	(1)	
5	0-6-0ST	IC	MW	1793	1912	(b)	(2)	
8	0-6-0ST	IC	MW	1079	1888			
	Reb		MW		1908	(c)	(2)	

(a) ex Barnt Green contract, Worcs ,by 1/1931   (1) to Midland Ironstone Co Ltd ,
(b) ex Barnt Green contract, Worcs ,by 3/1931   Scunthorpe, Lincs, BEAUCHAMP,
(c) ex Hattersley Tunnel contract, Mottram,   /1934
    Cheshire, by 3/1932   (2) s/s after 7/1934

SIR ROBERT McALPINE & CO. LTD.

C5   Construction of Cheddar Reservoir for Bristol and Minehead Corporations, 1933-7.

Gauge: 4ft 8½in

No.46		0-6-0ST	IC	HC	1539	1924	(a)	s/s
No.57		0-6-0ST	IC	HC	1586	1927	(b)	s/s
No.68		0-6-0ST	IC	HC	1608	1934	New	s/s
No.69		0-6-0ST	IC	HC	1609	1934	New	s/s

(a) ex Southampton Docks Extension contract
(b) ex Southampton Docks Extension contract,
    /1933

RENNIE, LOGAN & THOMSON

C6   Construction of the Taunton and Chard Railway, Chard-Ilminster, 1863-5

Ref: IRR 13 (3/1967) p.30; IRR 15 (9/1967) p.113; IRR 18 (4/1968) p.222

Gauge: 4ft 8½in

	BUSY BEE	0-4-0ST	OC	MW	79	1863	(a)	(1)
No.1		0-6-0ST	IC	MW	128	1864	New	(2)
No.2		0-4-0ST	OC	MW	156	1865	New	(3)

(a) ex James Rennie & Co , Rowsley-Buxton   (1) to J.Edwards, contr , Cosham, Hants
    Midland Railway contract (per MW   (2) to Logan & Hemingway, contrs , AJAX,
    records) but possibly new here   by 4/1870; later to Manchester,
                                    Sheffield & Lincolnshire Railway,
                                    408, /1876
        (3) to Logan & Hemingway, contrs ; later to
                  J.C.Billups, contr , /1874

PITTRAIL LTD.

C7   Lifting of the BR Taunton-Chard Junction line, 1964-5

Gauge: 4ft 8½in

No.3	0-6-0DM	AB	336	1939	(a)	(1)

(a) ex I.C.I. Ardeer Factory, Ayrshire   (1) to Aldridge Station depot, Staffs ,
                                      /1965

WALTER SCOTT & MIDDLETON LTD.

C8   Contract for the widening of the Cogload Junction-Norton Fitzwarren section of the GWR, 1930-2.

Gauge: 4ft 8½in

BRILL	0-6-0ST	IC	MW	1691	1907	(a)	(1)
STUBLICK	0-6-0ST	IC	MW	1425	1898	(b)	(1)
SIR WALTER SCOTT	0-6-0ST	IC	MW	1237	1892		
(f WALTER SCOTT)	Reb	MW			1917	(b)	(2)
ASHENDON	0-6-0ST	IC	MW	1733	1908	(b)	(1)
ALEXANDRA	0-6-0ST	IC	MW	1484	1901	(c)	s/s

(a) ex Wembley Exhibition contract,
    Middx
(b) ex Clydach contract, Glam , between
    8/1930 and 3/1931
(c) ex ? , by 11/1930

(1) to Stanmore Branch contract for
    Metropolitan Railway between 9/1931
    and 6/1932
(2) to Sir Lindsay Parkinson, contrs ,
    Chorley, Lancs , 290, after 7/1931

C.J.WILLS & SONS LTD.

C9   Construction of the Castle Cary-Langport cut-off line for GWR, 1903-6.

Gauge: 4ft 8½in

SOMERTON	0-4-0ST	OC	HC	656	1903	New	(1)
LORD MAYOR	0-4-0ST	OC	HC	402	1893	(a)	(2)

(a) (ex Price & Wills, contrs , Barry,
    Glam?)

(1) to Henley in Arden contract, Warwicks ,
    (1903?)
(2) (to Henley in Arden contract,Warwicks?)

THOS. W.WARD LTD.

C10   Tracklifting of the BR (ex S&DJR) Evercreech- Highbridge branch between
Bason Bridge and Glastonbury.

Gauge: 4ft8½in

-	0-4-0DM	JF	4210005	1949	(a)	(1)

(a) ex ? by 6/1967

(1) to ?

AE 2073 and other locomotives stored at Roads Reconstruction
Ltd., Cranmore Depot   (F.Jones)

820 (CF 1161) at New Mells Colliery   (F.Jones)

No.3 (HC 1815) at Imperial Smelting Co ,Avonmouth Works,
13/8/1949   (G.Alliez)

No.2 (KS 3128) at Imperial Smelting Co ,Avonmouth Works.
                                                      (F.Jones)

HUDSON (AE 1724) at Port of Bristol, Avonmouth Docks.
13/8/1949   (G.Alliez)

LESLIE (AE 1371) at Port of Bristol, Avonmouth Docks
       /1931   (Collection of R.A.Fox)

HALLEN (P 2035) at Port of Bristol, Avonmouth Docks.
13/8/1949   (G.Alliez)

26, D2006, DUBGLAS (HC D916) at Port of Bristol,
Avonmouth Docks.   13/12/1964   (R.K.Hateley)

FRY (S 7492) at Fry's Somerdale Works.

(Collection of R.A.Fox)

BONNIE PRINCE CHARLIE (RSH 7544) at Southern Wharves Ltd.,
Hamworthy (later Corrall Ltd)   (R.A.Fox)

SECUNDUS (B&S) at Pike Bros, Furzebrook Clay Mines.
18/9/1950   (G.Alliez)

TERTIUS (MW 999) at Pike Bros, Furzebrook Clay Mines
                              (Collection of F.W.Mabbott)

TERTIUS (MW 999) and MR 5242 at Pike Bros, Furzebrook
Clay Mines   (Collection of R.A.Fox)

OK 21160 and MR 5242 at Pike Bros, Fayle & Co , Norden
Clay Mines (Later E.C.C Ball Clays). 20/6/1965 (R.K.Hateley)

THAMES (MW 1552) at B.Fayle, Norden Clay Mines (later E.C.C
Ball Clays) /1948   (F.Jones)

AB 1475 at Admiralty, Holton Heath Factory.   (F.Jones)

Avon

Locomotive worked systems

ADMIRALTY, NATIONAL SHIPYARD NO.3, PORTBURY

1   A First World War project for a new shipyard commenced c/1914. Locomotives
worked on a temporary branch from Portbury Sidings on the GWR Portishead-
Bristol line to the extensive sidings at the shipyard site. The project was
abandoned c/1921 before completion and the railway installations dismantled.
The quarries at Frampton on Severn, Glos ,were opened to supply materials to
Portbury and to Beachley, Glos ,and equipment from all three sites was
auctioned 10/1921. This included two standard gauge 0-6-0 locomotives, one
by MW and the other by the 'Great Central Railway'. These may have operated at
Portbury.

Gauge: 4ft 8½in

-		0-4-0ST	OC	HE	282	1882	(a)	(1)
I.W.D. No.34	PORTBURY	0-6-0ST	OC	AE	1764	1917	New	(2)

(a) ex Orrell Colliery Co Ltd ,Wigan,
    Lancs ,by 9/1918

(1) to Tytherington Stone Co Ltd ,
        Falfield, Glos , 1/1919
(2) to Port of Bristol Authority,
        Avonmouth, Glos , after 12/1919

Gauge: 600mm

-		0-4-0PM	BgC	717	1917	New	s/s

AIR MINISTRY, FILTON AERODROME

2   Locomotives and tramway possibly used during the construction of these
installations (ST 600805 approx). Tramway closed and dismantled;the location
has since passed to the British Aircraft Corporation.

Gauge: 2ft 0in

-	0-4-0ST	OC	WB	2044	1917	New	s/s
-	0-4-0ST	OC	WB	2049	1918	New	(1)

(1) to Queenborough Cement Co Ltd ,
        Queenborough, Kent

ALBRIGHT & WILSON LTD., PORTISHEAD

3   A chemical works to the east of Portishead Docks with loco shed at ST 474769.
Products despatched by rail include phosphorus whose manufacture here
commenced in 1953.

Gauge: 4ft 8½in

-		0-4-0DM		P	5000	1956	New(a)	(1)
-		0-4-0DM		P	5002	1957	New	(2)
-		0-4-0ST	OC	P	1611	1923	(b)	Pvd on site
D2001	NORMAN	0-4-0DM		HC	D774	1950	(c)	Scr 7/1973
-		0-4-0DE		RH	381753	1955	(d)	

(a) ex P , hire, /1956
(b) ex P , hire, /1959;purchased 11/1961
(c) ex Port of Bristol Authority,
    Avonmouth, c /1969
(d) ex Thos W.Ward Ltd ,Templeborough
    Works, Sheffield, 6/1971

(1) ret to P , /1957
(2) to ? , Birmingham,for scr, c /1971

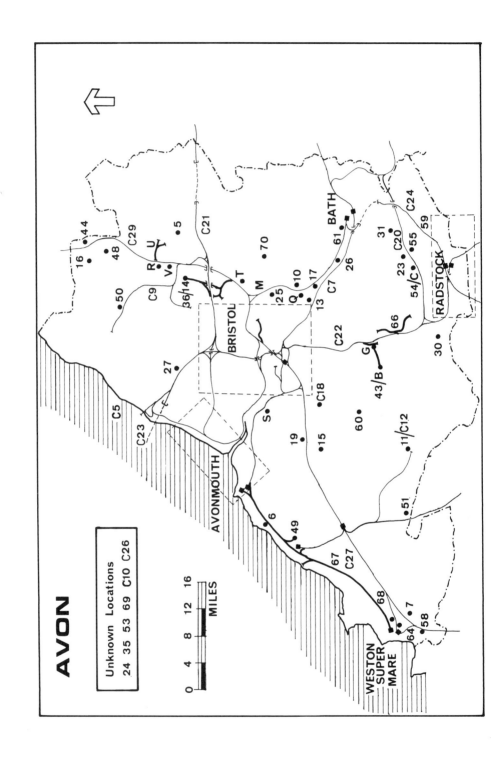

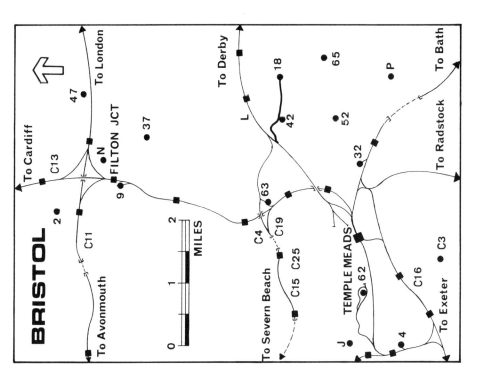

BRISTOL

AVONMOUTH

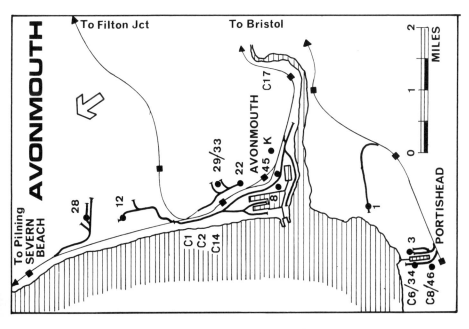

ASHTON CONTAINERS LTD., ASHTON GATE, BRISTOL (f Ashton Packing Co.)

4   Sidings serving the factory alongside the BR (ex GWR) Portishead branch at
ST 569710. Rail traffic ceased 13/5/1965.

Gauge: 4ft 8½in

-	0-4-0DM	JF	22288	1938	New	(1)

(1) to Pugsley, Stoke Gifford, c7/1965

JOHN ARNOLD & SONS LTD., BARN HILL QUARRY, CHIPPING SODBURY (Subsidiary of British
Quarrying Co Ltd until 31/10/1947 and subsequently of Amalgamated Roadstone
Corporation Ltd)

5   A quarry on the site of earlier workings (ST 725830?). A narrow gauge line
about 800 yards long was laid in 1928 and used to convey overburden from the
quarry to waste tip. The system was closed in 1938;the remaining loco was
stored until its disposal.

        Ref: IRR 20 (8/1968) p.275

Gauge: 2ft

-	4wDM	KS	4426	1930	New	(1)
-	4wPM	L	3864	1931	New	s/s

(1) to Penlee Quarries Ltd ,Cornwall,
10/1947

BLACK ROCK QUARRIES LTD., BLACK ROCK QUARRIES, NEAR PORTISHEAD (Subsidiary of Roads
Reconstruction (1934) Ltd ; Bryant & Langford Quarries Ltd until 7/12/1934)

6   A narrow gauge system connected two quarries (ST 451748 & 457747) with
standard gauge sidings (ST 455744) connecting with the Weston,Clevedon &
Portishead Light Railway. System closed and rails lifted c/1949.

Gauge: 2ft 0in

	-	0-6-0WT	OC	HC	1377	1919	(a)	s/s
	-	0-6-0WT	OC	HC	1378	1919	(a)	s/s
	-	4wPM		MR	400	1917	(b)	(1)
	-	4wPM		MR	587	1917	(c)	(1)
	-	4wPM		MR	1699	1918	(d)	s/s
D1	-	4wDM		KS	4427	1929	New	(1)
	-	4wDM		Crossley				(1)

(a) ex Leighton Buzzard Light Railway Ltd , (1) to Roads Reconstruction (1934) Ltd ,
    Beds , c /1922   Cranmore Depot
(b) ex WDLR, 2121
(c) ex S.Pearson & Son Ltd ,contrs;
    orig WDLR 2308
(d) ex WDLR, 2420

BRISTOL AEROPLANE CO. LTD., WESTON-SUPER-MARE

7   Aircraft factory (ST 337595) on the east side of the BR (ex GWR) Weston-super-
     Mare cut-off line. Served by sidings from the BR line laid c5/1943 by the
     Ministry of Aircraft Production. Rail traffic ceased c/1965 and track lifted.

Gauge: 4ft 8½in

-		4wDM	RH	237922	1946	New	(2)
-		4wDM	RH	237923	1946	New	(1)

        (1) to BR (SR), DS1169, 12/1948
        (2) to Thos W.Ward Ltd , Templeborough
              Works, Sheffield, /1965

BRISTOL CITY MUSEUM

8   A number of locomotives with associations with Bristol were collected for
     restoration and display in a proposed Transport Gallery at this museum.
     Storage was arranged in a warehouse at Port of Bristol Authority,Avonmouth
     Docks (ST 512785). However financial economies have caused the scheme to be
     abandoned and most of the proposed exhibits have been dispersed to alternative
     locations.

Gauge: 4ft 8½in

3		0-6-0ST	OC	FW	242	1874	(a)	(1)
S3	PORTBURY	0-6-0ST	OC	AE	1764	1917	(b)	(1)
S9	HENBURY	0-6-0ST	OC	P	1940	1937	(b)	(1)
2818		2-8-0	OC	Sdn	2122	1905	(c)	

(a) ex NCB South Western Division, No.4 Area,(1) to Somerset & Dorset Railway Circle,
      Abergorki Colliery,Mountain Ash,   Radstock, 11/1971
      Glam , 9/1963
(b) ex Port of Bristol Authority, Avonmouth
      Docks, /1964
(c) Withdrawn by BR, 10/1963; restored at
      Eastleigh Works, Hants , 1/1966-
      4/1967; moved to Bristol, 4/1967

BRISTOL MECHANISED COAL CO. LTD., FILTON COAL CONCENTRATION DEPOT

9   A modern coal concentration depot opened in 1965 on the west side of the BR
     (ex GWR) main line at ST 611788 just south of Filton Junction station.

Gauge: 4ft 8½in

MR. USEFUL	0-4-0DM	DC	2251/VF	D77	1947	(a)	(1)
(MR. USEFUL)	0-4-0DM	Bg		3410	1955	(b)	

The following locomotives were purchased by Renwick, Wilton & Dobson Ltd and stored
here. As far as is known none has been used here.

1	0-4-0DM	DC	2583/VF	D297	1956	(c)	(2)
2	0-4-0DM	DC	2588/RSH	7921	1957	(c)	(3)
3	0-4-0DM	DC	2723/Bg	2723	1961	(c)	(4)
4	0-4-0DM	DC	2652/Bg	2652	1958	(c)	(5)
(5)	0-4-0DM	DC	2655/Bg	2655	1959	(d)	(6)

(a) ex Barking Jetty Co Ltd , Creekmouth, Essex, 6/1965	(1) to Stonehouse Coal Concentration Co Ltd , 12/1966

(a) ex Barking Jetty Co Ltd , Creekmouth,
    Essex, 6/1965
(b) ex Marston, Thompson & Evershed Ltd ,
    Burton-on-Trent, Staffs, c12/1966
(c) ex South Eastern Gas Board, East
    Greenwich Gasworks, 10/1968
(d) ex South Eastern Gas Board, East
    Greenwich Gasworks, 11/1968

(1) to Stonehouse Coal Concentration Co Ltd ,
    12/1966
(2) to Berry, Wiggins & Co Ltd , Kingsnorth,
    Kent, c /1970
(3) to ?
(4) to Lancashire Fuel Co Ltd , Southport
    Coal Concentration Depot, Lancs ,
    /1970
(5) to Batchelor, Robinson & Co Ltd ,
    Hartlepool Tinplate Works,
    Co.Durham, 11/1971
(6) to Batchelor, Robinson & Co Ltd ,
    Hartlepool Tinplate Works,
    Co.Durham, 3/1973

BRISTOL SUBURBAN RAILWAY SOCIETY, BITTON STATION

10 This preservation group,hoping to restore rail services to a line in the Bristol
area, have obtained premises in the goods yard at Bitton station (ST 669704)
where storage and restoration of rolling stock is in hand.

Gauge: 4ft 8½in

	EDWARD HULSE	0-6-0ST	OC	AE	1798	1918	(a)
	-	4wDM		RH	235519	1945	(b)
45379		4-6-0	OC	AW	1434	1937	(c)
	GLENDOWER	0-6-0ST	1C	HE	3810	1954	(d)
3		0-6-0ST	OC	FW	242	1874	(e)
	FONMON	0-6-0ST	OC	P	1636	1929	(f)

(a) ex Imperial Smelting Co Ltd , Avonmouth to an
    employee of Avonmouth Engineers Ltd and
    stored there from c3/1972; moved to premises
    of J.S.Fry & Son Ltd , /1972; from there to
    Bitton station, 9/6/1973
(b) ex John Dickinson & Co Ltd , Keynsham, 1/1974
(c) ex Woodham Bros , Barry Dock, Glam , 17/5/1974
(d) ex NCB South Wales Area, Glyntillery Colliery,
    c6/1974

(e) ex Somerset & Dorset Railway
    Museum Trust, Radstock,
    c5/1975
(f) ex Somerset & Dorset Railway
    Museum Trust, Radstock,
    2/1976

BRISTOL WATERWORKS CO. LTD., BLAGDON RESERVOIR

11 A narrow gauge tramway was used in the maintenance of this reservoir. The
locomotive and other equipment remained on site (ST 507595) out of use for
many years until final disposal.

Gauge: 600 mm

-	0-4-0PM	BgC	736	1918	(a)	(1)

(a) ex BgC , 9/1921; prev WDLR 273   (1) to R.P.Morris, Longfield, Kent, 6/1971

BRITISH GAS CORPORATION, SOUTH WESTERN REGION, SEABANK GASWORKS, HALLEN,NEAR AVONMOUTH

(f South Western Gas Board)

12 A naphtha reforming plant opened 1968; liquid naphtha brought by sea is piped
into the works. Rail sidings were installed but the locomotive was used only
infrequently until 1/1970 and has been out of use since then. (ST 536823).

Gauge: 4ft 8½in

-	0-4-0DM	RH	418792	1959	(a)

(a) ex Gorse Hill Gasworks, Swindon, Wilts ,
    12/1968

CADBURY- SCHWEPPES LTD., SOMERDALE (f J.S.Fry & Sons Ltd ,subsidiary of Cadbury Bros Ltd.)

13   A factory served by an internal narrow gauge system (ST 658695) and standard gauge sidings (ST 660696) and branch to the north side of the BR (ex GWR) Bristol - Bath line adjacent to Keynsham station. Narrow gauge system closed c /1972.

Gauge: 4ft 8½in

-		4wVBT	VCG	S	7492	1928	New	(1)
	SOMERDALE	0-4-0DM		HC	D1009	1956	New	

(1) to Grove Scrap Iron & Steel Merchants, Grove Road, Fishponds, Bristol, 1/1964

Gauge: 1ft 11¾in

-	4wDM (f.PM)	L	8023	1936	New	(1)

(1) to R.J.King & Sons Ltd , Farrington Gurney, /1972

COALPIT HEATH CO. LTD., COALPIT HEATH COLLIERY (Coalpit Heath Coal Co Ltd until 2/1926;

Coal Pit Heath Co until c/1900)

14   Three collieries existed- Froglane, Mayshill and Nibley, the first two being known collectively as Coalpit Heath Colliery (ST 690819). They were producing coal prior to the opening of the Bristol & Gloucestershire Railway in 7/1832, which served them. Much of the route of this edge railway (which see) was used for the Midland Railway Bristol- Birmingham line and from the opening of this in 1846 a branch about a mile long ran from Westerleigh sidings to the collieries on the remainder of the route of the Bristol & Gloucestershire. A spur connected from this branch to the GWR line east of Coalpit Heath station. The colliery and railway installations passed to the NCB on 1/1/1947 (which see)

Gauge: 4ft 8½in

-		0-4-0T	OC	FJ	58	1866	New	s/s
-		0-6-0ST	OC	FW	326	1876	New	(1)
	LORD ROBERTS	0-6-0ST	IC	P	825	1900	New	Scr
	LORD SALISBURY	0-6-0ST	IC	P	1041	1906	New	(2)
-		4wDM		RH	242869	1946	New	(2)

(1) to P , /1906; resold to James Pain Ltd , Glendon North Ironstone Quarries, Northants , 8/1906
(2) to NCB, Division 7, Area 8, 1/1/1947

JOSEPH COLES & SON LTD., BACKWELL QUARRY, FLAX BOURTON

15   A quarry served by a narrow gauge tramway. Rail system closed c/1947 and lifted. Quarry later operated by Western Aggregates Ltd.

Gauge: 2ft 0in

-	4w(PM or DM)					s/s c /1947
-	4wPM	L	9791	1937	(a)	s/s c /1947

(a) ex L , 2/1941; prev Fosse Lime & Limestone Co Ltd , Glos

CROMHALL QUARRIES LTD., CHARFIELD

16   Quarry served by a narrow gauge system. Tramway closed and track lifted c/1952.

Gauge: 2ft 0in

		4wDM	MR	8756	1942	(a)	(1)

(a) ex Sanstone Ltd , King's Lynn, Norfolk   (1) to Joseph Arnold & Sons Ltd , Leighton
                                                             Buzzard, Beds , via Bungey, c /1953

JOHN DICKINSON & CO. LTD., KEYNSHAM PAPER MILLS (Keynsham Paper Mills Ltd ,branch of

E.S.& A.Robinson Ltd until c/1969)

17   Sidings served this paper mill alongside the north side of the BR (ex GWR)
        Bath - Bristol line. The locos stood in the open at ST 662687. Rail traffic
        ceased c /1969.

Gauge: 4ft 8½in

No.1		4wPM	AE	2013	1930	(a)	s/s c /1968
-		4wDM	RH	235519	1945	New	(1)

(a) ex AE , per Johseph Pugsley & Sons Ltd , (1) to Bristol Suburban Railway Group,
    Lawrence Hill, Bristol, 17/11/1932   Bitton station, 1/1974
    (Sold as "second-hand" locomotive
    and possibly used previously for
    demonstration purposes)

EAST BRISTOL COLLIERIES LTD., KINGSWOOD COLLIERY, BRISTOL (Bedminster, Easton,

Kingswood & Parkfield Collieries Ltd until 9/1914; Kingswood & Parkfield Collieries
Co Ltd until c/1900; Kingswood & Parkfield Coal Co Ltd until /1886; Kingswood Coal
& Iron Co Ltd until /1883.)

18   A company which operated a number of collieries including Parkfield and
        Belgium Pits (working in /1886) and South Pit (working in /1894). Latterly
        a standard gauge rail system connected Speedwell Colliery (ST 634746) and
        Deep Pit (ST 625746)(collectively known as Kingswood Colliery) with the LMS
        (ex Midland Railway) Bristol - Birmingham railway near Kingswood Junction
        (ST 620747). The colliery branch also served Peckett's Atlas Locomotive Works,
        (which see). Coal winding at Kingswood Colliery ceased 3/4/1936

Gauge: 4ft 8½in

(SPEEDWELL)	0-4-0ST	OC	FW	281	1875	(a)	(1)
MAY (f ATLAS)	0-6-0ST	OC	FW	286	1875	(b)	s/s
-	0-4-0ST	OC	P	520	1891	(c)	(2)

(a) ex AE after 1/1905; prev North Lincs   (1) to P , /1934
    Iron Co Ltd ,Scunthorpe, Lincs   (2) to Norton Hill Collieries Co , Radstock
(b) ex Darlaston Steel & Iron Co Ltd ,
    Staffs , by 6/1886
(c) ex Farrington Collieries Ltd ,
    Farrington

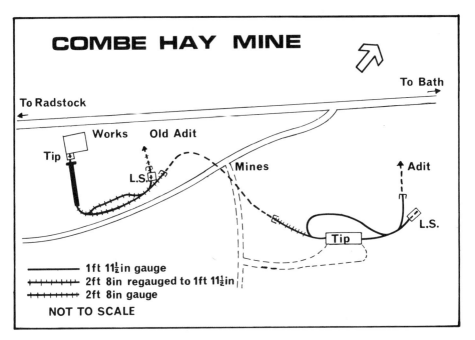

COMBE HAY MINE

To Bath

To Radstock

Works   Old Adit

Tip

L.S.

Mines

Adit

L.S.

Tip

——————— 1ft 11½in gauge
+—+—+—+—+ 2ft 8in regauged to 1ft 11½in
++++++++ 2ft 8in gauge

NOT TO SCALE

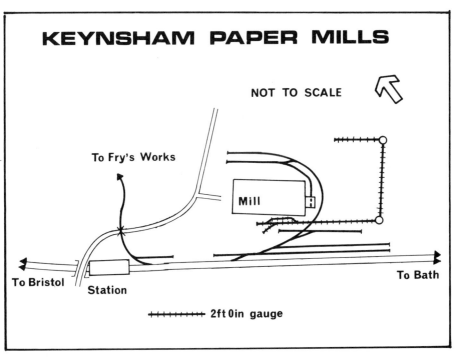

KEYNSHAM PAPER MILLS

NOT TO SCALE

To Fry's Works

Mill

To Bristol

Station

To Bath

++++++++ 2ft 0in gauge

ESSO PETROLEUM CO. LTD., FLAX BOURTON DEPOT

19   A petrol storage depot with sidings connecting to the north side of the BR
(ex GWR) Bristol - Taunton main line. The loco stands in the open at ST 508698.

Gauge: 4ft 8½in

-	0-4-0DM	JF	4210145	1958	(a)	(1)
-	0-4-0DM	JF	4210141	1958	(b)	

(a) ex Bowling Depot, Dunbartonshire, c /1968 (1) to Ministry of Fuel & Power, Oxspring
(b) ex Milford Haven Depot, Pembs   Depot, Yorks WR

WM. EVANS & CO. (OLD MILLS COLLIERIES) LTD., OLD MILLS AND SPRINGFIELD COLLIERIES,

FARRINGTON GURNEY (Old Mills Colliery Co and Wm Evans & Co until 1/7/1931)

20   Springfield colliery was served by standard gauge sidings (ST 651549)
adjacent to and on the north side of the GWR Bristol - Radstock line. Old
Mills colliery was north of the A362 road and connected to Springfield by a
narrow gauge tramway. The two pits were connected underground and Old Mills
shaft closed for coal winding 10/1941 and was then used for ventilation and
winding supplies only. Railway wagons were moved by horses prior to the
introduction of a locomotive. The combined colliery installation was vested
in the NCB on 1/1/1947.

Ref: 'The History of the Somerset Coalfield' by C.G.Down & A.J.Warrington; D&C

Gauge: 4ft 8½in

-	4wDM	RH	200793	1940	New	(1)

(1) to NCB, Division 7, Area 8, 1/1/1947

FARRINGTON COLLIERIES COMPANY, FARRINGTON COLLIERY (Also traded under the titles

Radstock Coal Co and Radstock Coal & Wagon Co)

21   A colliery at ST 641556 between Farrington Gurney and Paulton with recorded
workings prior to 1785. A railway line to the GWR Bristol - Radstock line
at Old Mills sidings was proposed 2/1871 and finally laid in 1882. After
interruptions to production because of strikes the colliery finally closed
10/1921.

Ref: 'The History of the Somerset Coalfield' by C.G.Down & A.J.Warrington; D&C

Gauge: 4ft 8½in

-	0-4-0ST	OC	BP	1736	1877	(a)	(1)
-	0-4-0ST	OC	WB	1432	1894	(b)	(2)
-	0-4-0ST	OC	P	520	1891	(c)	(3)

(a) ex Meakin & Dean, contrs ,(A BP loco, (1) s/s (after 8/1904?)
    works number unknown, was here by   (2) for sale 12/1921 and 7/1922; s/s
    /1885)   (3) to East Bristol Collieries Ltd
(b) ex M.W.Grazebrook Ltd , Netherton,
    Staffs
(c) ex G.Palmer, contractor, by 11/1912

FISONS LTD., AVONMOUTH

22 A chemicals factory at ST 519794 served by a siding off the Imperial Smelting Co's system of sidings. The works is also connected by aerial ropeway with the Port of Bristol Authority's Avonmouth Docks.

Gauge: 4ft 8½in

(FISONS NO.1)	0-4-0DM	JF	4200021	1948	New	(1)
(STOUR)	4wDM	FH	3677	1954	(a)	(2)
–	0-4-0DH	EEV	D1124	1966	New	

(a) ex Imperial Metal Industries (Kynoch) Ltd (1) to Joseph Perrin & Son Ltd ,
    Witton, Warwicks, /1963   Birkenhead, Cheshire, 1/1964
                                              (2) to EEV , 7/1966 ; resold to Tinsley
                                                  Wire Industries Ltd , Sheffield,
                                                  /1967

A.P.GARDNER, TUNLEY, NEAR RADSTOCK

23 A locomotive moved to this location for preservation; later resold.

Gauge: 4ft 8½in

FRY	4wVBT	VCG S	7492	1928	(a)	(1)

(a) ex Grove Scrap Iron & Steel Merchants   (1) to R.Finbow, Bacton, Suffolk, /1971
    Ltd , Grove Road, Fishponds, Bristol,
    11/1970; prev J.S.Fry & Sons Ltd

S.C.GILSON & SONS LTD., HOLCOMBE QUARRY, NEAR BATH

24 A narrow gauge tramway serving the quarry,location uncertain. System closed and dismantled(?)

Gauge: 2ft 0in

–	4wDM	RH	269290	1949	New	(1)

(1) to Westbere Ballast Pits (Ramsgate) Ltd ,
    Kent, /1958

HASKINS LTD., WARMLEY POTTERIES, NEAR BRISTOL

25 A tramway connected clay pits to the works at ST 670728. Works closed and rail system dismantled by 1965.

Gauge: 1ft 8in

–	4wPM	L	34024	1949	New	Scr c2/1960
–	4wPM	L	4366	1932	(a)	Scr c2/1960

(a) ex B.F.Poole, Sand & gravel pits,
    Lechlade, Glos , c2/1957 (converted
    from 2ft 0in gauge)

26   A locomotive and other light railway equipment were purchased and moved to this
      location (ST 689668) with the intention of laying down a pleasure railway.

Gauge: 2ft 0in

                            -              4wDM   HE   2207 1941 (a)

(a) ex Cotswold Light Railways, South
    Cerney, Glos , c12/1972

IBSTOCK BRICK (CATTYBROOK) LTD., CATTYBROOK BRICKWORKS, ALMONDSBURY (Cattybrook Brick

Co Ltd   until   /1973)

27   A works at ST 588833, opened c /1865, on the north side of the BR (ex GWR) main
      line between Patchway and Pilning. Standard gauge sidings were laid in off the
      GWR line under an agreement dated 16/4/1881 and removed 1965 after a period of
      disuse. The narrow gauge is used to bring clay from pits to the works, the
      section on the floor of the pits (ST 591835) being loco worked. The wagons are
      hauled individually up a cable worked incline from the pit floor to the works.

      Ref: IRR 20 (8/1968) p291-5   System closed by 4/1975.

Gauge: 2ft 10in

                            -              4wPM   Cattybrook c1916*   (1)
                            -              4wPM   Cattybrook c1920+   (1)
                            -              4wPM   L   507 c1932 New   s/s
                            -              4wDM   MR   5236 1930 (a)   (1)
                            -              4wDM   MR   5342 1931 (a)   (2)
                            -              4wDM   MR   9215 1946 (a)   (2)
                            -              4wPM   MR   5461 1937 (b)   (1)

* Originally fitted with a Benz engine, described as Belgian rather than German because
  of World War 1 patriotism; reb with Austro-Daimler engine; reb /1928 with a Morris
  Hotchkiss car engine; reb c /1940 with a Perkins diesel engine; reb with Morris
  Commercial petrol engine by /1965
+ Fitted with Morris Commercial engine

(a) ex Dinmor Quarries Ltd , Anglesey, per   (1) Scr by Lamb, Bristol, c /1972
    Madoc Jones, dealer, Denbighs,   (2) to A.M.Keef, Cote, Oxon, 5/1975
    12/1970 (re-gauged from 3ft 0in at
    Cattybrook)
(b) 3ft 0in gauge loco obtained as source of
    spare parts ex Dinmor Quarries Ltd ,
    Anglesey, per Madoc Jones, dealer,
    Denbighs , 12/1970

IMPERIAL CHEMICAL INDUSTRIES LTD., SEVERNSIDE WORKS, SEVERN BEACH

28   A modern works opened in 1963. Located to the east of the BR (ex GWR) Severn
      Beach - Avonmouth branch and the A403 road at ST 539828 with rail sidings
      connecting with the BR line.

Gauge: 4ft 8½in

            KILDALE   0-6-0DE   YE   2741 1959 (a)
            FARNDALE   0-6-0DE   YE   2719 1958 (b)   (1)
            IBURNDALE   0-6-0DE   YE   2725 1958 (c)

(a) ex Billingham Works, Co.Durham, 10/1962 (1) ret to Billingham Works, /1964
(b) ex Billingham Works, 9/1963
(c) ex Billingham Works, 9/1963

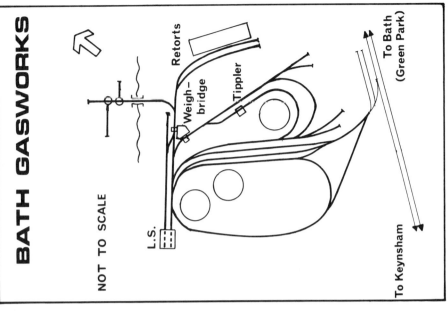

BATH GASWORKS

NOT TO SCALE

Retorts

Weigh-bridge

Tippler

L.S.

To Bath (Green Park)

To Keynsham

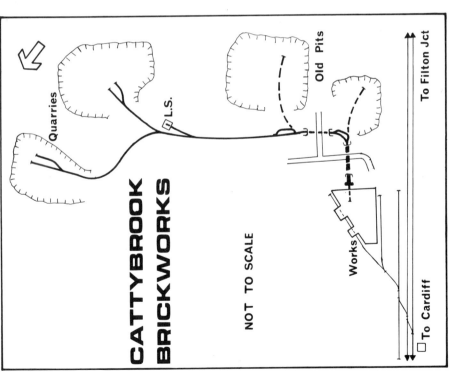

CATTYBROOK BRICKWORKS

NOT TO SCALE

Quarries

L.S.

Old Pits

Works

To Filton Jct

To Cardiff

IMPERIAL SMELTING (PROCESSES) LTD., AVONMOUTH WORKS (Subsidiary of Rio Tinto Zinc Ltd

and A.M & S. (Commonwealth Smelting) Ltd ; National Smelting Co Ltd , subsidiary of
Imperial Smelting Corporation Ltd until /1967)

29   Construction of this zinc smelting plant commenced c/1914 but from 10/1916
        the project was incorporated into the MoM Avonmouth Factory. This closed in
        1921 and was reopened for zinc production by the National Smelting Co in 1924.
        The plant is located to the east of St. Andrews Road station on the BR (ex GWR)
        Severn Beach - Avonmouth line,and has been extended and modernised in recent
        years. Standard gauge lines serve the works and connect with the BR line at
        Hallen Marsh Junction about half a mile to the north of the works. The narrow
        gauge system served the ingot plant of the older narrow gauge retort plant, the
        southern section of the works. This section was replaced and closed by the end
        of 1971 and the narrow gauge was lifted c /1972. The works is also connected
        by aerial ropeway with the Port of Bristol Authority, Avonmouth Docks. Loco
        sheds are at ST 524794 (narrow gauge) and ST 522797 (standard gauge).

Gauge: 4ft 8½in

No.1	ENGLISH CROWN	0-4-0ST	OC	P	1545	1919	(a)	(1)
No.2		2-4-2T	OC	HE	714	1900	(b)	Scr /1937
No.3		0-6-0ST	IC	HC	442	1895	(c)	Scr /1937
No.1		0-6-0T	IC	HC	1246	1916	(b)	Scr c12/1960
No.2		0-6-0ST	OC	AE	1798	1918	(b)	(5)
	FORWARD	0-6-0ST	OC	AE	1655	1913	(d)	(3)
No.3		0-6-0T	OC	HC	1815	1948	New	Scr c12/1960
	FORTH	0-6-0ST	OC	AB	1844	1924	(e)	(2)
"No.4"		0-6-0PT	IC	Wpn	657	1898	(f)	Scr c3/1961
	SANDRA	0-6-0ST	IC	MW	2046	1926	(g)	(4)
5		4wDH	S		10005	1959	New	
6		4wDH	S		10048	1960	New	
33		0-6-0DM	HC		D1193	1960	(h)	(6)
29		0-6-0DM	HC		D919	1956	(j)	
-		4wDH	S		10023	1960	(k)	

(a) ex Port Tennant Works, Glam , No.2
(b) ex MoM , Avonmouth Factory, /1924
(c) ex Chas. Wall, contr , Grays, Essex,
    DEVON
(d) ex Thos W Ward Ltd , Grays, Essex,
    c /1936; prev Checkland & Co Ltd ,
    Coleorton Colliery, Leics
(e) ex Thos W Ward Ltd , hire, c /1948
(f) ex BR , 2053 , 9/1954
(g) ex A.R.Adams Ltd , Newport, Mon , hire,
    /1957
(h) ex Port of Bristol Authority, Avonmouth,
    hire, /1973
(j) ex Port of Bristol Authority, Avonmouth,
    hire, c2/1974
(k) ex Swansea Vale Works, Glam , /1974

(1) to New Cheshire Salt Works Ltd ,
    Northwich, Ches
(2) ret to Thos W Ward Ltd , c/1948
(3) to J Cashmore Ltd , Newport, Mon ,
    3/1951
(4) ret to A.R.Adams Ltd , Newport, Mon ,
    4/1957
(5) to ?,at Avonmouth Engineering Ltd ,
    for preservation, c3/1971;later to
    Bristol Suburban Railway Society,
    Bitton
(6) ret to Port of Bristol Authority,
    Avonmouth, c12/1973

Gauge: 2ft 0in

–		4-6-0T	OC	HE	1246	1916	(a)	s/s
No.3	(No.1 until /1954)	0-4-0ST	OC	KS	3104	1918	(b)	Scr 11/1954
No.2		0-4-0ST	OC	KS	3128	1918	New	(1)
No.3		0-4-0ST	OC	HE	2384	1941	New	Scr 5/1954
–		4wPM		L	4763	1933	New	
					Reb	1954		Scr c /1962
–		4wPM		L	5568	1934	(c)*	s/s
–		4wDM		R&R	73	1936	New	Scr c /1949
–		4wDM		Bg	2108	1937	New*	s/s
4		4wDM		RH	200743	1940	New	Scr c9/1970
5		4wDM		RH	239381	1946	New	(2)
6		4wDM		RH	264239	1949	New	s/s c7/1970
7		4wDM		RH	287663	1950	New	s/s c /1972
8		4wDM		RH	354043	1953	New	(2)
"9"		4wDM		FH	3582	1954	New	(2)
–		4wBE		NSC	–	1960+	New+	Scr c /1969

(a) ex WDLR, 334
(b) ex Air Ministry, Ruislip, London , by 5/1924
(c) Supplied new to Improved Metallurgy Ltd, to L ; to National Smelting Co Ltd , 10/1934 after overhaul

(1) to C.H.Lambe & Son Ltd , Bromsgrove, Worcs , 5/1959; resold to C.Mathews, Ontario, Canada, 6/1959
(2) to M.E.Engineering Ltd , Cricklewood, London, /1972

* Not known whether here or at the Swansea Vale Works , Glam
+ Conversion of a fork lift truck

Conversion of one 2ft gauge steam locomotive (presumed KS 3104) to a petrol engined locomotive by apprentices was commenced but not completed and the loco was scrapped.

E.J.KING & SONS (SCRAP MERCHANTS) LTD., BELLE VIEW, PITWAY LANE, FARRINGTON GURNEY

30   Locomotive moved to this location for possible preservation.

Gauge: 2ft 0in

–	4wDM		L	8023	1936	(a)	(1)

(a) ex J.S.Fry & Sons Ltd , Somerdale, /1972

(1) to M.E.Engineering Ltd , Cricklewood, London, by 9/1974

LAPORTE INDUSTRIES LTD., COOMBE HAY MINE, NEAR BATH (Fullers Earth Union Ltd until 1/4/1968)

31   Fullers Earth has been obtained here by mining since before 1894. The 2ft 8in gauge system was loco worked within the mine and from the adit to the foot of an incline from where the wagons were cable hauled up to the works area (ST 729612). This system was replaced, c /1968, by a new 1ft 11½in gauge system serving another adit.

Gauge: 2ft 8in

–	0-4-0BE	WR	3867	1950	(1)

(1) converted to 1ft 11½in gauge

Gauge: 1ft 11½in

–	0-4-0BE	WR	G7174	1967	New
–	4wBE	WR	1277	1938	(a)
–	0-4-0BE	WR	3867	1950	(b)

(a) ex ?
(b) converted from 2ft 8in gauge

(John Lysaght Ltd until 1/10/1947; subsidiary of Guest Keen & Nettlefolds Ltd)

32   Steel works opened c /1858 on the north side of the BR (ex GWR) Bristol - Bath line, on the east side of the river, about one mile from Temple Meads station. Rail sidings at ST 615725 served the works; rail traffic ceased c /1964.

Gauge: 4ft 8½in

SIRIUS	0-4-0ST	OC	HL	2234	1891	(a)	
				Reb	1942		Scr c /1953
No.19	0-4-0ST	OC	HL	3333	1918	(b)	(2)
No. 8	0-4-0ST	OC	HL	2972	1912	(c)	Scr 4/1962
-	4wDH		TH	114V	1962	New	(1)

(a) ex Leicester Corporation Gas Department, (1) to Newman Industries Ltd , Yate ,
    via C.D.Phillips, dealer, Newport,   /1965; resold to NCB East Midlands
    Mon , /1936   Division, Area 3, Warsop Colliery,
(b) ex John Lysaght's Scunthorpe Works Ltd ,   Notts , 3/1966
    Lincs   (2) to ? , Fishponds, Bristol, 10/1967;
(c) ex John Lysaght's Scunthorpe Works Ltd ,   Scr 10-11/1967
    Lincs , /1953

MINISTRY OF MUNITIONS, AVONMOUTH FACTORY

33   In 8/1916 a site at Avonmouth was selected for a sulphuric acid plant to be supplied with concentrates from the adjacent zinc smelter of National Smelting Co then also under construction which was incorporated into the scheme. Plant was also installed for the production of picric acid but production of this was cancelled in favour of the manufacture of mustard gas. Rail sidings were installed and connected with the GWR Avonmouth - Severn Beach line. Output began in 1/1918,but full production was not reached before the Armistice Plant was auctioned 1/1920 and the factory had closed by /1921. The premises were taken over again by the National Smelting Co (which see) and reopened as a zinc smelter in /1924.

Gauge: 4ft 8½in

No.392	0-6-0ST	IC	MW	1153	1890	(a)	(2)
-	2-4-2T	OC	HE	714	1900	(b)	(1)
-	0-6-0T	IC	HC	1246	1916	New	(1)

(a) ex ? ; prev Thos.Oliver & Son ,   (1) to National Smelting Co Ltd ,
    Rugby-Charwelton (MS&LR) contract.   Avonmouth, /1924
(b) ex Bideford, Westward Ho & Appledore   (2) to P & W Anderson Ltd , North Devon &
    Railway, Devon, c/1917   Cornwall Light Railway contract,
                                        Devon

Gauge: 2ft 0in

-	4wBE	BE	16302	c1917	(1)
-	4wBE	BE	16304	c1917	(1)
-	4wBE	BE	16307	c1917	(1)
-	4wBE	BE		c1917	s/s

(1) to Hythe Pier Railway, Hants , /1922

MINISTRY OF POWER, PORTISHEAD DEPOT

34   An oil storage depot served by sidings from the BR (ex GWR) Bristol –
Portishead railway. Rail traffic ceased and track in depot lifted 1970.

Gauge: 4ft 8½in

M.O.P. No.7	0-4-0DM	JF 4210144	1958	New	(1)
M.F.P. No.6	0-4-0DM	JF 4210143	1958	(a)	(2)

(a) ex Purfleet Deep Water Wharf & Storage   (1) to Esso Petroleum Co Ltd , Purfleet,
    Co Ltd , Essex, c5/1965   Essex, c /1962
                                  (2) to G. Cohen Sons & Co Ltd , Cransley
                                       Depot, Kettering, Northants,
                                       c9/1969

NAILSEA COAL & COKE CO. LTD., WEST END COLLIERY, NAILSEA

35   Colliery closed /1879.

Gauge: 4ft 8½in

–	0-6-0ST	OC	FW	328	1877	New	(1)

(1) to Droitwich Salt Co Ltd , Droitwich,
Worcs , /1879

NATIONAL COAL BOARD

    This public body was constituted on 15/7/1946 , and as from 1/1/1947 ("vesting
day") collieries in Somerset and South Gloucestershire were grouped to form
Area 8 of Division 7 (South Western). A later reorganisation saw these
collieries become the Somerset & Bristol Group of No.6 (Monmouthshire) Area,
while from 26/3/1967 they became part of the East Wales Area and later the
South Wales Area.

    Ref: 'The History of the Somerset Coalfield' by C.G.Down & A.J.Warrington; D&C

Locomotives have been used at the following locations, all of which fall in the new
county of Avon:

Gloucestershire:

36   CH   COALPIT HEATH (ST 690819)   (f Coalpit Heath Co Ltd)
                Colliery served by a mile long branch, owned by BR (f LMS) from the
                BR (ex Midland Railway) Bristol – Birmingham line at Westerleigh. This
                branch passed under the BR (ex GWR) main line and a spur provided a
                connection near Coalpit Heath station. Colliery closed /1950 and
                dismantled; BR owned track lifted 3/1956.

37   HS   HARRY STOKE DRIFT MINE (ST 616786)

                A sinking undertaken by the NCB c /1953. The drift was served by an
                internal 3ft 6in gauge system although the locomotives delivered here
                saw little, if any, service on it. The mine closed 3/1963 and the site
                (about half a mile south-east of Filton Junction station) has been
                cleared.

Somerset:

38   K   KILMERSDON (or HAYDON) (ST 687538)   (f Writhlington Collieries Co Ltd)

                Colliery connected to the BR (ex GWR) Radstock– Frome branch by a standard
                gauge tramway of which part was a rope worked incline. Locomotives
                worked between the colliery and the incline head; they also worked a line
                serving dirt tips to the west of the colliery but this traffic was road
                worked from c /1940. Colliery closed 10/1973
                Ref: IRR 18 (4/1968) p.204

| 39 | NH | NORTON HILL (ST 668541)   (f Somerset Collieries Ltd)
Colliery on the south of the BR (ex S&DJR) Radstock- Shepton Mallet line
at a higher level with a steeply graded standard gauge line connecting the
sidings under the screens to BR. Coal winding ceased 11/2/1966 and track
subsequently lifted.

Ref: IRR 18 (4/1968) p.216

| 40 | OM | OLD MILLS (ST 651549)   (f Wm Evans & Co (Old Mills Collieries)Ltd)
Colliery on the north of the BR (ex GWR) Radstock - Bristol line with
standard gauge sidings serving the screens. Between 1953 and 1958 coal
for washing was brought here from Pensford Colliery by BR. Coal winding
ceased 1/4/1966, plant subsequently dismantled and site cleared.

| 41 | R | RADSTOCK (or LUDLOWS) (ST 692547) (f
Colliery served by sidings connecting with both the BR (ex S&DJR and
ex GWR) lines west of the Radstock stations. Horses used for shunting
until c /1947 when a road tractor was introduced. The locomotive is
believed to have only worked here for a short time on trials. Coal
winding ceased 19/3/1954 but part of the site remains in use as a store
for surplus machinery.

Other collieries taken over by the NCB in Somerset without locomotives were:

A   BRAYSDOWN (ST 704560). Served by a 2ft 6in gauge rope worked incline to
sidings on the BR (ex S&DJR) line opposite Writhlington Colliery. Closed
for coal winding c8/1956

B   BROMLEY (ST 606617) Served by a 2ft 0in gauge rope worked tramway taking
coal to the screens at Pensford Colliery. Coal winding ceased 18/5/1957
and tramway dismantled.

C   CAMERTON (ST 685581) Served by 4ft 8½in gauge sidings connecting with
the BR (ex GWR) Hallatrow- Limpley Stoke line. These were worked by
main line locomotives, horses, and (latterly) a road tractor. Coal
winding ceased 14/4/1950

D   CHARMBOROUGH (ST 678512) A small drift mine using road transport. Coal
winding ceased 2/8/1947

E   MARSH LANE (ST 631551) A small drift mine using road transport. Coal
winding ceased 4/11/1949

F   NEW ROCK (ST 648507) Two coal winding shafts, New Rock and Mendip, both
using road transport only. Coal winding ceased 28/9/1968

G   PENSFORD (ST 618627) Large colliery served by 4ft 8½in gauge sidings
at the head of an incline to the BR (ex GWR) Bristol - Radstock line.
Coal winding ceased 30/12/1958

H   LOWER WRITHLINGTON (ST 705553) Colliery latterly under the same
management as Kilmersdon and connected with it underground. The unit
was the last working colliery in Somerset. Served by sidings off the
BR (ex S&DJR) worked by a main line locomotive based at Radstock (ex
S&DJR) shed. Colliery ceased coal winding 10/1973

Gauge: 4ft 8½in

LORD SALISBURY	0-6-0ST	IC	P	1041	1906	(a)	CH-R 5/50-NH /53	(2)
-	4wDM		RH	242869	1946	(a)	CH-OM /53-K /68	(6)
-	4wDM		RH	200793	1940	(b)	OM-K-OM 10/61-	
							-K /64	(3)
GRAZEBROOK	0-4-0ST	OC	WB	1884	1908	(c)	NH	(1)
-	0-6-0ST	IC	HC	1029	1913			
			Reb		1931	(c)	NH	(1)
-	0-4-0ST	OC	P	1788	1929	(d)	K-NH /50-K /53-	
							-NH 7/58-K /59	(7)
LEONIDAS	0-4-0ST	OC	HL	3159	1916	(e)	NH	(4)
-	0-4-0T	OC	HE	1684	1931	(f)	NH-K 3/66	(5)

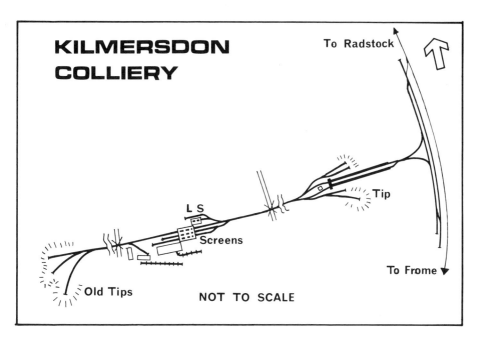

KILMERSDON COLLIERY

To Radstock

Tip

L S

Screens

To Frome

Old Tips

NOT TO SCALE

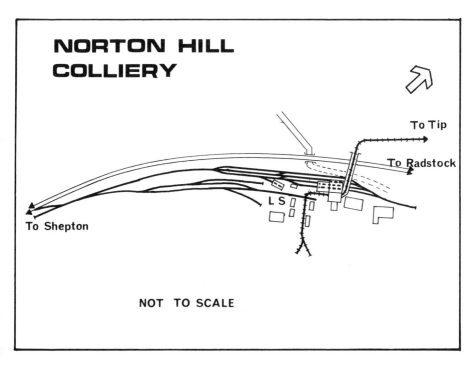

NORTON HILL COLLIERY

To Tip

To Radstock

To Shepton

L S

NOT TO SCALE

RADSTOCK

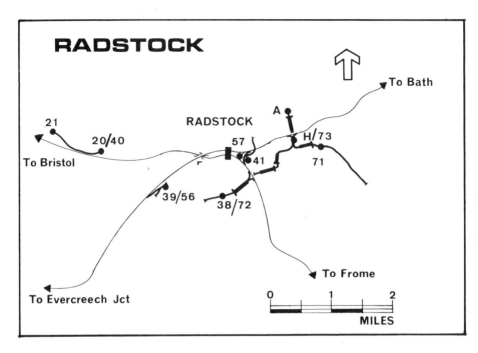

To Bath

21

20/40

To Bristol

RADSTOCK

A

57

H/73

41

71

39/56

38/72

To Frome

To Evercreech Jct

0   1   2
MILES

OLD MILLS COLLIERY

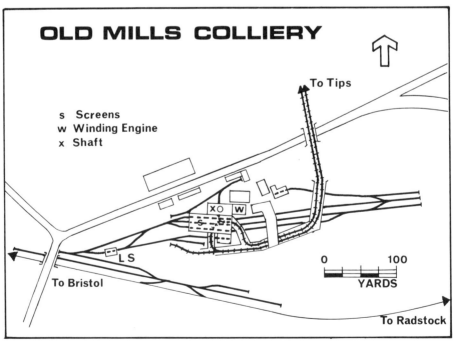

To Tips

s   Screens
w   Winding Engine
x   Shaft

X O   W

L S

To Bristol

0   100
YARDS

To Radstock

(a) ex Coalpit Heath Co Ltd , 1/1/1947
(b) ex Wm Evans & Co (Old Mills Collieries)
    Ltd , 1/1/1947
(c) ex Somerset Collieries Ltd , 1/1/1947
(d) ex Writhlington Collieries Co Ltd ,
    1/1/1947
(e) ex T.Hall, dealer, Llansamlet, Glam ,
    /1951; prev Royal Arsenal, Woolwich
(f) ex Phoenix Briquetting Works, Port
    Talbot, Glam , /1964

(1) to C.Whitlock, Wapping Wharf, Bristol,
    for scrap, 2/1951
(2) to Wm Pike Ltd ,
    scrap merchant, Trowbridge, Wilts,
    for scrap, 2/1965
(3) to Southern Counties Locomotive
    Preservation Co Ltd , Droxford,
    Hants , 7/1967
(4) scrapped on site, c /1955
(5) to Somerset Railway Museum, Bleadon &
    Uphill station, 10/1971
(6) to South Wales Area, Merthyr Vale
    Colliery
(7) to Somerset & Dorset Railway Circle,
    Radstock, 16/6/1974

Gauge: 3ft 6in

–	4wDM	RH	371382	1954	New	HS		(1)
–	4wDM	RH	371383	1954	New	HS		(2)

(1) to South Western Division, South Wales?
(2) to South Western Division, No.6 Area,
    New Rockwood Colliery, by 9/1963

Gauge: 2ft 8½in (previously 2ft 5½in)

–	4wBE	GB	2335	1951	New	R*-NH /51-GB 10/62+ - -K 4/63
–	4wBE	GB	2336	1951	New	NH-GB c11/62+ -K 4/63
–	4wBE	GB	2337	1951	New	NH-R* c6/64- +? -K 4/63

* - Stored at Radstock Central Stores
+ - Regauged (i.e. used on 2ft 5½in gauge at NH and on 2ft 8½in gauge at K)

PECKETT & SONS LTD., ATLAS LOCOMOTIVE WORKS, FISHPONDS, BRISTOL (Fox, Walker & Co
                                                                     until /1880)

42   Locomotive building works at ST 629746 established 1864. Served by the branch
     from the BR (ex Midland Railway) Bristol - Birmingham line to the East Bristol
     Collieries Ltd (which see). A colliery locomotive shunted the works until the
     collieries ceased work in 4/1936, after which Peckett used their own locomotive.
     The branch to BR was closed 6/1958 and lifted by 1960. The firm was taken over
     by Reed Crane & Hoist Co Ltd in 1961 and the last locomotive left the works
     2/1962. The works has since been closed completely and demolished and the
     site redeveloped.

     Ref: IRR 53 (4/1974)

Gauge: 4ft 8½in

NANCY	0-6-0ST	IC	P	1067	1905	(a)	Scr c7/1958

(a) ex Madeley Collieries Ltd , Staffs

PENSFORD & BROMLEY COLLIERIES LTD., BROMLEY COLLIERY (Bromley Colliery Ltd until 12/1909)

43   A narrow gauge line connected Bromley Colliery (ST 606617) with Pensford
      Colliery (ST 618627). Standard gauge locos were not used here but standard
      gauge sidings at Pensford Colliery were connected via a rope worked incline
      with the GWR Radstock - Bristol line. The narrow gauge loco proved to be
      underpowered and was replaced by main and tail rope haulage. Both collieries,
      latterly owned by Pensford & Bromley Collieries (1921) Ltd ,passed to the NCB
      (which see) on 1/1/1947

      Ref: 'The History of the Somerset Coalfield' by C.G.Down & A.J.Warrington; D&C

Gauge: 2ft 0in

    BROMLEY No.1   0-4-0T   OC   AE   1593 1910 New   (1)

                                    (1) to Old Delabole Slate Co Ltd ,
                                        Cornwall, c1/1913

PHORNIUM PATENT BRICK CO. LTD., CHARFIELD

44   A works served by a narrow gauge tramway. Works closed and tramway dismantled.

Gauge: 2ft 0in

            -                       4wPM   MR   5042 1929 New   s/s

PORT OF BRISTOL AUTHORITY. (f   Docks Committee of Bristol Corporation)

      Bristol has been a port from the earliest times but the first dock - a
      floating dock at Sea Mills, the third in the country - was not opened until
      about 1713; it was constructed by a group of Bristol merchants. Sundry
      extensions to the quay were made subsequently, and docks in the centre of
      Bristol (Cumberland Basin, etc) were constructed between 1804 & 1809 by the
      Bristol Dock Company. This company was taken over by Bristol Corporation on
      28/8/1848 and a Docks Committee formed. In 1854 the Bristol Port & Channel
      Dock Company was incorporated by an Act of Parliament and proceeded to construct
      the Avonmouth Dock which was opened in 1877. The first dock at Portishead was
      opened in 1879 by the Portishead Dock Co. This dock trade away from the
      Bristol Docks and in 1884 (by the Bristol Dock Act, 1884) both companies were
      purchased by Bristol Corporation. Considerable extensions were made at
      Avonmouth subsequently,including the Royal Edward Dock which was opened by
      King Edward Vll in 1908. Avonmouth concentrates on foreign trade, the City
      Docks on coastwise and near Continental trade and Portishead on coastwise
      trade. In 1973 construction commenced on the new East Dock complex near
      Portishead - it is not yet clear what rail facilities will be provided here.
      The City Docks are scheduled for closure in coming years.

Locomotives are used at:

45   A   AVONMOUTH DOCKS.   Situated on the north-east side of the confluence of the
          rivers Avon and Severn, with 94 acres of water area and a wharfage length
          of 17,000 ft. An extensive network of sidings serves the docks with
          three connections to the BR (ex GWR) Clifton - Severn Beach line running
          on the eastern boundary of the dock area. Locomotive depot and repair
          facilities at ST 513784

46   P   PORTISHEAD DOCKS.   Situated on the Severn about two miles south-west of
          Avonmouth with 16 acres of water area and a wharfage length of 4,000 ft.
          Rail facilities connect with the BR (ex GWR) Bristol - Portishead branch
          near its terminus. Loco depot at ST 472768 was closed c /1970 and is now
          used as a canteen; locos subsequently stabled in the open.

Storage facilities have been provided at Avonmouth Docks for locomotives intended for
preservation in Bristol City Museum (which see)

Gauge: 4ft 8½in

		Name	Type			Works No.	Date	History	Ref
		AVONMOUTH	0-6-0ST	OC	FW			A s/s after 4/1894	
		BRISTOL	0-6-0ST	OC	FW	180	1873	(a) A	(3)
		ALEXANDER	0-6-0ST	OC	FW	280	1875	New P Scr after /1934	
		HAROLD	0-6-0ST	OC	P	459	1887	New P Scr /1949	
		LIONEL	0-6-0ST	OC	P	466	1889	New A-P-A Sold 11/1951	
		LAURENCE	0-6-0ST	OC	P	526	1894	New A Scr /1949	
		PIONEER	0-6-0ST	OC	P	709	1898	(b) A	(1)
		LESLIE	0-6-0ST	OC	AE	1371	1898	New P	(2)
		KENNETH	0-6-0ST	OC	P	808	1900	New A-P c/18-A-P c/38-A	(6)
		FRANCIS	0-6-0ST	OC	AE	1431	1901	New A	(4)
		MURRAY	0-6-0ST	OC	P	1006	1904	New A-P c/47 Scr /1958	
		RONALD	0-6-0ST	OC	P	1093	1907	New A	(5)
		STRATHCONA	0-6-0ST	OC	P	1243	1910	New A	(7)
		MACKENZIE	0-6-0ST	OC	P	1244	1910	New A Scr /1960	
		HENRY	0-6-0ST	OC	P	1264	1913	New A	(5)
		EDWARD	0-6-0ST	OC	P	1377	1914	New A	(5)
		ALFRED	0-6-0ST	OC	AE	1679	1914	New A-P c/43-A	(6)
S 1		HUDSON	0-6-0ST	OC	AE	1724	1915	New A Scr c /1964	
S 2		WILLIAM	0-6-0ST	OC	AE	1725	1915	New P-A Scr c /1964	
S 3		(PORTBURY)	0-6-0ST	OC	AE	1764	1917	(c) A	(8)
S 5		(BRIAN)	0-6-0ST	OC	AE	1799	1918	New A	(9)
S 4		(PERCY)	0-6-0ST	OC	AE	1800	1918	New A	(9)
S 6		FYFFE	0-6-0ST	OC	P	1721	1926	New A Scr /1960	
S 8		WESTBURY	0-6-0ST	OC	P	1877	1934	New A	(10)
S 7		(ASHTON)	0-6-0ST	OC	P	1878	1934	New A	(10)
S 9		HENBURY	0-6-0ST	OC	P	1940	1937	New A	(11)
62			0-6-0T	OC	HC	1323	1918	(d) A	(12)
S10		HALLEN	0-6-0ST	OC	P	2035	1943	New A	(13)
S11		BRISTOL	0-6-0ST	OC	P	2036	1943	New A	(10)
S12		CLIFTON	0-6-0ST	OC	P	2037	1943	New A	(10)
S13		REDLAND	0-6-0ST	OC	P	2038	1943	New A	(10)
16	D3001	TINTAGEL	0-6-0DM		HC	D754	1952	New A	(14)
17	D3002	CAMELOT	0-6-0DM		HC	D755	1952	New A	(15)
18	D3003	CAERLEON	0-6-0DM		HC	D756	1952	New A	(15)
19	D3004	GLASTONBURY	0-6-0DM		HC	D757	1952	New A	(14)
20	(D1001)	GORDANO	0-4-0DM		HC	D894	1954	New P-A 5/66-P 11/66	(19)
21	D2001	NORMAN	0-4-0DM		HC	D774	1950	New A-P c/53-A /54	(16)
22	D2002	ARTHUR	0-6-0DM		HC	D760	1951	New A	(20)
23	(D2003)	MERLIN	0-6-0DM		HC	D761	1951	New A	(18)
24	D2004	LANCELOT	0-6-0DM		HC	D851	1955	New A	(17)
25	D2005	CELIDON	0-6-0DM		HC	D915	1956	New A	(21)
26	D2006	DUBGLAS	0-6-0DM		HC	D916	1956	New A-P /71	(21)
27	D2007	TRIBRUIT	0-6-0DM		HC	D917	1956	New A	(22)
28	D2008	GUINNION	0-6-0DM		HC	D918	1956	New A	(22)
29	(D2009)	AGNED	0-6-0DM		HC	D919	1956	New A	(23)
30			0-6-0DM		HC	D1171	1959	New A-P 1/72	
31			0-6-0DM		HC	D1172	1959	New A	
32			0-6-0DM		HC	D1192	1960	New A	(23)
33			0-6-0DM		HC	D1193	1960	New A	(23)
34			0-6-0DH		S	10148	1963	New A	
35			0-6-0DH		S	10149	1964	New A	
36			0-6-0DH		S	10150	1964	New A	
37			0-6-0DH		S	10151	1964	New A	
38			0-6-0DH		RR	10217	1965	New A	
39			0-6-0DH		RR	10218	1965	New A	
40			0-6-0DH		RR	10219	1965	New A	
41			0-6-0DH		RR	10220	1965	New A	
42			0-6-0DH		RR	10221	1965	New A	

(a) ex Chas Daniel, contr , by 7/1893
(b) ex Victoria Petroleum Co Ltd , Penarth
    Harbour, Cardiff, via Bute Works
    Supply Co
(c) ex Admiralty, Portbury Shipyard,
    after 12/1919
(d) ex Port of London Authority, Royal Docks
    11/1941

(1) Sold after 6/1918
(2) to ? , South Wales, for scrap, /1933
(3) to P , /1934
(4) to Pugsley, Stoke Gifford, for scrap,
    c10/1952
(5) to Warn
    Stapleton Road, Bristol, for scrap,
    10/1957
(6) Scr on site by Pugsley, /1959
(7) Scr on site by Rose (Iron & Steel) Ltd,
    Bristol, c12/1959
(8) Stored for preservation; to Somerset &
    Dorset Railway Circle, Radstock,
    11/1971
(9) to Godfrey & Sully, Metal & Steel Merch.
    Portishead, for scrap, /1964; Scr
    7/1964
(10) to Godfrey & Sully, Metal & Steel Merch.
    Portishead, for scrap, 3/1966; Scr
(11) Stored for preservation; to Somerset &
    Dorset Railway Circle, Radstock,
    11/1971
(12) ret to Port of London Authority, 1/1946
(13) to South Western Gas Board, Cheltenham
    Gasworks, 9/1964
(14) to Guest,Keen & Nettlefolds (South
    Wales) Ltd , Castle Works, Tremorfa,
    Glam , 10/1966
(15) to Guest,Keen & Nettlefolds (South
    Wales) Ltd , Castle Works, Tremorfa,
    Glam , 12/1966
(16) to Albright & Wilson Ltd , Portishead,
    c /1969
(17) to British Fuel Co , Carlisle Coal
    Concentration Depot, Cumbs , 7/1970
(18) to Boddy Industries Ltd , Carnforth,
    Lancs , c8/1970
(19) to Romford Scrap Metal Co Ltd , Essex ,
    c4/1973
(20) to Romford Scrap Metal Co Ltd , Essex ,
    c12/1973
(21) to Romford Scrap Metal Co Ltd , Essex,
    c12/1973; resold to ? , Belgium
(22) to Romford Scrap Metal Co Ltd , Essex,
    c12/1973; resold to W.R.Cunis Ltd ,
    Rainham, Essex
(23) to Birds' Commercial Motors Ltd , Long
    Marston, Worcs , c12/1974

JOSEPH PUGSLEY & SONS LTD., BEAUFORT PLANT DEPOT, STOKE GIFFORD

47   A firm of dealers with premises in use at St Phillips (Bristol) (in 1/1901), St Georges (Bristol) (in 4/1904) and at Cattybrook Iron Works, Lawrence Hill Bristol (in 1/1909 and 7/1920). The Stoke Gifford yard and plant depot was established on the site of a brickworks after the construction of the GWR Wootton Bassett - Patchway main line. Many locos of both standard and narrow gauges have passed through the yard being either resold or scrapped. Those indicated with an asterisk in the list below are not known to have been put into use while in the yard. All shunting was by BR &/or Pugsley's steam cranes from c /1965 at least; the depot closed in 1969 when the remaining stock was disposed of.

Gauge: 4ft 8½in

–	4wPM	MH	27	1927	(a)	Scr	/1969
–	4wDM	MR		c1928	(b)*	s/s	
–	4wDM	MR	4169	1927	(c)*	s/s	
–	0-4-0DM	JF	22888	1937	(d)*	(1)	

(a) ex W.D. & H.O.Wills Ltd , Swindon, Wilts   (1) to A.Robinson & Co (Westminster) Ltd ,
(b) ex Esso Petroleum Co Ltd , Fawley, Hants,   Woolston Tip, Hants , c /1969
    by /1957
(c) ex Esso Petroleum Co Ltd , Fawley, Hants,
    by /1958
(d) ex Ashton Containers Ltd , Bristol,
    /1965

Gauge: 2ft 0in

–	4wDM	DC/Bg	2104	1937	(a)*	s/s
–	4wDM	DC/Bg	2105	1937	(a)*	s/s
–	4wDM	RH	182153	1937	(b)*	Scr
181	4wDM	OK			(c)*	s/s
–	4wDM	RH			(c)*	Scr

(a) ex Cornwall County Council, Tolpetherwin
    Quarry, /1949
(b) ex Nuttall, contrs, by /1966
(c) ex ? , by /1966

QUARTZITE QUARRIES LTD., CROMHALL, CHARFIELD

48   Quarries served by a narrow gauge tramway, abandoned c /1940. One locomotive remained on site in an exceedingly decrepit condition for a further twenty years before disposal.

Gauge: 2ft 0in

–	0-4-0ST	OC	KS		(a)	(1)
–	0-4-0ST	OC	KS		(a)	(2)
–	0-4-0ST	OC	KS	4255 1922	(b)	(3)

(a) ex ? , /1935   (1) to P.Rodgers, Chipping Sodbury, for
(b) ex Aubrey Watson Ltd , contrs , c /1935   scrap, c /1940
    (2) to(Pugsley, Stoke Gifford?), c /1940
    (3) to Pearse & Co Ltd , Exeter, for scrap,
       2/1960 , per R.Morris, Pinhoe, nr
       Exeter

Conygar Quarry, near Clevedon (Roads Reconstruction Ltd until 17/2/1934)

49 A narrow gauge tramway (not locomotive worked) ran from the quarry (ST 422722) to a wharf and standard gauge sidings (ST 418724) connecting with the Weston Clevedon & Portishead Railway at Walton Park station. Rail traffic ceased c /1935 and railway and tramway lifted, quarry closed but later worked again by Amalgamated Limestone Corporation Ltd.

Gauge: 4ft 8½in

	FINETTA	0-4-0ST	OC	AE	1565	1911	(a)	(1)
292	NIDD	0-4-0ST	OC	KS	3112	1918	(b)	(2)

(a) ex Sandford Quarry   (1) to A.R.Adams & Son , Newport, Mon ,
(b) ex ICI, Billingham Works , Co.Durham,   /1934
    48   (2) to Vobster Quarries

Grovesend Quarries, Tytherington (Roads Reconstruction Ltd until 17/2/1934;

Tytherington Stone Co Ltd , until /1926)

50 There were originally three quarries at Tytherington; Grovesend (ST 658887), Church (ST 669884) and West (ST 665882). Grovesend was the last to be opened c /1894. Grovesend and Church (and almost certainly West) quarries were originally owned by H.L.Hardwick, trading as the Tytherington Stone Co. In 1901 Church quarry had a standard gauge connection to the Midland Railway Thornbury branch while West had a narrow gauge line to a loading wharf on the Midland Railway. Grovesend was not worked on a large scale until a later date. Almost certainly DAPHNE at first worked Church quarry and JF 7958 the West quarry, moving to Grovesend as it was developed. By 1915 a standard gauge line had been laid into West quarry, traffic being worked by a steam crane. Roads Reconstruction took over the three quarries. Internal rail traffic had ceased by 1948 in favour of road haulage and track had been lifted. The BR (ex Midland Railway) Thornbury branch was lifted c /1965 but was relaid 1972 by Eagre Construction Co Ltd (which see) for further use by Grovesend quarry traffic.

Gauge: 4ft 8½in

DAPHNE	0-4-0ST	OC	P	737	1899	New	(1)
CATHERINE	0-4-0ST	OC	HE	282	1882	(a)	s/s

(a) ex Admiralty, Portbury Shipyard, 1/1919 (1) to Pilkington Bros Ltd , Ravenhead
                                                   Works, St.Helens, Lancs , /1923

Gauge: 2ft 0in

	-	4wTG		JF	7958	1898	New	s/s
41		0-4-2ST	OC	KS	3065	1918	(a)	(1)
	-	0-4-0T	OC	AE	2073	1933	(b)	(3)
3		0-4-0WT	OC	AB	1855	1931	(b)	(3)
D8		0-4-0DM		Dtz	9898	1931		(2)

(a) ex Cranmore Depot, Somerset, by 12/1928 (1) to New Frome Quarry, Somerset, after
(b) ex Pugsley , c11/1941; prev Durham   7/1933
    County Water Board   (2) to Vobster Quarries, Somerset, c /1948
                                          (3) to Cranmore Depot, Somerset, 4/1949

Sandford Quarry, Banwell (Roads Reconstruction Ltd until 12/2/1934; Sandford
& Conygar Quarries Co ,subsidiary of Teign Valley Granite Co Ltd until 1/1924)

51   Quarry at ST 421591 operated by Sandford Quarries Co as a branch of Roads
Reconstruction (1934) Ltd. A narrow gauge tramway served the quarry while
standard gauge sidings connected with the BR (ex GWR) Yatton - Wells line.
The narrow gauge system closed c /1931; reopened c /1935 to serve the kilns
only (using the Dtz loco); finally closed c /1940 and lifted. Standard gauge
rail traffic replaced by road transport from 9/1964.

Gauge: 4ft 8½in

	BULFORD	0-4-0ST	OC	HC	1045	1914	(a)	(1)
	FINETTA	0-4-0ST	OC	AE	1565	1911	(b)	(2)
1700		0-4-0VBT	VCG	S	6219	c1927		
		Reb from 0-4-0PM	MW		1954	1918	(c)	Scr 8/1960
153		0-4-0DM		JF	19645	1932	New	(3)
758		0-4-0ST	OC	VF	798	1876	(d)	(4)
1262		4wVBT	VCG	S	9391	1949	New	(5)

(a) ex Sir John Jackson Ltd , Bulford Camp   (1) to Selby Oil & Cake Mills Ltd , Selby,
    construction contract, Wilts,   Yorks ER
    c /1915   (2) to Conygar Quarries
(b) ex WD , Codford, Wilts, 10/1919; prev (3) to Cranmore Depot, ex New Frome Quarries
    Teign Valley Granite Co Ltd ,   /1942; to Cranmore Depot, /1943
    Devon   (4) to New Frome Quarry, /1946
(c) ex Vobster Quarries, by 6/1926   (5) to New Frome Quarry, 9/1964
(d) ex A.R.Adams & Son Ltd , Newport, Mon ,
    /1942

Gauge: 2ft 0in

-	0-4-0T	OC	(AE?)				(1)
-	0-4-0T	OC	(AE?)				(1)
-	0-4-2ST	OC	KS	856	1904	(a)	(2)
-	0-6-0DM		Dtz	88153			(3)

(a) ex Cranmore Depot, by 1/1927   (1) to Cranmore Depot
                                (2) to Cranmore Depot, by 3/1931
                                (3) to Cranmore Depot, c /1942

ST. ANNES BOARD MILL CO. LTD., BRISTOL

52   A narrow gauge tramway connected the coal wharf on the River Avon and the
boiler house of this works at ST 620728. Tramway closed and lifted.

Gauge: 2ft 0in

-	4wPM	L	4483	1932	New	s/s
-	4wPM	L	4605	1932	New	s/s
-	4wPM	L	4882	c1932	New	(1)
-	4wPM	L	6955	1935	New	s/s
-	4wPM	L	10016	1938	New	(3)
-	4wPM	L	26476	1945	New	(2)

               (1) to L ; resold to Coleford Brick & Tile
                   Co Ltd , Cinderford, Glos , 7/1938
               (2) to P.G.Bale Ltd ,station sidings,
                   Brislington, Bristol c9/1967;
                   Scr c2/1968
               (3) to L c /1945 for repairs; ret 7/1945;
                   s/s

53   Sidings served an oil storage depot. Rail traffic ceased.

Gauge: 4ft 8½in

No.19	0-4-0DM	JF	4100014	1949	New	(2)
No.22	0-4-0DM	JF	22998	1943	(a)	(1)

(a) ex Salt End Refinery, Hull, Yorks (ER)   (1) to Salt End Refinery, Hull, Yorks (ER),
                                                       2/1950
                                               (2) to Wagon Repairs Ltd , Stoke-on-Trent,
                                               Staffs , 8/1968

SOMERSET COLLIERIES LTD.

       Somerset Collieries Ltd registered 26/9/1925 as a private company. A second
company of the same name was registered 5/12/1935 being a public company
formed to acquire the first company, Norton Hill Collieries Co , and other
companies.

       Ref: 'The History of the Somerset Coalfield' by C.G.Down & A.J.Warrington; D&C

Camerton Colliery

54   Colliery ,opened before 1800, later served by the GWR Hallatrow - Limpley
Stoke line,situated to the north of this branch at ST 684580. Horses were
used to move wagons except for the brief period when the locomotive was here
on trials. Colliery passed to the NCB on 1/1/1947; coal winding ceased
14/4/1950, and the plant later dismantled.

Gauge: 4ft 8½in

DUNKERTON	0-4-0ST	OC	P	1191	1910	(a)	(1)

(a) ex Dunkerton Colliery, c /1926   (1) to Walter, Scott & Middleton, contrs ,
                                                   c /1926

Dunkerton Colliery

55   Colliery opened in 1906 and served by sidings on the south side of the GWR
Hallatrow - Limpley Stoke line at ST 697586 after the extension of that line
east of Camerton by 4/1907. Colliery initially owned by Dunkerton Collieries
Ltd until closed 30/5/1925. Purchased by Sir Frank Beauchamp and reopened.
Transferred to Somerset Collieries Ltd , 23/12/1925 and finally closed 6/9/1927.

Gauge: 4ft 8½in

DUNKERTON	0-4-0ST	OC	P	1191	1910	New	(1)

                                       (1) to Camerton Colliery for trials, c /1926

Norton Hill Colliery, Midsomer Norton (Norton Hill Collieries Co until 5/12/1935)

56   Colliery opened 1903 with sidings at ST 668541 served by the LMS (ex S&DJR)
Radstock - Evercreech line. Colliery passed to NCB on 1/1/1947 (which see).

Gauge: 4ft 8½in

-	0-4-0ST	OC	P	520	1891	(a)	s/s
GRAZEBROOK	0-4-0ST	OC	WB	1884	1908	(b)	(1)
-	0-6-0ST	IC	HC	1029	1913		
			Reb	1931	(c)	(1)	

(a) ex East Bristol Collieries Ltd ,   (1) to NCB, Division 7, Area 8, 1/1/1947
     Kingswood Colliery
(b) ex M.W.Grazebrook Ltd , Netherton,
     Staffs
(c) ex McAlpine , contrs , No.33

Circle until /1974)

57   From 1970 to 1975 preserved locomotives and stock were kept at the former BR (ex S&DJR) Radstock loco shed (ST 693549) with infrequent operation over the BR line as far as Writhlington Colliery. In 1975 this project ceased and the stock was moved, principally to the West Somerset Railway (which see).

Gauge: 4ft 8½in

53808		2-8-0	OC	RS	3894	1925	(a)	(3)
	CRANFORD No.2	0-6-0ST	OC	WB	2668	1942	(b)	(1)
3		0-6-0ST	OC	FW	242	1874	(c)	(4)
S3	PORTBURY	0-6-0ST	OC	AE	1764	1917	(c)	(3)
S9	HENBURY	0-6-0ST	OC	P	1940	1937	(c)	(3)
	ISABEL	0-6-0ST	OC	HL	3437	1919	(d)	(3)
	LORD FISHER	0-4-0ST	OC	AB	1398	1915	(e)	(2)
24		4wDM		RH	210479	1941	(f)	(3)
47493		0-6-0T	IC	VF	4195	1927	(g)	(2)
	GLENFIELD	0-4-0ST	OC	AB	1719	1920	(h)	(2)
-		0-4-0ST	OC	P	1788	1929	(j)	(3)
No.1		0-4-0F	OC	WB	2473	1932	(k)	(3)
	FONMON	0-6-0ST	OC	P	1636	1929	(m)	(4)
900855		4wPMR		Wkm	6967		(n)	(3)

(a) ex Woodham Bros , Barry Dock, Glam ,
    10/1970
(b) ex Overstone Solarium, Northants, c8/1971
(c) ex Port of Bristol Authority, Avonmouth
    Docks, 11/1971 (where stored for
    Bristol City Museum)
(d) ex Keighley & Worth Valley Railway,
    Yorks (WR), 11/1971
(e) ex Longmoor Steam Trust, Hants , 11/1971
(f) ex South Western Gas Board, Bath Gasworks,
    11/1971
(g) ex Woodham Bros , Barry Dock, Glam ,
    11/1972
(h) ex NCB Northumberland Area, Backworth,
    5/1973
(j) ex NCB South Wales Area, Kilmersdon
    Colliery, 6/1974
(k) ex Great Western Preservations Ltd ,
    Didcot Depot, Oxon , c7/1974
(m) ex Aberthaw & Bristol Channel Portland
    Cement Co Ltd , Rhoose, Glam , 21/9/1974
(n) ex BR

(1) to Steamtown Museum, Carnforth, Lancs,
    6/1972
(2) to Cranmore Railway Co, Somerset,
    11/1973
(3) to West Somerset Railway Co Ltd,
    Somerset, various dates from 5/1975
    to 3/1976
(4) to Bristol Suburban Railway Society,
    Bitton, c5/1975 (FW 242) and
    2/1976 (P 1636).

SOMERSET RAILWAY MUSEUM, BLEADON & UPHILL STATION

58   The main buildings of this closed station on the BR (ex GWR) Taunton- Bristol main line have been converted into a museum of small railway relics. The locos are on static display on short sidings in the station yard at ST 325578.

Gauge: 4ft 8½in

1338		0-4-0ST	OC	K	3799	1898	(a)
	-	0-4-0T	OC	HE	1684	1931	(b)
1		4wVBT	VCG	S	9374	1947	(c)
	-	4wDM		FH	3057	1946	(d)
W 79976		4wDMR		A.CCars		1958	(e)

(a) ex BR (WR) , 4/1964
(b) ex NCB East Wales Area, Kilmersdon
Colliery, 10/1971
(c) ex ARC (Southern) Ltd , New Frome Quarry,
10/1971
(d) ex Plymouth Tar Distilleries Ltd ,Devon,
c1/1971
(e) ex BR (WR), Bristol, c6/1973

SOMERSETSHIRE COAL CANAL

59   The company of Proprietors of the Somersetshire Coal Canal Navigation
constructed a seven mile tramway from the collieries at Radstock to its main
canal at Midford, using the course of an unsuccessful canal. The tramway was
opened in 1815 using horses to haul the tubs. The gauge was 3ft 2in.
A steam locomotive built by William Ashman of Clandown Colliery, Radstock was
built in 1825 and put to work on the tramway in August 1827. It is believed
to have been relegated to a stationary hauler after frequent rail breakages;
later s/s.   The tramway remained in use with horse traction until sold in
1871 and its route used for the Bath Extension of the Somerset & Dorset Railway.

Ref: 'The Somersetshire Coal Canal & Railways' by Kenneth R. Clew; D&C , 1970
'The Somerset & Dorset Railway' by Robin Atthill; D&C , 1967

ST. KEVERNE & ASSOCIATED QUARRIES LTD., WINFORD QUARRY, NEAR BRISTOL (Subsidiary of

Amalgamated Roadstone Co Ltd)

60   A quarry (at ST 535638, about six miles south-west of Bristol) and crushing
plant opened in 1938. A tramway about 300 yards long connected the two.
Quarry closed 1954 and tramway dismantled.

Ref: IRR No.20   (8/1968) p.288

Gauge: 2ft 0in

LM 35		4wDM	OK	7736	1938	New	(1)
LM 37		4wDM	RH	177643	1936	(a)	(2)
LM 36		4wDM	RH	183078	1937	(b)	Scr /1954

(a) ex Cornish Road-Metal Ltd , Stepper Point(1) to British Quarrying Co Ltd , Borough
Quarry, Cornwall   Green Quarry, Kent, /1949
(b) ex British Quarrying Co Ltd , Allington (2) to St.Keverne Quarries, Cornwall,
Quarry, Kent   /1949

SOUTH WESTERN GAS BOARD

Bath Gasworks (Bath Gas Co until 1/5/1949; Bath Gas Light & Coke Co until 12/1927)

61   A large gasworks on the north side of, and served by sidings from, the BR
(ex S&DJR) line near Bath (Green Park) station, with a works loco shed at
ST 736650. Works established in 1818 and incorporated as the Bath Gas Light
& Coke Co by special act in 1856.   Production ceased 20/5/1971 and the rail
installations subsequently dismantled.

Gauge: 4ft 8½in

-	0-4-0WT	G	AP	4909	1901	New	(1)
No.1	0-4-0ST	OC	P	1267	1912	New	(2)
No.2	0-4-0ST	OC	AE	1978	1928	New	(3)
24	4wDM		RH	210479	1941	(a)	(4)
23	4wDM		RH	306089	1950	(b)	(5)

(a) ex Thos W Ward Ltd , Templeborough
    Works, Sheffield, c2/1964 ; f
    William Gray & Co Ltd , West
    Hartlepool, Co.Durham
(b) ex Thos W Ward Ltd , Templeborough
    Works, Sheffield, c2/1964 ; f ICI ,
    Winsford Works, Cheshire

(1) acquired by AE in 6/1928 in part
    exchange for AE 1978. No trace in AE
    records of resale, but reported locally
    as sent to the "Wickwar Quarry at
    Wootton" (sic), loaded up on a rail
    truck, possibly for stationary use.
    (see under Wickwar Quarries Ltd)
(2) Scr on site by Pugsley of Bristol,
    c2/1964
(3) Scr on site by W.G.Keen & Co of
    Salisbury, Wilts, c2/1964
(4) to Somerset & Dorset Railway Circle,
    Radstock, 11/1971
(5) to Stapleton Road Gasworks, Bristol,
    6/1971

Canons Marsh Gasworks, Bristol (Bristol Gas Co   until 1/5/1949)

62   Works, opened c/1820, near the Floating Harbour at ST 581725 served by standard
gauge sidings connecting with the BR (ex GWR) Temple Meads -- Ashton Junction
goods branch. Production ceased 1958 and the works was partly dismantled 1959.

Gauge: 4ft 8½in

3	FENWICK	0-4-0ST	OC	P	1221	1911	New	Scr c7/1960
1	J.W.S.DIX	0-4-0ST	OC	HL	2184	1891	(a)	(1)
	-	4wDM		RH	321731	1952	New	(2)

(a) ex Stapleton Road Gasworks, 6/1951

(1) ret to Stapleton Road Gasworks, 9/1954
(2) to Gloucester Gasworks, /1958

Stapleton Road Gasworks, Bristol (Bristol Gas Co   until 1/5/1949; Bristol

63   United Gas Light Co until /1891)

A large gasworks on the north-east side of the BR (ex GWR) line between
Stapleton Road and Ashley Hill stations. Extensive sidings served the works
and connected via a steeply graded line with the BR (ex GWR) line. There was
also a connection to the BR (ex Midland Railway) Kingswood Junction- Ashley Hill
Junction branch. The loco shed was at ST 606749. Works closed for production
26/3/1971,although the railway has seen occasional use since for the despatch
of material salvaged during the dismantling of plant.

Gauge: 4ft 8½in

	-	0-4-0ST	OC	P	451	1886	New	(1)
1	J.W.S.DIX	0-4-0ST	OC	HL	2184	1891	New(a)	Scr 7/1960
2	G.K.STOTHERT	0-4-0ST	OC	P	864	1901	New	Scr /1939
	J.FULLER EBERLE	0-4-0ST	OC	P	1967	1939	New	(3)
	-	0-4-0DM		RH	281268	1950	New	(4)
	-	0-4-0ST	OC	P	1611	1923	(b)	(2)
	-	0-4-0DE		RH	418602	1958	New	(5)
23		4wDM		RH	306089	1950	(c)	

(a) to Canons Marsh Gasworks, 4/6/1951;
    ret 24/9/1954
(b) ex P , loan, /1957; orig Courtaulds Ltd,
    Coventry, Warwicks
(c) ex Bath Gasworks, 6/1971

(1) to Pugsley, Stoke Gifford
(2) ret to P , c /1957
(3) to J.P.Vials & Sons, Haulage contrs ,
    Hardwick Garage, near Quedgeley,
    c5/1968
(4) to Tilsley & Lovatt Ltd , dealers,
    Trentham, Staffs, 8/1971; resold to
    Patent Shaft Steel Works Ltd,
    Wednesbury, Staffs, 1/1972
(5) to DowMac (Concrete) Ltd,Quedgeley,8/1971

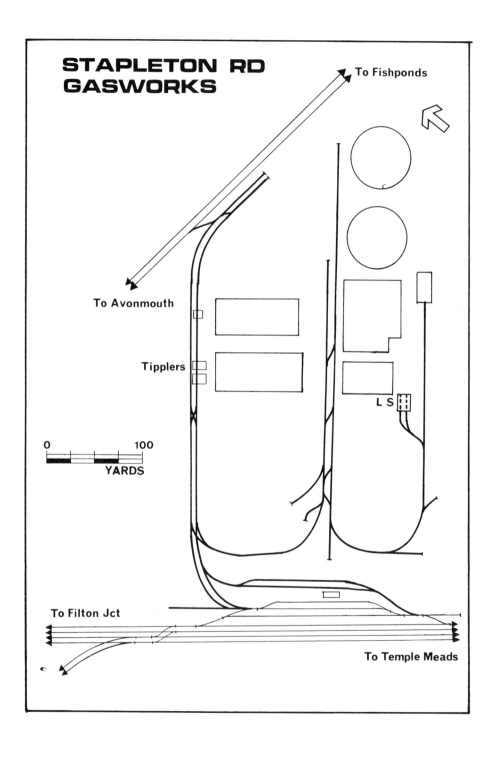

STAPLETON RD GASWORKS

To Fishponds

To Avonmouth

Tipplers

L S

0   100

YARDS

To Filton Jct

To Temple Meads

Weston-super-Mare Gasworks (Weston-super-Mare & District Gas Co until 1/5/1949;
Weston-super-Mare Gaslight Co from 1855 until 1934)

64   Works (at ST 607329) served by a rail siding from the BR (ex GWR) line just
north of Weston-super-Mare station. Rail traffic ceased c5/1968; works closed
and demolished.

Gauge: 4ft 8½in

WEASTE	0-4-0ST	OC	HC	302	1888	(a)	s/s	
-	0-4-0ST	OC	P	1612	1922	New	Scr	/1947
-	4wDM		FH	2914	1944	New	(1)	
-	4wDM		FH	3057	1946	New	(2)	

(a) ex J.T.Firbank, contr , Basingstoke,   (1) to Phoenix Timber Co Ltd , Rainham,
Hants, /1918   Essex
                                                (2) to Plymouth Tar Distilleries Ltd ,
                                                    Cattedown, Plymouth, Devon, /1968

UNITED ALKALI CO. LTD., NETHAM CHEMICAL WORKS, CREWS HOLE, BRISTOL

65   A works founded prior to 1859, in which year they were purchased by the
predecessors of United Alkali Co Ltd . By 1883 extensive narrow gauge tramways
- including a rope worked incline 150 yards long - had been laid on which
trucks were worked manually. The tramways also served a wharf on the River
Avon at ST 617728. It is believed that a steam locomotive worked on the
tramways up to the closure of the works, c /1926, but details are not known.

EARL OF WARWICK'S SOMERSET COLLIERIES

66   A standard gauge branch about ¾ mile long was laid from Clutton station on
the GWR Bristol - Radstock line (ST 628593) to Frys Bottom Colliery (ST 629604)
and was opened 3/9/1873. Frys Bottom Colliery had been sunk before 1858 and
closed 31/7/1895. Greyfield Colliery (ST 639587) commenced after 1833 and
from c /1842 was trading under the name of Greyfield Coal Co , which by 1913
had become the Greyfield Colliery Co Ltd. From 1873 this colliery was served
by a standard gauge branch about ¾ mile long connecting with the Frys Bottom
branch at Clutton station. Greyfield Colliery ceased coal winding 28/5/1911
and was dismantled shortly afterwards. In 1908 the Clutton Coal Co was formed
as a subsidiary of the Greyfield Coal Co Ltd to sink the Clutton Colliery
(ST 627596) which opened by 1912 and was served by a siding off the Frys Bottom
line. This colliery closed in 8/1921.

   Ref: 'The History of the Somerset Coalfield' by C.G.Down & A.J.Warrington; D&C

Gauge: 4ft 8½in

FRANCES	0-4-0ST	OC	RWH	2040	1885	New	(1)
DAISY	0-4-0ST	OC	P	581	1894	New	(2)
EMLYN	0-4-0ST	OC	?			(a)	(3)

(a) ex C.D.Phillips, Newport, Mon , hire   (1) Scr on site c /1895
by c /1900   (2) to Wynnstay Collieries Ltd , Denbighs,
                                                   c /1922
                                               (3) ret to C.D.Phillips off hire, c /1910

67   A fourteen mile long light railway connecting the towns named. The line had
junctions with the GWR at Clevedon and Portishead and provided rail outlets
for Conygar and Black Rock quarries (which see). Loco and carriage sheds were
at Clevedon (ST 407709). The Weston – Clevedon section was opened to traffic
1/12/1897, the extension to Portishead on 7/8/1907. Closure was on 18/5/1940;
the assets passed to the GWR on 22/6/1940 and track lifting commenced 11/12/1942.

Ref: 'The Weston Clevedon & Portishead Railway' by Colin Maggs; Oakwood 1964
'The Locomotives of the GWR, Part 10'; RCTS , 1966

Gauge: 4ft 8½in

45	HAROLD	0-6-0ST	IC	K	1829	1872	(a)	(1)	
	CLEVEDON	0-6-0T	IC	WkB			(b)	(2)	
2	CLEVEDON	2-2-2WT	IC	Sharp	1017	1857	(c)	(3)	
1	WESTON	2-2-2WT	IC	SS	1707	1866	(d)	(4)	
3	PORTISHEAD	2-4-0T	IC	RS	2383	1879	(e)	(5)	
1	CLEVEDON	2-4-0T	OC	D	1222	1879	(f)		Scr /1940
	(GENERAL DON until /1906)								
2	PORTISHEAD	0-6-0ST	IC	MW	1134	1890	(g)	(6)	
	EMLYN No.82	0-6-0ST*	IC	K			(h)	(7)	
	–	2-4-0T	IC	SS			(j)	(8)	
	EMLYN No.96	0-6-0ST	IC	BH			(k)	(7)	
3	WESTON	0-6-0ST*	IC	MW	731	1881	(m)		Scr /1940
(4)	WALTON PARK	0-6-0ST	OC	HC	823	1908	New	(9)	
4	HESPERUS	2-4-0T	IC	SS	2578	1876	(n)		Scr 6/1937
2	NORTHIAM	2-4-0T	OC	HL	2420	1899	(p)	(10)	
5		0-6-0ST	IC	MW	1970	1919	New		Scr /1940
	–	4wPMR		DC	1252	1922	New		Scr /1940
	–	4wPM		MH		1925	New		Scr /1926
	–	4wPM		MH	A137	1926	New		Scr /1940
2	PORTISHEAD	0-6-0T	IC	Bton		1877	(q)	(11)	
4		0-6-0T	IC	Bton		1875	(r)	(12)	
5		4wPMR		DC	1650	1928	(s)		Scr /1940

*   These locos ran at times as 0-4-2ST on the WC&PR

(a) ex C.D.Phillips, Newport, Mon ,hire,
   /1897
(b) ex ? , /1897
(c) ex Furness Railway, 12A, /1898
(d) ex Furness Railway, 35 , /1899
(e) ex ? , contrs , Freshwater Yarmouth
   & Newport Railway construction, IoW ,
   (/1899?) as 0-6-0T
(f) ex AE , /1901 ; orig Jersey Railway
(g) ex Jackson & Co , contrs , Stowmarket,
   Suffolk, /1907
(h) ex C.D.Phillips, Newport, Mon ,hire ,
   summers of /1902/5/6/7
(j) ex ? , loan, /1903-5
(k) ex C.D.Phillips, Newport, Mon , hire,
   /1905
(m) ex AE after /1904; prev Burry Port &
   Gwendraeth Valley Railway, CWM MAWR
(n) ex Bute Works Supply Co , /1911; orig
   Watlington & Princes Risborough Railway;
   then GWR 1384
(p) ex Kent & East Sussex Railway, loan, /1918
(q) ex SR, B643 , 12/1925; orig LBSCR 43 GIPSY HILL
(r) ex SR, 2653 , 4/1937; orig LBSCR 53 ASHTEAD
(s) ex SR, No.5 , /1934

(1) ret to C.D.Phillips off hire, /1898
(2) to ? , after 2/1899
(3) s/s after c /1904
(4) to Pugsley, Bristol, /1904 for scrap
(5) to Renishaw Iron Co Ltd , Derbys , /1900
(6) to William Cowlin & Son Ltd , Portishead
   Power Station contract, /1926
(7) ret to C.D.Phillips off hire
(8) ret to ? off loan
(9) to Shropshire & Montgomeryshire Railway,
   /1913
(10) ret to Kent & East Sussex Railway, off
   loan, /1921
(11) to GWR , 5 , 7/1940; Scr 3/1954
(12) to GWR , 6 , 7/1940; Scr 1/1948

WESTON-SUPER-MARE POTTERY, BRICK & TILE CO. LTD., ROYAL POTTERIES, WESTON-SUPER-MARE

68   Production commenced at a works and claypits at Locking Road, c /1836 and was later transferred to a new site about ¼ mile to the south at ST 332607 which was purchased 9/1898, the limited company of the title being formed in this year. A narrow gauge tramway was later in use at this site, where production of bricks and flower pots continued until 8/12/1961 when the company went into voluntary liquidation. The track was then lifted and the remaining locos stored until disposal. The site remained partially intact and was later taken over by Ansar Mosaics.

Gauge: 2ft 0in

-	4wDM	OK				(1)
-	4wDM	OK				(1)
-	4wDM	HE	2805	1943	(a)	s/s c /1965
-	4wDM	OK	6191			s/s c /1965

(a) ex ? , orig WD   (1) to A.J.Quick, Scrap merchant, Weston-Super-Mare for scrap, 8/1959

WICKWAR QUARRIES LTD., TANHOUSE QUARRY, NEAR WICKWAR

69   A narrow gauge tramway served this quarry which closed c /1936; tramway lifted. There is no evidence of standard gauge track here. The AP loco was reported at Bath Gasworks to have been sent to the "Wickwar Quarry at Wootton" (sic). It is possible that it was adapted for stationary use at this location.

Gauge: 4ft 8½in

-	0-4-0WT	G	AP	4909	1901	(a)	s/s

(a) ex Bath Gas Co , per AE , c6/1928

Gauge: 1ft 11⅝in

-	4wPM	L	3964	1931	New	s/s
-	4wPM	L	4026	1931	New	s/s

WOTTON BROS. LTD., WICK QUARRY, MARSHFIELD

70   A quarry at ST 710730 served by a narrow gauge tramway. Tramway closed and track lifted.

Gauge: 2ft 0in

-	4wPM	L	5142	1934	(a)	s/s by 9/1959
-	4wPM	L	8030	1936	New	s/s by 9/1959
-	4wPM	L	10839	1939	(b)	s/s by 9/1959

(a) New to Jolly & Son, Bath, who may have been a dealer purchasing on behalf of Wotton Bros; later here.
(b) Exhibited 17/2/1939 at British Industries Fair, Birmingham. Sold 1/4/1939 to Stanley Engineering Ltd , Bath, who were agents for Wotton Bros Ltd

WRITHLINGTON COLLIERIES CO. LTD.

The group comprised five major collieries, three of which used locomotives (below). The other two were Upper Writhlington (ST 699550) (closed c1/1898) and Huish (closed 2/1912).

Ref: 'The History of the Somerset Coalfield' by C.G.Down & A.J.Warrington; D&C

Foxcote Colliery, Radstock (Writhlington Colliery Co until 6/4/1897;

Writhlington, Huish & Foxcote Colliery Co by /1894; Foxcote Colliery Co until c /1890)

71   Colliery at ST 710553 connected to Lower Writhlington by a rope worked incline. Loco FOXCOTE worked coal trains from the depot to Turners Tower Coal Depot (ST 719538). Loco believed transfered to Lower Writhlington in c /1928 when the line to Turners Tower was closed and lifted. Colliery opened /1859; closed 2/1931.

Gauge: 2ft 8½in

FOXCOTE	0-6-0ST	OC	HC	369	1890	New	s/s

Kilmersdon Colliery, Radstock (Kilmersdon Colliery Co Ltd until 6/3/1924; Kilmersdon Colliery Co until 6/4/1897)

72   Colliery at ST 687538 served by standard gauge sidings via a cable worked incline to the GWR Radstock - Frome line at ST 694544. Colliery vested in the NCB, Division 7, Area 8 (which see) on 1/1/1947

Gauge: 4ft 8½in

KILMERSDON	0-4-0ST	OC	HC	464	1896	New	s/s
-	0-4-0ST	OC	P	1788	1929	New	(1)
ALBERT	0-6-0ST	?				(a)	(2)

(a) ex "The Docks, at Bristol" , loan, c/1936 (1) to NCB, Division 7, Area 8, 1/1/1947
                                   (2) ret to ? , off loan, c /1937

Lower Writhlington Colliery

73   Colliery at ST 705553. Originally served by the 3ft 2in gauge Somersetshire Coal Canal tramroad from Radstock to Midford. Standard gauge sidings off the S&DJR opened in 1886. The 2ft 8½in gauge lines connected the colliery with the incline up to Foxcote Colliery and also ran eastwards to the foot of another incline (serving Upper Writhlington Colliery, Frome Hill coal depot and sidings on the GWR Radstock - Frome line). Locomotives were only used between the colliery and the foot of the Foxcote and Frome Hill inclines. The 2ft 8½in gauge system was closed c /1940; the colliery was vested in the NCB, Division 7 Area 8 (which see) from 1/1/1947.

Gauge: 2ft 8½in

ENTERPRISE	0-4-0ST	IC	HE	279	1882	New	(1)
WRITHLINGTON	0-6-0ST	OC	HC	546	1900	New	(1)
-	0-4-0ST	OC	P	1546	1920	New	(1)

(1) Believed sold to William Evans, Writhlington Foundry (adjacent to the colliery) for scrap, c /1940

Non-locomotive systems

Letters A to H inclusive are used as location codes for installations operated without locomotives by the National Coal Board. Details are to be found of these sites on page H. 93.

ASHTON VALE COLLIERY & IRONWORKS, BRISTOL

J   A works area (ST 566716) owned by the Ashton Vale Iron Co Ltd ; blast furnaces were in operation by 1861 and a colliery in 1886- 1894. A tramway ran from these to a wharf on the River Avon at the New Cut (ST 568721). Tramway closed and partly dismantled by 1902.

AVONMOUTH LIGHT RAILWAY

K   A standard gauge railway ran from the GWR/Midland Railway Joint Bristol - Avonmouth line at ST 519777 to an electricity substation in St. Andrews Road, Avonmouth (ST 517785) owned by Bristol Corporation. Railway laid 1906, motive power not known. Closed.

AVON & GLOUCESTERSHIRE RAILWAY

L   4ft 8in gauge edge railway opened 7/1832 to carry coal from collieries in the Mangotsfield area, and from the Coalpit Heath area via the Bristol & Gloucestershire Railway (which see), south to Londonderry Wharf on the River Avon (ST 662698) and Keynsham (Avon) Wharf (ST 666694). Traffic was horse worked. Line taken over by the GWR 7/1851 and the northern part of the railway closed 1865. The section south of California Colliery (ST 666714) was closed 1904.

BRISTOL & GLOUCESTERSHIRE RAILWAY

M   4ft 8in gauge edge railway built to carry coal from the Coalpit Heath area to Avon Street Wharf, Bristol (ST 598726). A junction with the Avon & Gloucestershire Railway (which see) was at Mangotsfield (ST 672757). The section north of Mangotsfield opened 7/1832; the route south to Bristol opened 6/8/1835. Traffic was horse worked. The route between Bristol and Westerleigh was incorporated into the Bristol and Gloucester Railway and reopened as a broad gauge line 6/7/1844. It became part of the Midland Railway Bristol-Birmingham line in 1846. The remaining track in the Coalpit Heath area was retained for colliery traffic (see under Coalpit Heath Co Ltd)

FILTON LIMEKILN, BRISTOL

N   A narrow gauge tramway connected the limekiln (ST 613790) with a small quarry. Tramway closed and lifted.

HANHAM COLLIERY, BRISTOL

P   A colliery at ST 637720 operating by 1886, owned then by Leonard, Boult & Co Ltd. A narrow gauge tramway including a rope worked incline ran from this colliery to a wharf on the River Avon (ST 635718). Tramway closed and dismantled 1926.

LONDONDERRY LIMESTONE QUARRY, NEAR BRISTOL

Q   A 300-yard long narrow gauge tramway ran from the quarry at ST 663700 to a lime kiln by the River Avon. Line opened by 1902. Closed and dismantled.

OLD WOOD COLLIERY, RANGEWORTHY, NEAR YATE

R   A standard gauge railway ran from the Midland Railway Bristol- Birmingham line to a colliery at ST 703852. Colliery and railway closed by 1900.

PARADISE BOTTOM TRAMWAY, BRISTOL

S   A 2ft 0in gauge tramway, including a rope worked incline, was constructed in 1795 and was later owned by the Bristol Strontia Co. Used to transport celestine from pits at Leigh Court (ST 543745) to Miles Dock (ST 549752) on the River Avon. Tramway closed c /1912 and dismantled.

       Ref: IRR No.22 (12/1968), p.352

SHORTWOOD BRICKWORKS, BRISTOL

T   A long established brickworks (ST 680769) owned by the Shortwood Brick & Tile Co until taken over by the Cattybrook Brick Co Ltd in 1903. A ropeworked tramway of 1ft 6in gauge connected the quarry with the works. The works and tramway closed 6/1959 but remained intact for some time subsequently; the quarry remains open supplying clay to Almondsbury brickworks by road. Shortwood Colliery, in operation by 1894 and owned by the Shortwood Colliery Co Ltd , was adjacent to the brickworks and the tramway served this also until the 1920's.

YATE LIMEWORKS, NEAR BRISTOL

U   A one mile long tramway connected the limekilns (ST 705860) alongside the Midland Railway Bristol- Birmingham line with Yate Court Quarry (ST 718859) (closed by 1901) and a quarry at Bury Hill (ST 718855). Limeworks closed and tramway lifted c /1920.

YATE COLLIERIES, NEAR BRISTOL

V   Separate standard gauge branches from the Midland Railway Bristol- Birmingham line served No.1 Pit (ST 702836) and No.2 Pit (ST 701843). Narrow gauge tramways served and connected the two pits. The collieries were operating before 1854; later the .owners were Long, Nowell & Co (in 1869-1871 at least) and then F.H.Jones (by 1886). All railways and collieries were closed by 1901 (probably by 1894).

Contractors lines

JOHN AIRD & CO.

C1   Construction of the Royal Edward Dock, sheds and granary at Avonmouth for the Port of Bristol , 1902-8

Gauge:4ft 8½in

–	0-4-0ST	OC	MW	786	1881	(a)	(1)
507	0-6-0ST	IC	MW	1579	1902	New	(2)
508	0-6-0ST	IC	MW	1584	1902	New	(3)
6	0-6-0ST	IC	MW	1585	1902	New	(4)
28	0-6-0ST	IC	MW	1586	1902	New	(5)
509	0-4-0ST	OC	MW	1587	1902	New	(6)
510	0-4-0ST	OC	MW	1588	1902	New	(7)
30	0-6-0ST	IC	MW	1592	1902	New	(8)
36	0-6-0ST	IC	MW	1593	1902	New	s/s
138	0-6-0ST	IC	MW	1601	1903	New	(9)

Four other locos, details unknown, were used on this contract.

(a) ex Aswan contract, Egypt   (1) to Metropolitan Water Board, Battersea, London, /1914
          (2) to Topham, Jones & Railton Ltd , contrs , Crymlyn Burrows, Glam , 53
          (3) to Derwent Valley Water Board, Derbys , FRENCH
          (4) to Topham, Jones & Railton Ltd , contrs , Crymlyn Burrows, Glam , 52
          (5) later Caffin & Co Ltd , contrs
          (6) to Topham, Jones & Railton Ltd , contrs
          (7) to contract at Singapore
          (8) to WD , Palestine, 30 , c /1917
          (9) to Perry & Co (Bow) Ltd , contrs ; later to APCM Kent Works, Stone, Kent, ARTHUR

Additionally, two locomotives from this contract are believed to have been sold to John Wainwright & Co Ltd , Mells, Somerset, c /1908-10.

SIR WILLIAM ARROL & CO. LTD.

C2   Construction of Avonmouth Dock Extension for the Port of Bristol Authority, c /1924- .

Gauge: 4ft 8½in

FORTH	0-6-0ST	OC	AB	1844	1924	New	(1)
CLYDE	0-6-0ST	OC	AB	1845	1924	New	(2)
TOWER	0-6-0ST	OC	AB	1846	1924	New	(3)
TAY	0-4-0ST	OC	AB	1828	1924	New	(4)

(1) to C.J.Wills & Sons Ltd , contrs , Becontree, Essex
(2) to Thos W Ward Ltd , Sheffield, 38648
(3) to Thos W Ward Ltd , Sheffield, 38649
(4) to Smeed, Dean & Co Ltd , Highsted, Kent, /1927

BOVIS CIVIL ENGINEERING LTD. (A.E.Farr Ltd. until 1/1/1973)

C3   Construction of flood water relief tunnels at Headley Lane, Hartcliff Way,
      Bedminster, Bristol (ST 579697), 1972-5.

Gauge: 2ft 0in

-	4wBE	WR	4815		(a)	s/s
1	4wDM	HE	7270	1972	New	(1)
2	4wDM	HE	7271	1972	New	(1)
3	4wDM	HE	7272	1972	New	(1)
4	4wDM	HE	7273	1972	New	(1)
5	4wDM	HE	7312	1973	New	(1)
6	4wDM	HE	7313	1973	New	(1)
7	4wDM	HE	7317	1973	New	(1)
8	4wDM	HE	7320	1973	New	(1)
9	4wDM	HE	7321	1973	New	(1)

(a) ex Thyssens Ltd , contrs, hire   (1) to Westbury Station Plant Depot,
                                              Wilts , by 5/1976

C4   Contract, details unknown, with plant depot at Albion Road, Stapleton Road,
      Bristol, 1972-4

Gauge: 2ft 0in

-	4wDM	HE	7266	1972	New	(1)
-	4wDM	HE	7267	1972	New	(1)

                        (1) one loco to Westbury Station depot,
                            Wilts, the other to Lawrence Weston
                            Depot, Avonmouth

CHARLES BRAND & SON LTD.

C5   Construction of the tunnel for CEGB high voltage electricity cables under the
      Severn,   -1972. Depots at Aust (ST 573902) on the Avon bank of the river and
      at Beachley (ST 549903) and Newbridge (ST 538904) on the Chepstow bank.

Gauge: 2ft 0in

-	4wBE	WR	6761	1963	(a)	(1)
-	4wBE	WR	6762	1963	(a)	(1)
-	4wBE	WR	6763	1963	(a)	(1)
-	4wBE	WR	6764	1963	(a)	(1)
-	4wBE	WR	6765	1963	(a)	(1)
-	4wBE	WR	6766	1963	(a)	(2)
-	4wBE	WR	6767	1963	(a)	(1)
-	4wBE	WR	6768	1963	(a)	(1)
-	4wBE	WR	6806	1965	(a)	(1)
-	4wBE	WR	6807	1965	(a)	(2)

(a) ex Merton Plant Depot, London
    by 4/1971
                        (2) to Fleet Line tunnel contract for
                            London Transport, London, /1973
                        (1) later at Kier Ltd , Setchey Plant Depot,
                            near Kings Lynn, Norfolk , 5/1974

WILLIAM COWLIN & SON LTD.

C6   Construction of Portishead Power Station for the North Somerset Electric
      Supply Co Ltd , c /1926-9.

Gauge: 4ft 8½in

        PORTISHEAD   0-6-0ST IC MW   1134 1890 (a) (1)

(a) ex Weston, Clevedon & Portishead   (1) Scr by Pugsley after 2/1929
    Railway, 2 , /1926

        Contract at Portishead; possibly the same work as above.

Gauge: 2ft 0in

           -                    0-4-0ST OC KS   3090 1917 (a) (1)

(a) ex Balfour, Beatty & Co Ltd ,   (1) to Somerdale contract by 1/1931
    Kinlochleven contract, Argyllshire,
    by 8/1927

C7   Contract at J.S.Fry & Sons Ltd , Somerdale.

Gauge: 2ft 0in

           -                    0-4-0ST OC KS   3090 1917 (a) (1)

(a) ex Portishead contract by 3/1931   (1) later A.Waddington & Sons Ltd , contrs ,
                                          after 5/1931

CHAS. DANIEL

C8   Contract at Portishead.

Gauge: 4ft 8½in

                        0-6-0ST IC MW   16 1860 (a) s/s
        FAREHAM   0-6-0ST IC MW   51 1862 (b) s/s

(a) ex J.T.Leather, Waterloo Main Colliery, Leeds, Yorks, WR
(b) ex T. & C.Walker, Somerset & Dorset Railway contract, c /1874
    (May not have been to this contract)

EAGRE CONSTRUCTION CO. LTD.

C9   Reinstatement and relaying of the BR Yate- Thornbury line to renew rail access
      to ARC Tytherington Quarry, 1972-3.

Gauge: 4ft 8½in

        ALFRED HENSHALL   0-4-0DM   RH 313392 1952 (a) (1)

(a) ex Scunthorpe Depot, 4/1972; f North   (1) ret to Scunthorpe Depot, /1973
    Western Gas Board, Denton, Lancs

LOGAN & HEMINGWAY

C10 Construction of Dry Dock for Chas Hill & Son, Bristol, c /1883.

Gauge: 4ft 8½in

		ST	MW				s/s

H. LOVATT & CO. LTD.

C11 Construction of the GWR Avonmouth- Filton line, 1907-10.

Gauge: 4ft 8½in

	0-6-0ST	IC	MW	817	1881	(a)	s/s

(a) ex Lucas & Aird , contrs

MEAKIN & DEAN

C12 Construction of the Blagdon Reservoir for the Bristol Waterworks Co.

Gauge: 4ft 8½in

-	0-6-0ST	IC	MW	21	1861	(a)	(1)
-	0-4-0ST	OC	BP	1736	1877	(New?)	(2)

(a) ex Birkenhead contract, Cheshire

(1) to Hundred of Manhood and Selsey
Tramway, Sussex, 2 SIDLESHAM, /1907
(2) to Farrington Collieries Co , Somerset,
(possibly by /1885)

SIR ROBERT McALPINE & SONS LTD.

C13 Construction of the Brabazon Runway, Filton, Bristol for Bristol Aeroplane Co Ltd , 1946-7

Gauge: 4ft 8½in

No.40	0-6-0ST	IC	HC	1525	1924	(a)	(1)
No.74	0-6-0ST	IC	HC	1669	1936	(b)	(2)
No.82	0-6-0ST	IC	HC	1674	1937	(c)	(3)
No.92	0-6-0ST	IC	HC	1697	1938	(a)	(4)
No.200	0-6-0ST	IC	HC	1749	1946	New	(4)
No.201	0-6-0ST	IC	HC	1750	1946	New	(4)

(a) ex Great Stanney Depot, Cheshire
(b) ex Caerwent contract, Mon
(c) ex Gloucester contract

(1) to Great Stanney Depot, Cheshire,
after 8/1946
(2) to Hayes Depot, Middx , after 8/1946
(3) to Hayes Depot, Middx, /1947
(4) to Great Stanney Depot, Cheshire,
after 8/1946 and by 4/1948

MITCHELL & THOMPSON

C14 Construction of extension to Avonmouth Dock, Port of Bristol, 1891-4.

Gauge: 2ft 7¾in

-	0-4-0ST	OC	AB	702	1891	New	(1)

(1) for sale, 26/7/1894

NOTT, BRODIE & CO. LTD.

C15   Construction of Bristol to Avonmouth Portway road, 1922–

Gauge: 4ft 8½in

TRANMERE	0-6-0ST	IC	HC	654	1903	(a)	(1)
SHARPNESS	0-6-0T	IC	SS	3472	1888	(b)	s/s

(a) ex Beaufort contract, Mon   (1) to Shirehampton Plant Depot
(b) ex Ministry of Munitions, f Sir John
     Jackson, contr

Gauge: 2ft 0in

–	0-6-0WT	OC	HC	1314	1918	(a)	(1)
TATTOO	0-4-2ST	OC	KS			(b)	(2)
OLD BILL	(0-4-2ST	OC	KS?)			(b)	(3)

(a) ex WDLR 3204   (1) to P & W Anderson Ltd, North Devon &
(b)(ex Beaufort contract, Mon?)   Cornwall Light Railway construction,
         Devon
        (2) to Shirehampton Depot
        (3) s/s after 8/1930

C16   Reconstruction of Parson Street Station for GWR, Bristol, 1932

Gauge: 4ft 8½in

C.J.WILLS 28	0-6-0ST	IC	HC	671	1904	(a)	(1)

(a) orig C.J.Wills, contrs   (1) to Shirehampton Depot,

C17   Shirehampton Plant Depot

Gauge: 4ft 8½in

15	TRANMERE	0-6-0ST	IC	HC	654	1903	(a)	(1)
27	TRYM	0-4-0ST	OC	HE	287	1883	(b)	(2)
	C.J.WILLS 28	0-6-0ST	IC	HC	671	1904	(c)	(3)
	JOHN	0-6-0ST	IC	HC	327	1889		
			Reb	HC		1908	(d)	(2)
26	AVON	0-6-0T	IC	MW	1005	1887	(e)	(4)
	BATTLE	0-6-0ST	IC	MW	1392	1898	(g)	s/s
29	DYNEVOR	0-6-0ST	IC	MW	1726	1908	(f)	(2)

(a) ex Avonmouth contract; to E.Nuttall Sons   (1) to Adams, Nuttall, Notts
     & Co, contrs , Bartley, Worcs , hire;   (2) to Sir Robert McAlpine & Sons Ltd ,
     & ret   Otterspool, Lancs
(b) ex H. Arnold & Son, conts   (3) to Vauxhall Motors Ltd , Luton Works,
(c) ex Parson Street Station contract,   Beds , /1941
     Bristol   (4) to Furness Shipbuilding Co Ltd ,
(d) ex Price, Wills & Reeves, contrs,   Haverton Hill, Co.Durham
     BROMBOROUGH
(e) ex Pauling & Co Ltd , contrs
(f) ex Topham, Jones & Railton Ltd , contrs,
     Crymlyn Burrows, Glam , 36
(g) orig John Price, Crowhurst Park Siding,
     Sussex

THOMAS OLIVER

C18 Construction of Barrow Gurney Reservoirs for the Bristol Waterworks Co ,1885-8

Gauge: 4ft 8½in

ANNIE	0-4-0ST	OC	HE	17	1866	(a)	(1)
NELLIE	0-4-0ST	OC	HE	29	1868	(a)	(1)
FRED	0-4-0ST	OC	HE	137	1875	(a)	(1)

(a) ex Lawrence Hill contract, Bristol   (1) to Dore & Chinley Railway construction
                                                      contract, Derbys

C19   Contract for GWR at Lawrence Hill, Bristol, c /1883-7 (?).

Gauge: 4ft 8½in

ANNIE	0-4-0ST	OC	HE	17	1866	(a)	(1)
NELLIE	0-4-0ST	OC	HE	29	1868	(a)	(1)
FRED	0-4-0ST	OC	HE	137	1875	(a)	(1)
WILLIE	0-6-0ST	IC	HE	65	1871	(a)	(2)
FRANK	0-6-0ST	IC	HE	161	1876	(a)	(2)
NENE	0-6-0ST	IC	HE	242	1881	(a)	(2)
FLORENCE	0-6-0ST	OC	BH	466	1878	(a)	(2)
GIBBON	0-6-0ST	IC	HE	545	1891	(New?)	(2)

(a) ex Wellingborough contract, Northants   (1) to Barrow Gurney contract
                                             (2) to Dore & Chinley Railway construction
                                                     contract, Derbys

PAULING & ELLIOTT

C20   Construction of the Limpley Stoke- Dunkerton branch for the GWR, 1908-10

Gauge: 4ft 8½in

26	TYERSALL	0-6-0ST	IC	MW	1068	1888	(a)	(1)
56	NORTHOLT	0-6-0ST	IC	MW	1555	1902	(a)	(2)

(a) ex Northolt Jct-High Wycombe construction (1) to Greenford contract; later to
    contract   J.Lyons & Co Ltd , Greenford,
                                                      /1919
                                              (2) to Freshwater, Yarmouth & Newport
                                                      Railway, IoW, 2 , /1913

C21   Construction of the Patchway - Wootton Bassett main line (33 miles) for the GWR, 1897-1903.

Gauge: 4ft 8½in

22	WOODSIDE	0-6-0ST	IC	HE	266	1881	(a)	s/s
	HAROLD	0-4-0ST	OC	HE	400	1886	(b)	(1)
	CHESTERFIELD	0-6-0ST	IC	HE	571	1892	(a)	(2)
10	CLIVE	0-6-0ST	OC	HE	573	1893	(c)	(3)
13	TRUDY	0-6-0ST	OC	HE	574	1893	(c)	(4)
15	LINCOLN	0-6-0ST	IC	HE	578	1893	(c)	(5)
	TUXFORD	0-6-0ST	IC	HE	579	1893	(c)	(6)
	GEOFFREY	0-6-0ST	OC	HE	581	1893	(a)	(7)
11	BOLSOVER	0-6-0ST	IC	HE	584	1894	(a)	(8)
	SPINKHILL	0-6-0ST	IC	HE	585	1894	(a)	(9)
	FRANCIS	0-6-0T	IC	HE	586	1894	(a)	s/s
	BERNARD	0-6-0T	IC	HE	587	1894	(a)	(5)
	ANNIE	0-6-0ST	OC	HE	593	1893	(a)	(10)
	ERNEST	0-6-0ST	OC	HE	594	1893	(d)	(11)
	ABERAVON	0-6-0T	IC	HE	607	1895	(c)	(12)
46	SCARCLIFFE	0-6-0ST	IC	HE	625	1895	(a)	(13)
51	RUSSIA	0-6-0ST	IC	HE	626	1895	(c)	(11)
	MAESTEG	0-6-0ST	IC	HE	627	1895	(c)	(7)
	DICK	0-4-0ST	OC	HE	628	1895	(c)	(14)
	TORPEDO	0-4-0ST	OC	P	449	1886	(a)	s/s
	SAM	0-4-0ST	OC	HC	444	1895	(e)	(15)
	TALBOT	0-4-0ST	OC	MW	1279	1895	(c)	(16)
	JACK	0-4-0ST	OC	MW	1300	1895	(c)	s/s
	GARTH	0-6-0ST	IC	MW	1302	1895	(c)	(17)
39	MARGAM	0-4-0ST	OC	MW	1306	1895	(c)	(18)
66	FILTON	0-4-0ST	OC	P	690	1898	New	(10)
67	GEORGE	0-4-0ST	OC	P	729	1898	New	(19)
68	FRANK	0-4-0ST	OC	P	730	1898	New	(20)
69	YATE	0-6-0ST	OC	P	718	1898	New	(21)
70	CHIPPING SODBURY	0-6-0ST	OC	P	719	1898	New	(7)
71	SOMERFORD	0-6-0ST	OC	P	720	1898	New	(7)
72	BADMINTON	0-6-0ST	OC	P	721	1898	New	(7)
73	WOOTTON BASSETT	0-6-0ST	OC	P	722	1898	New	s/s
74	PATCHWAY	0-6-0ST	OC	P	723	1898	New	(22)
	URMSTON	0-4-0ST	OC	HE	450	1888	(f)	(23)
81	THE AUDITOR	0-6-0ST	OC	CF	1105	1895	(g)	(7)
	-	0-6-0ST	IC	HE	63	1871	(h)	(24)
	CORSTON	0-6-0T	IC	MW	1196	1890	(j)	(7)
	SULLY	0-4-0ST	OC	HE	367	1885	(k)	(25)
133		0-6-0ST	IC	MW	595	1877	(m)	s/s
84	SALTBURN	0-6-0ST	OC	BH	511	1883	(m)	s/s
	ANNIE	0-4-0ST	OC	MW	1135	1891	(n)	(18)

Approximately fifty locomotives were used on this contract. Subsequently, the first sale of plant, held at Sodbury Tunnel, on 8/7/1902 included thirty locos. The second sale, on 11/11/1902, included eleven locos and the third sale, held at the contractors yard, Wapley, near Yate (Midland Railway) on 13/3/1903 included seven locos.

Sixteen of the locos were sold to C.D.Phillips, dealer, Newport, Mon.

(a) ex contract for Chesterfield- Warsop railway construction, Derbys
(b) ex contract for Langwith- Beighton railway construction, Derbys
(c) ex contract for Maesteg- Port Talbot railway construction, Glam

(1) to contract for Queens Dock branch construction, Liverpool
(2) to Fison, Packard & Prentice, Burwell, Cambs
(3) to P.Baker & Co, c /1902
(4) to Morrison & Mason, /1903

(d) ex contract for Lambourne Valley
    railway construction, Berks
(e) ex Contract for Cardiff Graving Dock
    construction, Glam
(f) ex Bispham Brick & Tile Co , Lancs
(g) ex Walter Scott & Middleton, contrs,
    Heaton Mersey, Cheshire
(h) ex T.M.Brown , /1899
(j) ex Logan & Hemingway, contrs , Renishaw
    Derbys , 22
(k) ex J.S.Peters, Merstham Lime Quarry,
    Surrey, c /1899
(m) ex Walter Scott & Middleton, contrs
(n) f Pethick Bros , contrs

(5) to Kirk & Randall, contrs, c /1902
(6) to L.P.Nott, contrs , Birkenhead, Ches
(7) to contract for Dover Harbour breakwater
    construction
(8) to William Moss & Sons, /1902; later
    Thos W.Ward, Sheffield, 17428
(9) to United Alkali Co Ltd , /1902
(10) to J.F.Wake, dealer, Darlington,c /1903
(11) to contract for King George V Dock
    construction, Hull
(12) to Moss Bay Iron & Steel Co Ltd ,
    Cumbs , 9 , /1903
(13) to contract for Finsbury Park –
    Moorgate railway construction,
    London
(14) to contract for Seaham Harbour New
    Dock construction; then to Seaham
    Harbour Dock Co Ltd , Co.Durham
(15) to Aitken & Morcom, Pontypridd, Glam
(16) to London County Council, Barking,
    Essex
(17) to Hutchinson & Co , contrs, Leek
    Brook, Staffs
(18) to West Thurrock Depot, Essex
(19) to Jas Byrom, Heaton Park contract,
    Manchester; later to Hardwick
    Colliery Co , Derbys
(20) to P & W McLellan, S.America, /1906
(21) to contract overseas ?
(22) to C.D.Phillips, dealer, Newport, Mon ,
    /1903; later to Electrode Alkali Co
    Ltd , Middlewich, Cheshire
(23) to contract for Seaham Harbour New
    Dock construction; later to MoM
    Gretna Factory, Dumfries
(24) to Mackay & Davies, contrs , c /1902
(25) to Pauling & Co Ltd , contrs

J. PERRY & CO.

C22   Construction of the Bristol & North Somerset railway,   –1873
Gauge: ?

0-6-0ST	(1)
0-6-0ST	(1)

(1) for sale at Hallatrow, on completion of
    contract, 22/7/1873

C23   Construction of the Severn Tunnel for the GWR,   1879-85.

Gauge: 7ft 0¼in

		0-6-0	IC	Sdn		1848	(a)	s/s

(a) ex Severn Tunnel Railway, /1879 ;
     f GWR, CALIBAN

Gauge: 4ft 8½in

	-	2-2-2		Charles Tayleur,				
				Vulcan Foundry	1845	(a)	s/s	
	SEVERN	0-6-0ST	IC	MW	746	1880	New	(1)
	SUDBROOK	0-6-0ST	IC	MW	891	1883	(b)	(2)

(a) ex GWR, 115 , /1876   (1) to Manchester Ship Canal Co , Lancs
(b) ex T.Nelson, contr , by /1887   (2) to Topham, Jones & Railton Ltd ,
                                         contrs

T. & C.WALKER

C24   Construction of the Somerset & Dorset Railway extension, Evercreech Jct-
         Bath, 1872-4.

Gauge: 4ft 8½in

BORTH	0-6-0ST	IC	MW	66	1863	(a)	(1)
FAREHAM	0-6-0ST	IC	MW	51	1862	(b)	(2)
	0-6-0ST	IC	Worcester Engine Co				(3)
	0-6-0ST	OC	FW				(3)
	0-6-0ST	IC	?				(3)
	0-4-0ST	OC	?				(3)

(a) ex Henry Jackson, c /1872; orig   (1) later T.Docwra & Son, contrs,
    T.Savin, BORTH, working of Cambrian   Rotherhithe, London
    Railway   (2) to Chas Daniels, contr , (at Portishead
(b) ex William Tredwell, contr ,   ?)
    Portsdown Hill Forts contract,   (3) Offered at auction, 11/8/1874
    Fareham, Hants, c /1872

WARING BROS.

C25   Construction and working of the Clifton (Hotwells) - Avonmouth railway for
         Bristol Port Railway & Pier , -1869.

Gauge: 4ft 8½in

	0-4-2T	IC	St Helens	1856	(a)	(1)
	0-4-2T	IC	St Helens	1853	(b)	(1)

(a) ex J.Cross & Co , ST Helens, Lancs,   (1) to Bristol Port Railway & Pier , /1869
    orig LNWR 1370 (reb Cross from 0-4-2)
(b) ex J.Cross & Co, St Helens, Lancs,
    orig LNWR 1389

WELDON & CO. (of Birmingham)

C26   Contract at St Phillips Station, Bristol, -1904, and at Congresbury Goods Yard.
Gauge: ?

0-4-0ST	(1)
0-6-0ST	(1)

(1) for sale, 18/2/1904

UNKNOWN CONTRACTOR (Possibly W.Jackson)

C27   Construction of the Weston, Clevedon & Portishead Railway, 1896-7
Gauge: 4ft 8½in

0-4-0ST						s/s
0-6-0T	IC	RS	2383	1880	(a)	(1)

(a) ex W.Jackson, contr, Freshwater,   (1) to Weston, Clevedon & Portishead
    Yarmouth & Newport Railway construction,   Railway, No.3 PORTISHEAD
    IoW

UNKNOWN CONTRACTOR

C28   Construction of the Camerton - Limpley Stoke branch for the GWR, c /1908
Gauge: ?

Six locomotives in use on this contract, 7/1908

UNKNOWN CONTRACTOR

C29   Construction of Bristol & Gloucester Railway, 1842-4.
Gauge: 7ft 0¼in

0-6-0	IC	Charles Tayleur,				
		Vulcan Foundry	163	1842	New	s/s
0-6-0	IC	Charles Tayleur,				
		Vulcan Foundry	164	1842	New	s/s

Dorset

Locomotive worked systems

ADMIRALTY   (See also Ministry of Defence, Navy Department for installations operating
rail systems after 1/4/1964)

Inland Waterways & Docks, Poole

1   Admiralty operated harbour installations, 1918-1920 period.

Gauge: 4ft 8½in

-	0-4-0ST	OC	KS	3123	1918	New	(1)

(1) to Inland Waterways & Docks, Portsmouth,
Hants

Royal Naval Cordite Factory, Holton Heath

2   A large factory and storage depot on the north side of the BR (ex LSWR) line
between Hamworthy and Wareham. Served by standard gauge sidings and an
extensive narrow gauge system. A line also ran alongside BR for about a mile,
crossing over this to serve a jetty in the Wareham Channel at SY 971908. The
factory was opened by 1914; closed and normal rail traffic ceased c /1961.
Part of the site was used by the Decca Record Co Ltd (which see), the remainder
being dismantled during 1963. Additionally the Material Laboratory section of
the works remained with the Admiralty for some time and some locomotives were
retained, and occasionally used, in this section after the main closure. The
site was almost fully cleared by 1967.

Gauge: 4ft 8½in

R.N.C.F. No.3		0-6-0ST	IC	MW	1228	1895	(a)	(1)	
R.N.C.F. No.4		0-6-0ST	IC	MW	1620	1903	(b)	(2)	
R.N.C.F. No.3		0-4-0ST	OC	AE	1976	1925	New	(4)	
No.16		0-4-0ST	OC	HL	3360	1918	(c)	(3)	
YARD No.1596		0-4-0ST	OC	WB	2596	1938	New	(6)	
YARD No.1627	RELIANCE	0-6-0ST	IC	HE	1659	1930			
		Reb		HE		1938	(d)	Scr	3/1963
		2-2-0PMR		Bg	3017	1938	New	s/s	
YARD No.1339		4wDM		RH	207103	1941	(e)	(5)	

(a) orig Walter Scott & Co , contrs ,
Quainton Road, Bucks, J.R.WRIGHT
(b) ex Walter Scott & Middleton Ltd ,
(Ashendon-Aynho (GWR) contract,Oxon ?)
(c) ex Portsmouth Dockyard, Hants
(d) ex HE , c6/1938; prev Haifa Harbour
Works Department, Palestine,
H.H.W.D. No.11
(e) ex Ministry of Aircraft Production,
Morris Motors Ltd factory, Cowley,
Oxon

(1) s/s after 11/1917
(2) to Chatham Dockyard, Kent, /1925
(3) to Stephenson Clarke & Associated Co.s
Ltd , Poole, c /1935
(4) to ROF Creekmoor, c /1950
(5) to Wrabness Depot, Essex, c /1953
(6) to George Cohen Sons & Co Ltd , Northam
Ironworks Depot, Southampton, Hants,
c /1961

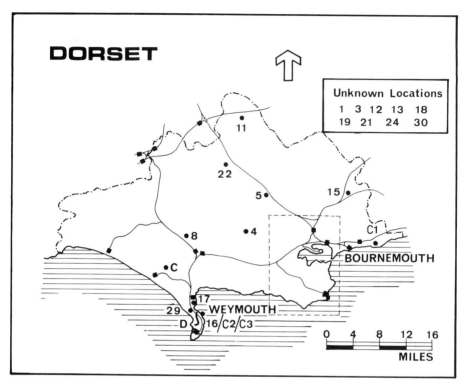

DORSET

Unknown Locations
1 3 12 13 18
19 21 24 30

11

22

5

15

8

4

C1

C

BOURNEMOUTH

17

29 WEYMOUTH

D 16/C2/C3

0 4 8 12 16

MILES

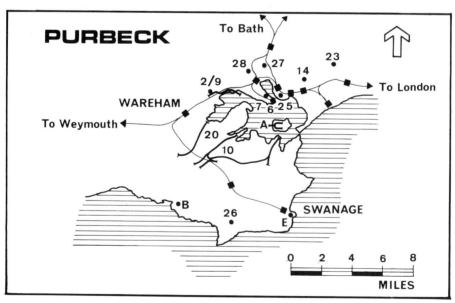

PURBECK

To Bath

28 27

23

14

2/9

WAREHAM

To London

7 6 2 5

To Weymouth

A

20

10

B

26

SWANAGE

E

0 2 4 6 8

MILES

Gauge: 2ft 6in

No.	Name / Yard	Type		Builder	Works No.	Year		Note
1		0-2-4F	OC	AB	1474	1916	New	s/s
2		0-2-4F	OC	AB	1475	1916	New	s/s
–		0-4-0PM		RP	52124	1918	New	(1)
–		4wDM		RH	168829	1933	New	s/s
–		4wDM		RH	168830	1933	New	s/s
–		4wDM		FH	2337	1940	New	(3)
–		4wDM		RH	246794	1947	New	(2)
	YARD No.2066	4wDM		RH	246795	1947	New	(3)
1		4wBE		Electromobile				(3)
2		4wBE		GB	1103	1928	New	(3)
3		4wBE		GB	1102	1928	New	(3)
4	YARD No.1201	4wBE		GB	1139	1929	New	(3)
5		4wBE		GB	1140	1929	New	(3)
6	YARD No.1208	4wBET		GB	480			(3)
7		4wBET		GB	481			(3)
8	YARD No.1210	4wBET		GB	482			(3)
9	YARD No.1211	4wBET		GB	483			(3)
10	YARD No.1212	4wBET		GB	484			(3)
11	YARD No.1213	4wBET		GB	485			(3)
12		4wBE		GB	1220	1931	New	(3)
13		4wBE		GB	1221	1931	New	(3)
14	YARD No.1479	4wBET		RS&J	2145			(3)
15	YARD No.1381	4wBET		W&B				(3)
21	YARD No.1372	4wBE		GB	1455			(3)
22	YARD No.1573	4wBE		WR	1195	1938		(3)
23	YARD No.1574	4wBE		WR	1194	1938		(3)
24	YARD No.1570	4wBET		GB	853			(3)
25	YARD No.1571	4wBET		GB	854			(3)
26	YARD No.1572	4wBET		GB	855			(3)
27		4wBET		GB	3183			(3)
28		4wBET		GB	3184			(3)
29		4wBE		GB	1867	1943	New	(4)
30		4wBE		GB	1975	1944	New	(4)
31	YARD No.2001	4wBET		GB	3281			(3)

(1) to Pounds Shipowners & Shipbreakers
    Ltd , Hants, c /1956; to B. Clifford,
    London, for preservation, 4/1974
(2) to RNAD Ernesettle, Devon, c /1956
(3) to Bowman,
    for scrap, c /1961
(4) to Decca Record Co Ltd , Holton Heath

F.J.BARNES LTD., PORTLAND QUARRIES

3   System served quarries, location uncertain. Quarries closed and track lifted.

Gauge: 2ft 0in

Name	Type		Builder	Works No.	Year		
EXCELSIOR	0-4-2 T	OC	WB	970	1888	(a)	s/s

(a) ex J.Nuttall, Lynton & Barnstaple Railway
    construction , Devon, c /1898; orig
    C.J.Naylor, Kerry, Montgomeryshire

BEDFORD & JESTY LTD., WATERCRESS GROWERS (Bedford & Jesty until 1937; William Bedford until 1920)

Ref: NGI No.60 (Spring 1972), p.4

Doddings Farm, Bere Regis

4   Narrow gauge line laid c /1919 from watercress beds (SY 852934) to a packing shed at the farm (SY 852937). Later considerably extended across fields to a new packing shed near Bere Regis village at SY 848946, to give a total length of about one mile.

Gauge: 1ft 6in

–		4wPM		(Lott & Walne?)	c1928	New(a)	s/s
–		4wPM		(Lott & Walne?)	c1930	New(a)	s/s
–		4wPM		(Lott & Walne?)	c1930	New(b)	s/s
No.2	EXPRESS	4wPM		B.J.Fry	c1936	New(c)	(1)
–		4wPM		Jesty	1948	New(c)	
		4-2-2	OC	Regent St.Poly.	1898	(d)	

(a) Dodge engine
(b) Rover 8 engine
(c) Austin 7 engine
(d) Preserved locomotive; ex ? , Ipswich,
    c /1970

(1) Parts,including engine, used in the Jesty loco; remainder scr on site, 3/1961

Spetisbury Watercress Beds

5   A line of length about ¼ mile runs from packing sheds (ST 907029) to watercress beds also on the south west side of the A350 road and BR (ex S&DJR) rail route between Blandford and Poole.

Gauge: 1ft 6in

–	4wPMT	Jesty	c1964 New

CORRALL LTD. (Subsidiary of P.D.Fuels Ltd.)(Southern Wharves Ltd until 1/10/1962; prev Stephenson Clarke & Associated Companies Ltd ; orig Hamworthy Wharf & Coal Co Ltd)

Ballast Wharf, Hamworthy

6   A coal wharf at Poole Harbour (SZ 010901) served by sidings at the end of the BR (ex LSWR) Hamworthy goods branch.

Gauge: 4ft 8½in

No. 4	IRIS	0-4-0ST	OC	WB	1496	1896	(a)	(1)
No.16	LITTLE AUDREY	0-4-0ST	OC	HL	3360	1918	(b)	(1)
No. 1	BONNIE PRINCE CHARLIE	0-4-0ST	OC	RSH	7544	1949	New	(2)
No. 2	WESTERN PRIDE	0-4-0ST	OC	RSH	7645	1949	New	(3)
–		4wDM		FH	2054	1938	(c)	
(1136)		4wDM		RH	242867	1946	(d)	

(a) ex Admiralty, Portland Dockyard, c /1929
    via C.J.Smith, dealer, Hamworthy
(b) ex Admiralty, Royal Naval Cordite
    Factory, Holton Heath, c /1935
(c) ex Southern Gas Board, Poole Gasworks,
    c /1966
(d) ex Southern Gas Board, Poole Gasworks,
    2/1973

(1) Scr on site by Baker (of Southampton),
    /1950
(2) to Dible's Wharf, Northam, Southampton,
    Hants , 9/1965
(3) to Pollock Brown & Co Ltd , Northam,
    Hants, for scrap, 3/1966

Railway Wharf, Hamworthy

7 A small quayside installation west of Ballast Wharf at SZ 006902. A siding from the BR (ex LSWR) Hamworthy goods branch served this wharf and oil storage sidings.

Gauge: 4ft 8½in

(EDITH)		4wPM	MH	33	1927	New	s/s	c /1966

CROCKWAY LIGHT RAILWAY GROUP, CROCKWAY FARM, FRAMPTON, NEAR DORCHESTER

8 A private narrow gauge preservation group constructing an operating line (SY 613959). Until c5/1973 the group, then known as the Creekmoor Light Railway Group, were working at a site at Creekmoor, Poole (SY 999941).

Gauge: 2ft 0in

No.1	SAMSON	4wDM		FH	1887	1934	(a)
No.2	DELILAH	4wDM		MR	9778	1953	(a)
No.3	BRUNEL	4wDM		RH	179880	1936	(b)
No.4	DAVID	4wDM		MR	8644	1941	(c)
	FOJO	0-6-0WT	OC	OK	9239		(d)

(a) ex Upton Brickworks Ltd , near Poole, c12/1968
(b) ex L.W.Vass Ltd ,dealer, Ampthill, Beds ,
       12/1969
(c) ex Pollock, Brown & Co Ltd , Northam,
       Hants , 5/1971
(d) ex Empresa Carbonifera do Douro,
       Portugal, per A.M.Keef, Oxon , 8/1972

DECCA RECORD CO LTD., HOLTON HEATH

9 Factory established on part of the site of the Admiralty Royal Naval Cordite Factory, served by a tramway taken over with the site. Rail traffic ceased and track lifted c /1961.

Gauge: 2ft 6in

D1	DECCA No.1	4wBE		GB	1975	1944	(a)	(1)
	DECCA No.2	4wBE		GB	1867	1943	(a)	(1)

(a) ex Admiralty, Holton Heath   (1) to Bowman,
                                              for scrap, c /1961

E.C.C. BALL CLAYS LTD., NORDEN CLAY MINES, CORFE CASTLE (Pike Bros, Fayle & Co Ltd
until c8/1970 (subsidiary of English China Clays Ltd from 1967); B.Fayle & Co Ltd
until 29/4/1949; prev B.Fayle & Co from foundation in 1795)

10   A line of 3ft 9in gauge was opened about 1806 to connect clay pits at Norden
(SY 950828 approx) with a quay at Middlebere Creek (SY 975865) three miles away.
Another short line was opened about 1868 and ran from Newton Heath (SZ 005845
approx) to Goathorn Pier (SZ 016864). About 1900 the Middlebere line was
abandoned and replaced by a new line from Norden to Goathorn. The section from
Goathorn to a point just east of the exchange sidings with the SR (ex LSWR)
Wareham- Swanage branch (SY 957828) was disused from 1936, leaving about four
miles of lines in use in the Norden area. In 1948 this remaining system was
relaid to 1ft 11½in gauge and new motive power introduced, remaining in use
until c /1968. Then road transport was introduced and most of the track had
been lifted by 1969. The loco shed was at SY 958829, while diesel locos were
also left near a tipping dock at SY 952827.

Ref: 'The Railways of Purbeck' by R.W.Kidner; Oakwood Press, 1973

Gauge: 3ft 9in

"TINY" (f. CORFE)	0-4-0T	OC	Lewin		1868		Scr 11/1948
THAMES	0-4-0ST	OC	MW	1552	1902	(a)	(1)

(a) ex London County Council, Barking   (1) Sold for scrap, 9/1948
    Outfall, Essex, THAMES (rebuilt
    from 3ft 6in gauge) via J.Stiff &
    Sons, London, 5/1909

Gauge: 1ft 11½in

RUSSELL	2-6-2T*	OC	HE	901	1906	(a)	(1)
–	0-4-0DM		OK	20777	1936	(b)	(3)
–	0-4-0DM		OK	21160	1938	(b)	(3)
–	4wDM		RH	175413	1936	(c)	(2)
–	4wDM		RH	179889	1936	(d)	(2)
–	4wPM		MR			(e)	Scr c /1961
–	4wDM		MR	5242	1930	(f)	Scr c /1967
–	4wDM		RH	392117	1956	(g)	(3)

  * Soon altered here to 0-6-2T owing to trouble with the leading pony truck

(a) ex Brymbo Steel Co Ltd , Hook Norton,   (1) purchased by the Birmingham Locomotive
    Oxon, /1948   Club and to the Talyllyn Railway,
(b) ex Bungey, Hayes;   Narrow Gauge Museum, Towyn, Merioneth,
(c) ex Hine Bros.(Ringwood) Ltd , Gillingham 8/1955
    Pits   (2) to A.M.Keef, Bampton, Oxon, 8/1972
(d) ex Severn River Catchment Board   (3) to Hampshire Light Railway Society &
(e) ex Standard Steel Co Ltd , dealers,   Museum Co Ltd , Durley, Hants, 11/1972
    Croydon, Surrey
(f) ex Furzebrook Clay Mines, 10/1959
    (converted to 1ft 11½in gauge from
    2ft 8in gauge at Furzebrook, /1959)
(g) ex Charles Brand & Son Ltd , contrs,
    Merton Depot, Surrey, c /1961

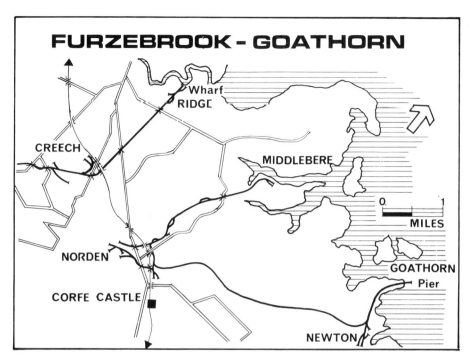

FURZEBROOK - GOATHORN

Wharf
RIDGE
CREECH
MIDDLEBERE
0 1
MILES
NORDEN
GOATHORN
Pier
CORFE CASTLE
NEWTON

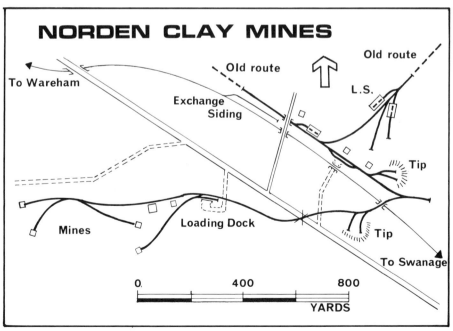

NORDEN CLAY MINES

To Wareham
Old route
Old route
Exchange
Siding
L.S.
Tip
Mines
Loading Dock
Tip
To Swanage
0 400 800
YARDS

GILLINGHAM POTTERY, BRICK & TILE CO.LTD., GILLINGHAM

11   A line some 200 yards long ran from pits on the east side of the B3092 road
      which it tunnelled under to reach the works at ST 809259. Works closed and
      railway dismantled.

Gauge: 2ft 0in

-	4wDM	RH	189972	1938	New	(1)
-	4wDM	MR	2059	1920	(a)	(2)
-	4wPM	OK	4470	c1931		(3)

(a) ex Hendre-ddu Slate Quarries Ltd ,   (1) to Moor Park Venture Scout Group,
    Merioneth, c /1939   Farnham, Surrey, 2/1971 (prop rty
                                                    of P.Briddon)
                                             (2) to Robin Pearman, Potters Bar, Herts
                                                    2/1971, for preservation
                                             (3) to Brockham Museum, Surrey, 2/1971
                                                    for preservation (property of
                                                    P.D.Nicholson)

HINE BROS. (RINGWOOD) LTD.

Gillingham Pits

12   Pits served by a narrow gauge tramway. Site closed by 1959 and system dismantled.

Gauge: 1ft 11½in

-	4wDM	RH	166032	1933	New	(1)
-	4wDM	RH	175413	1936	New	(2)
-	4wDM	RH	211678	1942	New	s/s

(1) to Lytchett Brick Co Ltd , Upton
(2) to Pike Bros , Fayle & Co Ltd , Corfe
       Castle

Binnegar Pits, Wareham

13   Pits served by a tramway abandoned c /1948, although the pits remained in use
      until after 1960.

Gauge: 2ft 0in

-	4wPM	Hine Bros.		s/s c /1962

GEORGE JENNINGS, SOUTH WESTERN POTTERY, PARKSTONE (Subsidiary of Thos. Wragg & Sons Ltd)

14   Works at SZ 037908 served by a standard gauge line about ¼ mile long from
Parkstone station (BR, ex LSWR). The narrow gauge system connected the clay
pits to the works. By 1967 all track had been removed and the premises were
for sale.

Gauge: 4ft 8½in

–		0-4-0ST	OC	FW	159	1872	New	(1)
GEORGE JENNINGS		0-4-0ST	OC	P	528	1893	New	(2)
GEORGE JENNINGS		0-4-0ST	OC	P	920	1902	New	(3)

(1) to G.Palmer, contr , /1893
(2) to P , /1902, in part payment for P 920;
resold to Hutchinson & Co, contrs,
Leek Brook, Staffs
(3) to W.Turner, Parkstone, 25/11/1963 for
preservation, but scr on site, /1966

Gauge: 2ft 0in

–	4wPM	FH				s/s c /1966
–	4wPM	L	3355	1930	New	s/s c /1966
–	4wBE	VE	6712	1948	New	s/s c /1966
–	4wDM	FH	3790	1956	New	(1)

(1) to Thos W Ward Ltd , Ringwood, Hants,
c /1965

MINISTRY OF DEFENCE- ARMY DEPARTMENT, WEST MOORS DEPOT (War Department until 1/4/1964)

15   A storage depot for oil products and other goods covering a wooded area between
the BR (ex LSWR) Ringwood and Fordingbridge lines east of West Moors station,
with exchange sidings at SU 083033. Depot closed with final rail traffic in
7/1974.

Gauge: 4ft 8½in

Worked by standard locomotives of the War Department and Army Department.

MINISTRY OF DEFENCE- NAVY DEPARTMENT (Admiralty until 1/4/1964)

Portland Dockyard

16   Construction of Portland Breakwater commenced in 8/1847 and railways and
locomotives were then used by the contractor, J.T.Leather. The Breakwater
was completed in 8/1872. The GWR and LSWR jointly constructed for the Admiralty
the line from Portland station to the Breakwater and was completed (per GWR
records) by 2/1876. From 1/1/1899 this railway was owned by the Admiralty,
although maintained and managed by the GWR and LSWR jointly. Standard gauge
sidings from the end of this line (at the commencement of the Easton & Church
Hope Railway) served the Dockyard. Latterly locomotives stabled near the main
gate at SY 695744. Goods traffic over the BR Weymouth - Portland branch
ceased 5/4/1965 and Admiralty rail traffic ceased on or about this date.

Ref: 'The Railways of Dorset' by J.H.Lucking, RCTS, 1968
IRR No.49 (8/1973), p.87

Gauge: 4ft 8½in

No.1		0-4-0ST	OC	WB	1493	1896	(a)	s/s
No.2		0-4-0ST	OC	WB	1494	1896	(a)	(1)
No.3		0-4-0ST	OC	WB	1495	1896	(a)	(2)
No.4		0-4-0ST	OC	WB	1496	1896	(a)	(3)
	–	0-4-0ST	OC	P	686	1898	(a)	(4)
No.6		0-4-0ST	OC	P	687	1898	(a)	Scr c /1959
No.8		0-4-0ST	OC	AB	1570	1917	New	(5)
	YARD No.111	0-4-0DM		JF	22920	1940	(b)	(6)
	YARD No.113	0-4-0DM		JF	22935	1941	(b)	(7)

(a) ex W.Hill & Co Ltd , Portland Dockyard
    construction contract
(b) ex Admiralty, Risley Yard, Lancs ,
    12/1960

(1) to Barrow Haematite Steel Co Ltd ,
    Barrow, Lancs
(2) to Hastings & St.Leonards Gas Co ,
    Sussex, c /1925, via J.Smith,
    Hamworthy
(3) to Hamworthy Wharf & Coal Co Ltd ,
    c /1929, via J.Smith, Hamworthy
(4) to Admiralty, Grosnez Fort, Alderney,
    Channel Islands
(5) to Thos W Ward Ltd , Ringwood, Hants ,
    for scrap, 1/1963
(6) to Bird's Commercial Motors Ltd ,
    Long Marston, Warwicks , /1967
(7) to Bird's Commercial Motors Ltd ,
    Pontymister, Mon , /1967

Royal Naval Underwater Weapons Establishment, Bincleaves, Weymouth

17   Narrow gauge tramway serving the establishment at SY 684780, at the northern-
most end of Portland Breakwater.

Gauge: 2ft 0in

–		4wDM	RH	209429	1943	New	
YARD No.351		4wBE	GB	1584	1939	New	Scr /1964
–		4wBE	GB	2345	1950	New	

MINISTRY OF SUPPLY, ROYAL ORDNANCE FACTORY, CREEKMOOR

18   Factory closed and rail system dismantled.

Gauge: 4ft 8½in

–	0-4-0ST	OC	P	2012	1941	New	(1)
R.N.C.F. No.3	0-4-0ST	OC	AE	1976	1925	(a)	(2)

(a) ex Admiralty, Holton Heath, c /1950

(1) to ROF Llanishen, Cardiff, Glam ,
    c /1944
(2) to NCB, East Midlands Division, No.4
    Area, Sutton Colliery, Notts, 6/1956
    via W.Bush & Co Ltd , dealers,
    Alfreton

<u>OMNIUM MANUFACTURERS LTD., MANNINGS BRICKFIELDS, NEWTOWN, PARKSTONE</u>

19   Narrow gauge tramway including an incline served the works. Works closed c /1946
although the locomotive and rail system remained in part until after the site
was taken over by Bluebird Caravans in 1959.

Gauge: 2ft 0in

–	4wDM	RH	168791	1933	(a)	(1)

(a) ex East Surrey Water Co   (1) s/s after /1959 but by 8/1967

<u>PIKE BROS., FAYLE & CO.LTD., FURZEBROOK CLAY MINES, NEAR WAREHAM</u> (Pike Bros. (Wareham)
Ltd until 29/4/1949)

20   Long established ball clay workings on Creech Heath. The tramway was
established (with horse traction) by 1863. Its route was from West Creech
(SY 920833) via Furzebrook to Ridge Wharf (SY 938871) at Wareham Harbour –
about six miles. At Furzebrook was the loco shed (SY 931840) and exchange
sidings with the BR (ex LSWR) Wareham – Swanage branch. By 1939 most of the
clay produced was being shipped via these exchange sidings. In 1940 the area
to the east of Furzebrook was requisitioned for training purposes by the War
Department resulting in the complete closure and lifting of the section of
tramway in this area. The remainder of the system was replaced by road transport
from 1954, being sold for scrap to Abelson & Co (Engineers) Ltd in 4/1955.
Pending completion of the replacement roadways some rail traffic continued until
final closure in 7/1957. All track was lifted by 1959.

   Ref: 'Pike Bros., Fayle & Co Ltd ' by W.J.K.Davies, NGRS, 1957.
         'The Railways of Purbeck' by R.W.Kidner, Oakwood Press, 1973

Gauge: 2ft 8in

PRIMUS	0-4-2T*	OC	B&S		1866	New	(1)	
SECUNDUS	0-6-0WT	OC	B&S		1874	New		
	Reb Lewin 1880 & P			1936			(2)	
TERTIUS	0-6-0ST	OC	MW	999	1886	New		
	Reb MW	1911	& Pike	1951			Scr	/1959
QUARTUS	0-4-2T**	OC	JF		1885	(a)		
			Reb		1921		Scr	/1934
QUINTUS	0-4-0ST	OC	MW	1854	1914	New		
		Reb P			1934		(4)	
SEXTUS	0-4-2ST	OC	P	1692	1925	New	(4)	
SEPTIMUS	0-4-2ST	OC	P	1808	1930	New	(3)	
–	4wDM		MR	5242	1930	(b)	(5)	

 * Uncertain whether 0-4-2T or 0-6-0T
** Uncertain whether 0-4-2T or 0-4-2WT

(a) ex JF , /1889
(b) ex Bungey, Hayes, Middx, 10/1951

(1) converted to a stationary winding
    engine at Creech Grange Mine by /1888;
    Scr c /1900
(2) to Museum of Science & Industry,
    Birmingham, via Abelson & Co (Engineers)
    Ltd , 7/1955
(3) to P , 3/1956 for overhaul for the
    proposed North Somerset Light Railway
    Co ; when this scheme fell through
    Scr at P by Pugsley, /1962
(4) Scr on site 12/1956 by Keen & Co of
    Salisbury, Wilts
(5) Reb to 1ft 11½in gauge at Furzebrook,
    /1959; to Norden Mines, 10/1959

REDLAND PIPES LTD., WIMBORNE (f Norcon Ltd.)

21   Works served by narrow gauge tramway. Line closed and dismantled.

Gauge: 2ft 0in

| | - | 4wDM | MR | 7604 | 1939 | (a) | (1) |

(a) ex Durham County Water Board   (1) to Ripley Works, Surrey, /1968

SIR THOS. SALT, BART, SHILLINGSTONE MANOR ESTATE

22   A miniature gauge line laid down to serve the needs of the estate, including the conveyance of pig food, which thus qualified its inclusion as an industrial line. System closed and sold by auction, 10/7/1975.

Gauge: 10¼ in

1	BELLE	0-4-0DM	C&N	1954	New	(1)
2	CYCLOPS	Bo-BoPM*	Guest	1960	New	(1)
	WASP	4wPM	Shillingstone	1963	New	(1)
4	JASON	2-6-0+0-6-2	K	1938	(a)	(1)

  * Bo-Bo.DM until /1961

(a) ex   (1) to ? , /1975

SHARP, JONES & CO LTD., BOURNE VALLEY POTTERIES, BRANKSOME

23   A works at SZ 055921 was established in 1853. In 1886 a line some 1¼ miles long was laid to bring clay to the works from new pits at SZ 067933 approx. This line was horse worked for the first three years. Later a connection was laid from the works to the LSWR line near Branksome station. The clay pits tramway, which included a gradient of 1 in 22, was closed in 1948 and lifted by 8/1948. The siding connection to the works has since 1948 been shunted by a Muir-Hill road tractor.

    Ref: IRR No.1 (11/1962), p.18

Gauge: 4ft 8½in

| PIONEER | 0-4-0ST | OC | HC | 336 | 1889 | New | (1) |
| MARS | 0-4-0T | OC | AE | 1701 | 1915 | New | (2) |

(1) to WD , Poole, c /1915; ret ; to Trent
    & Co , Parkstone, for scrap, 9/1948
(2) to British Periclase Co Ltd , West
    Hartlepool, Co.Durham, per MoS,
    /1942

JAMES SMITH, IRONWORKS, HAMWORTHY

24   Locomotives were kept at the works by this dealer pending resale. Locos known are listed.

Gauge: 4ft 8½in

No.3		0-4-0ST	OC	WB	1495	1896	(a)	(1)
No.4		0-4-0ST	OC	WB	1496	1896	(a)	(2)
	BEXHILL	0-6-0ST	IC	MW	1365	1898		
				Reb Wake			(b)	(3)

(a) ex Admiralty, Portland Dockyard
(b) ex S.Pearson & Son Ltd , contrs

(1) to Hastings & St.Leonards Gas Co ,
    Sussex, c /1925
(2) to Hamworthy Wharf & Coal Co Ltd ,c /1929
(3) to British Sugar Corporation Ltd ,
    Ipswich, c /1937

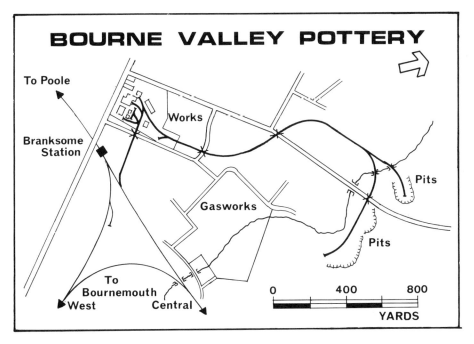

BOURNE VALLEY POTTERY

To Poole

Branksome
Station

Works

Gasworks

Pits

Pits

To
Bournemouth
West   Central

0   400   800

YARDS

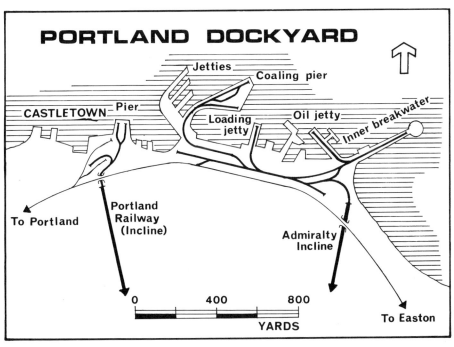

PORTLAND DOCKYARD

Jetties

Coaling pier

CASTLETOWN Pier

Loading
jetty

Oil jetty

Inner breakwater

To Portland

Portland
Railway
(Incline)

Admiralty
Incline

To Easton

0   400   800

YARDS

SOUTHERN GAS BOARD, POOLE GASWORKS (Bournemouth Gas & Water Co until 1/5/1949)

25   A small works at SZ 015907 south of the BR (ex LSWR) line east of Poole station served by standard gauge sidings off this line. The narrow gauge line served the retort houses and was taken out of use c /1968. The standard gauge was retained to serve a new gas reforming plant from c /1968 until 4/1972. Works closed 4/1972 and was being demolished in 3/1973.

Gauge: 4ft 8½in

	No.1	4wPM	HU		c1924	(New?)	Scr 12/1946
1136	(f No.2)	4wDM	FH	2054	1938	New	(1)
1135	(f 3)	4wDM	RH	242867	1946	New	(2)

(1) to Corralls Ltd , Hamworthy, c /1966
(2) to Corralls Ltd , Hamworthy, 2/1973

Gauge: 2ft 0in

–	4wDM(f PM)	L	18557	1942	New	(2)
–	4wDM(f PM)	L	25919	1944	New	(1)

(1) to Alan Keef, dealer, Bampton, Oxon ,
    /1968
(2) to Alan Keef, dealer, Bampton, Oxon ,
    /1970

SWANWORTH QUARRIES LTD., WORTH MATRAVERS, NEAR SWANAGE

26   A quarry at SY 969783 served by an internal narrow gauge tramway. System replaced by dumpers, closed and lifted.

Gauge: 2ft 0in

–	4wPM	L	24811	1944	New	Scr
–	4wDM	HE				Scr
–	4wDM	RH				Scr

SYKES & SON (POOLE) LTD., CREEKMOOR POTTERIES, POOLE

27   A narrow gauge system was used to transport clay from pits on the east and west to the works at SZ 002939. This traffic from the clay pits ceased c12/1964 and most of the track was lifted by 5/1965 but about 50 yards of track in the works was retained to handle sand traffic at the kilns for some time afterwards.

Gauge: 2ft 0in

–	4wDM	RH	168836	1933	New	s/s c /1962
(No.2)	4wDM	RH	172894	1934	(a)	(1)
(No.3)	4wDM	RH	181806	1936	(b)	(1)
1210	4wDM	RH	192878	1939	(c)	(1)
–	4wDM	RH	193964	1939	(c)	(2)
–	4wDM	RH	200780	1941	(d)	(2)
–	4wDM	RH			(d)	(2)
–	4wDM	RH	200786	1941	(e)	s/s c /1963

(a) ex John A Cook, dealer, Bristol   (1) Sold for scrap, c1/1965
(b) ex John Lysaght's Scunthorpe Works Ltd ,(2) to Harman of Poole for scrap, c1/1967
    Lincs
(c) ex J.B.Edwards, dealer,Whyteleaf, Surrey, c /1962
(d) ex Edmund Nuttall Ltd , contrs, c /1962
(e) ex Lytchett Brick Co Ltd , Upton, c /1962

UPTON BRICKWORKS LTD., UPTON, NEAR POOLE (f Lytchett Brick Co Ltd)

28 A tramway served clay pits (SY 984940) and brought the clay about half the distance to the works which were at SY 982934, a conveyor belt being used for the remainder of the distance. Locomotives, derelict and under repair, were to be found at the works also. Brickworks closed c /1968; tramway lifted and works demolished 1969.

Gauge: 2ft 0in

–		4wDM	RH	166032	1933	(a)	Scr /1956
–		4wDM	RH	178990	1936	(b)	s/s c /1966
–		4wPM	MR	1826	1918	(c)	s/s /1967
–		4wPM	MR				s/s by /1966
H 16		4wPM	MR	4716	1936	(d)	s/s c /1966
H 10		4wPM	MR			(d)	s/s
1	BUGSY	4wDM	MR	20057	1949	(e)	(3)
–		4wDM	MR	9778	1953	(f)	(2)
–		4wDM	FH	1887	1934	(g)	(2)
–		4wDM	FH	1896	1934	(h)	(4)
–		4wDM	RH	200876	1941	(j)	(1)
–		4wPM	L	3587	1930	(k)	s/s

(a) ex Hine Bros (Ringwood) Ltd ,
    Gillingham Pits
(b) ex Moorhouse Sand & Gravel Pits,
    Westerham, Kent, via Cohen, /1953
(c) ex Cohen, Brighton Road contract,
    c /1955; f H.Sabey & Co Ltd ,
    Yiewsley, Middx
(d) ex Esso Petroleum Co Ltd , Fawley,
    Hants, /1957
(e) ex MR , /1962; f Birmingham Corporation
    Water Department, Elan Aqueduct
    construction
(f) ex Great Ouse River Board,
    9/1961
(g) ex Bournemouth Plant Hire, /1964;
    prev M.E.Engineering Co Ltd ,
    Cricklewood, London
(h) ex ? , /1964
(j) ex Edmund Nuttall Ltd, contrs, c /1960
(k) ex St.Albans Gravel Co , Herts ,
    by 3/1939

(1) to Sykes & Son (Poole) Ltd ,
    Creekmoor, /1964
(2) to Creekmoor Light Railway Group,
    Poole, /1968
(3) to J.J.A.Evans, Launceston, Cornwall
    for preservation, /1968
(4) to J.J.A.Evans, Launceston, Cornwall,
    for preservation, c /1969

VICKERS (ENGINEERING) LTD., WEYMOUTH WORKS, WYKE REGIS

29 A torpedo factory at SY 668764 with an internal tramway serving the works and running to a pier. Works closed and factory site taken over by Wellworthy Ltd by 1967.

Gauge: 2ft 0in

–	4wBET		1929	Scr c10/1967

<u>WAR DEPARTMENT, POOLE DEPOT</u> (See also Ministry of Defence - Army Department for location with locomotives in use after 1/4/1964)

30   Rail sidings served this depot to the west of Poole station during the 1914-1920 period. Depot closed and track lifted.

Gauge: 4ft 8½in

PIONEER	0-4-0ST	OC	HC	336	1889	(a)	(1)

(a) ex Sharp, Jones & Co Ltd , Bourne   (1) ret to Sharp, Jones & Co Ltd
     Valley Potteries, Branksome, c /1915

Non·locomotive systems

BROWNSEA ISLAND TRAMWAY

A   A line was laid round most of the western perimeter of the island to connect clay pits with pottery works and with a pier at SZ 009881. The tramway, of unknown gauge, was laid before 1857 and probably closed about 1877.

KIMMERIDGE TRAMWAYS

B   An act was obtained in 1848 to construct tramways to serve oil shale pits. An early line seems to have run from Yellow Ledge (SY 909787) for some way parallel to the coast line. A later line ran from a pier at SY 908788 for about a mile as far as a shale mine at SY 915787. It's gauge is uncertain, and it was closed by 1906.

PORTESHAM TRAMWAY

C   Tramway built by William Mansfield in 1885 connecting a stone quarry at SY 612860 with the GWR Abbotsbury branch by a double track incline and further line into Portesham station. Quarry and tramway leased to Sir George Elliot in 1887 but disused by 1901.

PORTLAND RAILWAY

D   This 4ft 6in gauge line was incorporated in 1825 and opened in 10/1826 to convey stone from Priory Corner (SY 688730) to Castletown Pier (SY 688745). The upper section was horse worked and the descent to Castletown was by a self acting incline. By 1850 a network of lines connected many quarries to the line, while from 1865 stone was transhipped at Castletown to the Weymouth and Portland Railway. The line closed in 9/1939 and the majority of the track was lifted in 1957.

SWANAGE PIER TRAMWAY

E   A line about one third of a mile long ran from the pier (SZ 036788) westward to a coal yard and to stone bunkers. The tramway was horse worked, was probably opened about 1859 and finally became disused in the 1930's.

Contractors lines

C.V.BUCHAN LTD.

C1   Contract for the construction of a sewerage tunnel in Bournemouth from Pier to Alum Chine, with a plant depot at SZ 078904. 1971-2.

Gauge: 1ft 6in

-	4wBE	CE	5882	1971	New	s/s
-	4wBE	CE	5882C	1971	New	s/s

COODE, SON & MATHEWS (f. JOHN COODE)

C2   Construction of the Admiralty Breakwater, Portland, 1847-1872.

      Ref: 'The Chronicles of Boulton's Siding' by A.R.Bennett ; Loco Publishing Co.
        IRR No.49 (8/1973) p.86

Gauge: 7ft 0in

QUEEN	0-4-0WT	IC	EBW	(329	1852?)	(New	(2)?)
	0-4-0WT	IC	EBW	454	1853	(New?)	(1)
	0-4-0WT	IC	EBW			(New?)	(1)
	0-4-0WT	IC	EBW			(New?)	(1)
	0-4-0WT	IC	EBW			(New?)	(1)

(1) to I.W.Boulton, Ashton-under-Lyne,
      Lancs, /1875
(2)(to Torbay & Brixham Railway, Devon,
      /1868?)

Gauge: 4ft 8½in

LORD ROBARTES	0-6-0	IC	RS	619	1847	(a)	(1)
LORD WARDEN	0-6-0	IC	(RS	620?)		(b)	(1)

(a) ex Grissel & Peto, contrs , Cornwall   (1) to I.W.Boulton, Ashton-under-Lyne,
(b) ex S.M.Peto, contr   Lancs, /1875

W.HILL & CO. LTD.

C3   Construction of Portland Dockyard for Admiralty, -1896.

Gauge: 4ft 8½in

No.1	0-4-0ST	OC	WB	1493	1896	New	(1)
No.2	0-4-0ST	OC	WB	1494	1896	New	(1)
No.3	0-4-0ST	OC	WB	1496	1896	New	(1)
No.4	0-4-0ST	OC	WB	1496	1896	New	(1)
	0-4-0ST	OC	FW			(a)	s/s
	0-4-0ST	OC	MW	503	1875	(b)	(2)
	0-4-0ST	OC	P	686	1898	New	(1)
	0-4-0ST	OC	P	687	1898	New	(1)
No.9	0-6-0ST	OC	P	751	1898	New	(3)

(a) ex ?
(b) ex Butterley Co Ltd , Silverdale,
    Staffs, PEPLOW

(1) to Admiralty, Portland Dockyard
(2) to Joseph Pugsley & Son Ltd , Stoke
    Gifford, Glos
(3) to Joseph Pugsley & Son Ltd , Stoke
    Gifford, Glos ; later to Ebbw Vale
    Steel & Iron Co Ltd ,Mon